D0562406

# THE MINORS

THE

# MINORS

## The Struggles and the Triumph
## of Baseball's Poor Relation
## from 1876 to the Present

# NEIL J. SULLIVAN

St. Martin's Press   New York

*With gratitude to Dan Fenn and Peter Woll*

THE MINORS: THE STRUGGLES AND THE TRIUMPH OF BASEBALL'S POOR RELATION FROM 1876 TO THE PRESENT. Copyright © 1990 by Neil J. Sullivan. All rights reserved. Printed in the United States of America. No part of this book may be used or reproduced in any manner whatsoever without written permission except in the case of brief quotations embodied in critical articles or reviews. For information, address St. Martin's Press, 175 Fifth Avenue, New York, N.Y. 10010.

*Design by Judith Stagnitto*

Library of Congress Cataloging-in-Publication Data

Sullivan, Neil J.
The minors.
p.   cm.
ISBN 0-312-03864-X
1. Baseball—United States—Clubs—History—19th century. 2. Baseball—United States—Clubs—History—20th century. I. Title.
GV875.A1S95 1990 796.357'64'0973—dc20 89-24148

First Edition

10  9  8  7  6  5  4  3  2

# CONTENTS

# PREFACE

THE MINOR LEAGUES play a secondary role in professional baseball that unfortunately hides the richness of their game. Such teams as the Albuquerque Dukes, the Toledo Mud Hens, and the Pawtucket Red Sox entertain their fans and communities, but their more significant purpose is usually thought to be as a training ground for future major leaguers. Even television ads for the minor leagues encourage people to come out to see the major league stars of tomorrow.

While New Yorkers think of the minor leagues in terms of Met phenoms at Tidewater and beleaguered Yankees on the shuttle to Columbus, the minors from time to time have been more than vassals of the majors. In fact, the power brokers of the major leagues periodically have had to crush the growth of minor leagues to prevent them from gaining parity with the American and National Leagues. Without that coercion, the face of professional baseball might be very different from what we know today.

This book is a history of minor league baseball that examines how the battles of the game's moguls, especially club owners and league executives, have shaped professional baseball over the past 110 years. It is also a celebration of the minor league players and teams who have given fans in hundreds of communities so much enjoyment despite the white-collar wars that occasionally threaten to destroy the minor league game.

The theme of this book is that the minor leagues are minor because the major leagues have wanted them so. The majors have continually made decisions about personnel policies, franchise relocation, expansion, and broadcasting that were indifferent or damaging to the minors. The survival of minor league baseball is a testament to the spirit of the players and the loyalty of their fans.

The history of minor league baseball cannot be covered completely in one book, so the effort here has been to present a sample of memorable players, teams, and games against the backdrop of front office battles.

THE YEARS OF minor league baseball will be considered over three historical periods. The first era extends from 1877 to 1920, when professional baseball tried to become organized baseball. The entrepreneurial spirit of player unions and maverick ball clubs was crushed by the owners of self-proclaimed major league franchises whose superiority over the minors was more evident in their monopoly of big city markets than in the quality of their baseball. Major and minor league owners recognized their need for each other and made agreements to govern their affairs, but these agreements were trashed whenever the majors felt their privileged position was threatened.

In spite of this bullying, the minor leagues represented the true foundation of baseball as a *national* pastime. The Pacific Coast League, established in 1903, continued the half-century tradition of professional baseball in California. The International League brought baseball to Canada in the 1880s, and seventy years later fielded a team in Cuba. Other minor leagues in this first era extended the game from Orlando, Florida, to Victoria, British Columbia. The Blue Grass League, the Copper-Country Soo League, and the Kitty League (Kentucky, Illinois, and Tennessee) suggest even by their names the diversity and romance of the minor league game in those first decades.

From 1921 through 1950, the minor leagues achieved their peak popularity. These chapters cover an era of great teams and leagues that has never been equaled in the minors' history. Interest in baseball grew phenomenally during those years, yet the major leagues remained locked into ten cities in the east and midwest. The minors responded to the new opportunities by creating higher classifications for their most successful leagues. The range from Class D to Triple A permitted organized ball to be played in towns as remote as Pauls Valley, Oklahoma, and Glace Bay, Nova Scotia.

Some of the finest teams in organized baseball played in the high minors at Baltimore, Los Angeles, and Newark during these years. A few local heroes went to the majors and wound up in baseball's Hall of Fame. Many others of comparable ability spent almost their entire careers in the minors in relative obscurity, but they are now getting the appreciation they deserve.

The remarkable growth of the minors occurred as a debate raged over the purpose of these leagues. Branch Rickey contended that the minors could survive only as wards of major league patrons, who would use the minors in a farm system of player development. Rickey was opposed by baseball's commissioner, Kenesaw Mountain Landis, who countered that the integrity of the minor league game required independence from major league franchises. In appearance and moral fervor, Rickey and Landis were baseball's version of rival prophets, and their battles over the minors had something of the air of a religious war.

By the end of World War II, the Pacific Coast League was trying to win acceptance as a third major league. Despite the pressures of wartime, the PCL and other Triple-A leagues had narrowed the distance between themselves and the major leagues. Organized baseball could have incorporated some minor leagues as new, competing major leagues; instead, the majors used franchise shifts, expansion, and television to raid the growing minor league markets and perpetuate an artificial hierarchy.

From 1949 to 1963, attendance at minor league games dropped from almost forty-two million to less than ten million, while the number of leagues fell from fifty-nine to eighteen. The independent minor leagues favored by Commissioner Landis had been routed by the major leagues' hot pursuit of postwar riches. The security that the majors extended robbed the minors of the vitality and romance that had put teams in remote towns and given professional baseball much of its color.

In recent years the ownership of minor league teams has been profitable enough to attract new investors and restore integrity to the minor league game. This book concludes by considering the new era that may be emerging in professional baseball—a period when the major leagues are so embroiled in their battles over wealth that fans turn to the minors to rediscover the beauty of the game.

# ACKNOWLEDGMENTS

THE IDEA FOR this book was first suggested to me by Jane Dystel, my agent, whose encouragement was instrumental in my completing the project. Her partner, Jay Acton, is an impresario of baseball and a former owner of the Utica Blue Sox. Ardie Deutsch brought author and agency together, and I am grateful for his interest in my work.

Tom Heitz and the staff of the National Baseball Library at Cooperstown could not have been more gracious and efficient in providing me with the books and articles that I needed.

I appreciate the information and opinions that several baseball officials offered about the relationship between the major and minor leagues. Peter O'Malley, Fred Claire, and Charlie Blaney of the Los Angeles Dodgers took time from spring training in what would prove to be a championship season. Joe McIlvaine and Frank Cashen of the New York Mets shared their thoughts on their estimable farm system. Bud Selig and Harry Dalton of the Milwaukee Brewers provided interesting analyses of some of the current issues in baseball.

In the minor leagues, Harold Cooper and Randy Mobley of the Triple-A Alliance graciously discussed the changes in their leagues on several occasions. Bill Cutler of the Pacific Coast League was very helpful in explaining minor league baseball in the west. Carl Sawatski and Jimmy Bragan offered valuable lessons on how baseball operates at the Double-A level in Texas and the south. Max Schumacher, Jim Burris, and Frank Harraway were generous in explaining the travails of the American Association and its hopes for the future.

At St. Martin's, George Witte has been patient, constructive, and encouraging—the finest traits an editor can own.

Friends are indispensable in helping a writer maintain a healthy perspective about his work. Roger Hannon shares my delight with baseball, and he manages to steer between innocence and cynicism when discussing its front office games. Ron Yoshida helps me to put baseball in the proper academic light. Jim Sugrue, Joel Cardillo, and Jack Burke keep me aware of how fortunate I am to be able to do this work, and Sister Geraldine McCullagh assures me that God loves baseball too.

Most important, my family is a great source of help and encouragement. Joyce is primarily responsible for that terrific state, and Kaitlin and Timothy are my fellow beneficiaries. Barbara Trick has provided indispensable order to the house when Kate and Tim have demanded fresh diapers over a completed paragraph.

Finally, none of my current work would be possible without the assistance and inspiration of Peter Woll and Dan Fenn. I am happy to dedicate this book to them with deep appreciation for their friendship.

# · Part One ·

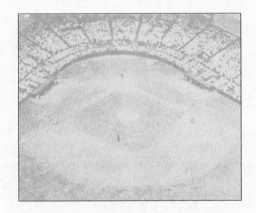

# GETTING
# ORGANIZED

*T*HE ORGANIZATION OF *baseball is one of the principal legacies*
*of the nineteenth-century game. During that era many leagues were*
*established that proved unable to complete a single season. Their com-*
*mon flaw, regardless of location or ambition, was a desire for immedi-*
*ate gain without the recognition that sacrifices by every team were*
*necessary for each league's success. Instead, rosters were raided,*
*schedules were not honored, corruption was prevalent, and rowdy*
*play was condoned.*

*To its great credit, the National League solved these problems. Able*
*officials disciplined, cajoled, and persuaded owners and players to*
*work for a common purpose. The first major league was a model of*
*how to create a commercially successful association for baseball. Had*
*the League's magnates been content with that great achievement, base-*
*ball might have developed in a very different form. But these officials*
*and owners were determined to be not tough competitors but exclusive*

*rulers. Because they viewed any other league as a potential threat, baseball was organized around the fundamental principle that any new association must be subordinate to the National League.*

*A number of leagues refused to accept the NL's dictates, and within their own markets they operated as independently as possible from the National League owners. When the Western League successfully challenged the NL monopoly, the stranglehold of organization became, ironically, even more secure. This happened because the new American League preferred not to lead other competitors into a new era of multiple majors, independent and freely associated. They instead favored sharing the monopoly with the National League, which profited from the infusion of new energy and wealth.*

*The leagues that were left out of the major league accord bonded into a new association that was eager to accept the scraps from the majors. Within this new group, however, were teams and leagues that bowed to no one, and by 1920 American baseball was again in a position to organize itself in a way that protected the diversity of the national pastime.*

# One

# UNORGANIZED BASEBALL

In 1876 BASEBALL became a permanent part of American culture when some enterprising gentlemen began to make an honest buck off the game.

In the second half of the nineteenth century, baseball leagues were forming all over America, but few were planned with much thought for the future. These were spontaneous associations content to enjoy the game at the moment, without the distraction of long-term planning. In 1876 the National League of Professional Baseball Clubs was established, and it began the modern organization of baseball into a business of such mesmerizing appeal that the most basic principles of the commercial market are dismissed as intrusions.

By posing as a romantic diversion instead of a profitable business, organized baseball has been able to intimidate competing leagues and has denied players the freedom to choose

their employers; the major leagues have raided the best players
of minor league teams and compensated those clubs with a pittance. These abuses are permitted because baseball operates
outside antitrust law; left to their own devices, the major league
owners have historically followed a strategy of bullying weaker
rivals without regard for the game's ultimate health.

Corruption, franchise instability, strikes, and collusion are
some effects of the owners' behavior. These aggravations, so
familiar to modern fans, were part of the business of baseball
from its beginnings.

Then, as now, some of the owners were admirable fellows
while others were outrageous. Some were talented and ener-
getic while others were lazy and ineffective. Some were devoted to developing a grand future for baseball while others
were committed to greed. Despite their personal differences,
baseball owners have tended throughout the game's history to
unite around the proposition that power was best left to them
alone. Individual players, unions, competing leagues, commissioners, and league presidents were all tolerated as long as
they did not interfere with the interests of the major league
owners. That principle would prove to be the foundation and
hallmark of the majors' relationship with the minor leagues.

THE NATIONAL LEAGUE created minor league baseball by
arrogating to itself alone the status of major league. Robert
Obojski, among others, was persuaded that "there must be a
major league before there can be a minor league," but that conclusion begs the question, in what sense was the National
League a major league?[1]

As far as the game itself was concerned, this nineteenth-century "primitive baseball," as Harvey Frommer calls it, was too
unstable to permit useful comparisons with baseball as we
know it.[2] Scouting that relied on gossip, contracts that few respected, and payrolls that were not always met led to a hap-

hazard distribution of talent all over the country. Playing conditions were extremely varied, press coverage was unreliable, and schedules were uncertain. Without question, the National League included some of the best teams and players in the country, but whether they were in a class by themselves is arguable.

Harold Seymour is one historian who has rejected the Nationals' claim of superiority: "During these first few years there were plenty of clubs outside the League as good or better than those who were members. In 1877, for example, about fifty professional non-League clubs were in action, and they succeeded in beating League teams no fewer than seventy-two times. Many games between clubs outside the League were just as well played as those in it, and League teams were even accused of avoiding the strong independent clubs."[3] So, was the NL's boast of major league status utterly false? Not exactly.

What the National League created was not so much major league baseball as monopoly baseball: a business that would be characterized by the club owners' total control of major markets, players, and competing franchises. The lasting effect of monopoly baseball has been that organizational games in the offices of club owners, league presidents, and eventually, union officials became as much a part of American baseball as the sport whose beauty lies in its intricately balanced rules and baffling physics.

The first attempt at an effective business structure for baseball was the National Association of Baseball Players, created in New York in 1858. This group was the outgrowth of elite gentlemen's clubs such as the New York Knickerbockers. The Association thought of baseball as Avery Brundage thought of the Olympics, as a recreation unsullied by commercial intrusions and thus limited to the wealthy.

The popularity of baseball spread so remarkably that in a few years the game was also played by teenagers in tattered uniforms in the camps of the Civil War. By the time of Lee's surrender in 1865, the National Association represented over 300 clubs across the country—a reflection of the ability of the rich to avoid military service.

But this culture of privileged amateurism could not prevent the game's appeal from reaching the working class, and the Association foundered in its inability to accommodate commercial interests. The National Association of *Professional* Base Ball Players was thus organized in 1871 to try to turn a popular game into a prosperous business.

While the amateur association had numbered more than 300 clubs, the new organization limited membership to seven teams in an obvious attempt to enhance value by limiting supply. But having recognized the commercial appeal of baseball, the National Association could not control the seamier elements that threatened the future of this new phenomenon.

From its beginning, baseball encompassed a range of American values. With its pastoral setting and languid season, the sport comforted a nation that had barely survived the Civil War. Reflecting the tempo of small towns and farms, its games had no place for the timekeeper who set the frantic pace of the new industrial life. The mythical heroes of the game inspired the author of "Casey at the Bat" in 1888, and even trenchant souls such as Mark Twain were enthralled by the sport.

Less happily, baseball's popularity also attracted gamblers, pickpockets, and other marginal characters who found the opportunities for easy money irresistible. In the early 1870s, games were routinely fixed, and few but the rowdy bothered to attend. Magazine sketches from that period pictured baseball first in lovely bucolic settings and later in caricatures of financial vice.

While corruption threatened the genteel character of baseball's early years, the National Association was unable to meet even its most basic commercial needs. "Revolving," or contract jumping, was rampant. Scheduled games were not played, and boredom quickly set in as the Boston Red Stockings dominated the pennant races. This first professional association staggered through five years until a revolt of western owners led to the creation of the National League of Professional Baseball Clubs. William Hulbert of Chicago was the principal instigator of the new league. He was assisted by Al Spalding, whom Hulbert lured from Boston back to his native Illinois. Spalding was an outstanding pitcher and manager who also possessed the organizational skills that Hulbert recognized were necessary to the new league (and that Spalding put to good use in establishing a sporting goods empire that bore his name and continues to thrive).

For the first time, baseball was organized by owners rather than players. Hulbert's strategy for succeeding where others had failed turned on the effective exercise of authority within the League and the domination by the NL of any rival clubs. Hulbert and his colleagues saw the protection of their rosters and the limiting of salaries as paramount objectives. They developed specific tools for securing their control over both the players and rival leagues, and these devices became the focus of revolt by players and leagues who challenged the National League's domination.

The reserve clause was Hulbert's instrument for controlling players. This provision bound a player to a team even after a contract had expired. By the unilateral action of the club owner, a player was kept out of competitive bidding and reduced to the choice of playing for a comparatively low salary or not playing at all. A condition of League membership was respect for other teams' rosters, including its "reserved" players. Failure to comply could mean expulsion from the League.

While the reserve clause corralled the players, other techniques restricted the non-League clubs. The draft and the option gave League teams some influence over the rosters of their potential competitors. The draft allowed NL teams to select players from non-League franchises in return for a fixed payment that had no relationship to the player's value on an open market. The draft effectively precluded non-League teams from developing and keeping their best players. To the contrary, once a player was ready to contribute to the club that had refined his game, a League team would likely seize the man for a nominal draft fee.

The option allowed League teams to send players to non-League clubs, subject to recall. The non-League roster could thus become cluttered with the NL's marginal players, reducing the opportunity for other players to develop.

The reserve clause, the draft, and the option were championed for years as necessary for the economic stability of baseball. In truth, they were necessary only for the economic advantage of the major league owners who could undermine leagues that tried to resist. No doubt without those controls, professional baseball would have developed very differently as a business, but as a game it would have been just as appealing.

Bound by the reserve clause, the players had to endure the owners' paternalism. Contracts required players to behave according to the standards of the club owners. (The story is told of Mike "King" Kelly being upbraided for drinking lemonade in a saloon during the small hours. Kelly himself was offended, insisting that he had had liquor in his glass and that he would never drink lemonade at such an hour.) The owners' sanctimonious dictating of off-field behavior was extremely presumptuous, but the owners were also acutely aware of how severely corruption had damaged the National Association.

In more sensible efforts to bolster the League, Hulbert insisted that schedules be honored and that the umpire be given more respect. His success in these areas further stabilized commercial baseball, as well as helping to market the game to a wider, more wholesome audience.

WHILE THE COMMERCIAL problems of organizing baseball were being solved, the basic rules of the game were being refined. As far back as 1845, the bases had been separated by ninety feet, a decision that Red Smith thought represented the closest thing to perfection in human history. Not until almost fifty years later was the pitching rubber moved back to the sixty feet six inches that represents the center of the diamond.

In the years between these geometric adjustments, the number of balls triggering a walk was dropped from nine to four, one-bounce outs were eliminated, fielders began wearing gloves, pitchers started throwing overhand without a running start, batters could no longer request a location for the pitch, ground balls had to stay in fair territory past first or third to be hits, and the sizes of bats and balls were regulated.

The development of uniform playing rules was a critical part of the struggle to organize baseball. The game had initially developed with so many local variations that baseball was not a national sport in any true sense. By the 1890s a common set of rules enabled the delightful and inevitable comparisons to begin: Who has the best team? Who is the best pitcher? Who is the greatest offensive threat?

As the fundamental elements of the sport matured, the business of baseball settled its essential organizational issues. Hulbert, Spalding, and other magnates rescued baseball from the anarchy that disrupted schedules and rosters and allowed games to be fixed. In that way they contributed to baseball's future success as surely as Kelly, Brouthers, Keeler, and other stars of the nineteenth-century game.

But establishing a stable economic base for the game was not enough for the early owners. Consistent with the business culture of their time, they would be satisfied with nothing short of total control of every economic aspect of the game. In their effort to eradicate the anarchy of baseball's early years, the National League owners rejected a market of several competitive leagues in favor of a monopoly that stifled every other association of clubs. It remains ironic that by equating security with monopoly, the National League owners provoked the very rebellions by players and other owners that kept organized baseball in a state of turmoil in its early decades.


OCCASIONALLY THE LEAGUE owners became so intoxicated with their own power that they abandoned the veil of their draft and option clauses. In postseason barnstorming tours that ranged from coast to coast, League teams raided the best players from local clubs. Moreover, they did not hesitate to schedule games in smaller markets without regard for the financial effects on local teams.

Responding to these provocations, L. C. Waite of the St. Louis Red Stockings called for a convention of fellow non-League teams to meet in February 1877 in Pittsburgh to organize against the monopoly. Notice of the meeting apparently alerted the NL owners to the effects of their arrogant behavior, for Hulbert, Spalding, and A. G. Mills quickly hatched a plan to convince the opposition to accept an affiliated status with the National League. The so-called League Alliance represented one of the first three nominal minor leagues, since one of the conditions of membership was an acknowledgment of the National League's exclusive claim to being a major league. That genuflection plus ten dollars would extend the League's protection against "revolving" and would further discipline the members by prohibiting them from playing teams who had signed a blacklisted player.

Waite and his followers rejected the Alliance as a sham. They proceeded to meet in Pittsburgh, and created the International Association. This league, ostensibly independent of the National League, initially fielded teams in Pittsburgh, Rochester, Columbus, and Lynn, Massachusetts, in the United States, and London, Guelph, and Manchester in Canada. The London Tecumsehs won the championship that first year with a 14–4 record with two ties, edging the Pittsburgh Alleghenies by one game.

William Arthur "Candy" Cummings, who claimed credit for inventing the curveball, pitched for Lynn while also serving as the League president. "Pud" Galvin, the first 300-game winner, got his start in the International Association.

One of Cummings's teammates on the Lynn club was a black player, John W. "Bud" Fowler. Fowler played for a number of teams in both the United States and Canada. He appeared in only three games for Lynn; no record of his playing appears again until six years later, when he cropped up again in the Northwestern League. Fowler was one of several black players who were able to compete in organized baseball in the nineteenth century until the game resolved its ambivalence about blacks in favor of a racist ban that lasted until 1946.

The best team in the International Association was the Buffalo Bisons of 1878. In fact, an article by Joseph Overfield in the 1977 issue of the *Baseball Research Journal* contends that the Buffalo Bisons of 1878 were the greatest minor league team of the nineteenth century. Buffalo had played a number of National League and International Association teams in 1877 with some success as an unaffiliated franchise. Before joining the IA in 1878, Buffalo hired a completely new team. Even such stars as John Montgomery Ward were dropped from the roster. The most prominent new Bison was Davey Force, an eight-year veteran. Pud Galvin was signed and became the first minor league pitcher to throw a shutout.

The 1878 Bisons played a 116-game schedule, finishing with a record of 81–32 with three ties. Their record against National League teams was a very impressive 10–7, and they had beaten every team in that league at least once. In those days of limited rosters, Galvin's pitching record was almost unbelievable. He started 101 of the Bisons's games and completed 96 of them! In games that he did not start as pitcher, he played right field and then came on in relief. His record was 72–25 with three ties, 10–5 against National League opponents. He beat Boston in a twelve-inning game on October 2, beat another NL team, Providence, in a thirteen-inning game on the next day, and pitched and lost to Boston on October 4. Estimates are that he pitched approximately 900 innings that season, more than three times the number that would lead the major leagues today. Such a comparison, however, is misleading, as pitching in those days was a different craft. With a much deader ball, pitchers could allow batters to make contact, since the chance of driving the ball for extra bases was remote. The terrible physical strain that now is a part of every pitch in organized ball was reserved at that time for crucial moments in a game.

The Bisons's great success on the field netted a profit for the front office of $248.94. The owners applied for admission to the National League, and they were accepted. Buffalo remained a League franchise until 1886 and had three third-place finishes during those years. All of the Bisons continued with major league careers.

The defection of the Bisons was just one of the International Association's problems. Membership was a casual commitment, and schedules and rosters were often ignored. The resulting financial chaos left its teams helpless before the National League. Even after the IA notified the National League of its willingness to consider joining the Alliance, several IA teams bolted to the Alliance, accepting the NL's terms without condition or discussion.

The International Association proved to be so inept that it survived only two seasons. At the same time, the League Alliance embraced thirteen clubs from Brooklyn to Memphis. The Indianapolis Hoosiers won the Alliance championship in 1877, led by Ed "The Only" Nolan, who reputedly threw thirty shutouts that year.

The New England League, the third minor league formed in 1877, was established around a group of amateur and semipro teams that had played during the Civil War. This league survived in various forms until 1949. It neither challenged the National League directly as the International Association had, nor did it try to accommodate the League through the League Alliance. In this league Napoleon Lajoie and Wilbert Robinson began their distinguished careers.

Other leagues were soon established in other parts of the country. Baseball organized in the midwest in 1879. Owner, manager, and promoter Ted Sullivan was the major architect of the Northwestern League, which initially consisted of teams in Davenport and Dubuque, Iowa; Rockford, Illinois; and Omaha, Nebraska. This particular association was short-lived, but it led to the Western League, which in turn spawned both the American Association and the American League.

Ted Sullivan was perhaps the principal figure in minor league baseball during the nineteenth century. No one was more responsible for spreading professional baseball beyond the northeast. He provided the skills that organized baseball in the south and midwest, stabilizing the game into thriving leagues.

Another league, the Eastern Championship Association began operating in 1881. It placed three clubs in New York City, another in the independent city of Brooklyn, and the final two in Philadelphia and Washington. This league collapsed after two seasons, but some of its members joined the Inter-State League, which survived in various forms into the 1950s.

After reviewing the formation of these early leagues, Robert Obojski concludes, "It should be emphasized that soon after the first minor leagues were established almost every responsible executive in professional baseball recognized that a spirit of cooperation must exist between the minor circuits and the major teams of the National League. The administration of baseball at all its levels eventually came to be so carefully structured—after early trials and tribulations—that it won the admiration of business and political leaders throughout the nation."[4]

This assessment glosses over the nature of the "spirit of cooperation," which in fact resembled a kind of Pax Romana— surrender or die. The League Alliance, which has been characterized as a "sop" by Harold Seymour and "a pooling scheme" by historian David Voigt, was a kind of protection racket whose major purpose was to safeguard the NL's monopoly.

The initial division of leagues into major and minor was the result of organizational intimidation, not a disparity of talent. The hierarchy of leagues was created for commercial reasons, specifically the National League owners' commitment to monopoly. Today one of the most natural features of baseball is its business structure: an elaborate hierarchy that distinguishes the majors from Triple-A, Double-A, Class-A, and Rookie leagues. Some remember categories of B, C, and D ball and even the special Open Classification, a limbo for the Pacific Coast League of the 1950s. We take for granted that these various leagues reflect the disparity of talent in the sport: as young players improve, they move up the ladder until they get a shot at the big leagues. Major leaguers who fail to measure up are "sent down." To a degree, that assumption of disparity holds throughout the history of the game, but in general, the status and purpose of minor league baseball has reflected organizational battles among owners rather than competition on the ball field.

BY 1883 THE first challenges to the National League had been routed, and having served its purpose, the League Alliance was disbanded. The National League was at a peak of power, having eliminated its competitors or brought them to heel. But while the National League's organizational advantages usually allowed it to crush its foes with little effort, it was just as easy for the vanquished to rebound and launch a new challenge. The American Association was a rival to the NL from 1882 to 1891. The AA began with significant advantages, including more populous markets than even those in the National League. In its inaugural season, the AA included teams in Baltimore, Cincinnati, Louisville, Philadelphia, Pittsburgh, and St. Louis. At the same time, the NL was represented in Boston, Buffalo, Chicago, Cleveland, Detroit, Providence, Troy, and Worcester. In the 1883 season, both leagues expanded into New York City.

The American Association modeled its constitution after that of the National League, but some popular exceptions boosted its prospects. Admission was priced at twenty-five cents rather than the fifty cents charged by the NL. Games were permitted on Sunday, and liquor could be sold at the park. As in the National League, strict penalties were imposed against gambling, but the AA's magnates seemed to have a clearer sense that the game was supposed to be fun.

Apparently amicable relations between the two leagues ended quickly when two American Association players were raided by the National League. Responding to protests from the aggrieved clubs, Hulbert issued a condescending statement that barely acknowledged the existence of the other league and denied completely its legitimacy.

The NL's conceit was a blunder, since AA teams were generally well financed and strong attractions. The Association was denounced as the "Beer and Whiskey Circuit" because of the principal businesses of several of the owners, but snide references could not change the fact that the National League monopoly was now seriously threatened. The AA had shown that they could compete for players by ignoring the reserve clause and creating a freer labor market, the eternal bête noire of baseball owners. The American Association struck a market balance between anarchy and monopoly.

To the rescue of the National League owners came, ironically, a minor league. The Northwestern League, which had disbanded after the 1879 season, was trying to reestablish itself in 1883. To improve its chances, the Northwestern League wanted to secure protection against predatory raids by the competing majors.

The National League leaped at the opportunity. It had a new president, A. G. Mills, who had succeeded Hulbert after his death in 1882. Mills saw the Northwestern invitation as an opportunity to reach a truce with the American Association. He suggested a three-party conference to iron out differences, restore the integrity of contracts and rosters, and not coincidentally, restore the owners' preeminence.

Harold Seymour records some of Mills's professions in favor of independent leagues all across America, loosely affiliated but free to govern their internal affairs. If sincere, this was a very different vision of organized baseball from that which the National League had pursued to that point. Only a year before, Hulbert had acknowledged the League Alliance as the only appropriate place for any organization outside of the National League. If true, Mills's remarks would mean that the goal of a major league monopoly was being abandoned in favor of a truce among competitors.

In the "Harmony Conference" called by Mills, the National

League, the American Association, and the Northwestern League drafted the first National Agreement for baseball. The pact established the relationships among the various leagues, and it has remained the charter of organized baseball. Its most essential elements were the codification of the reserve clause, established time periods for contract negotiations, an agreement to honor expulsions of players, and an administrative mechanism to resolve disputes among the parties.

For the moment, the National League had lost its monopoly, but it had secured an even more important objective: owners still controlled players. Reserve lists were submitted each year by every club committed to the National Agreement, and those players were then ignored by the Agreement's signatories.

This respect for the reserve clause ended the free labor market for players. Competition that raised salaries was controlled once again, so that players had the option of accepting an owner's offer or finding another line of work. The National League's monopoly had been not so much broken as extended. As long as the American Association cooperated in the labor policy, the principal financial threat to the owners was gone.

The players tried to protect their interests by establishing a third major league, the Union Association, in 1884. That twelve-team circuit included clubs in familiar markets such as Boston and Chicago, as well as in new towns including Kansas City and Milwaukee.

The Union Association directly challenged the National League and the American Association because it rejected the National Agreement and attempted to raid players from other clubs. Despite some important financial backing, it could not buck the organizational power of the National League. Spalding was particularly active in preventing the raiding of White Sox ace Larry Corcoran and in undercutting any gains that the Union Association was making.

Unable to crack the major league markets, the Union Association disbanded after the 1884 season. Although ineffective, it demonstrated the players' resentment of their diminished status and their willingness to challenge the owners over the notorious reserve clause.

THE MAJOR LEAGUE game stabilized through the 1880s, with the National League established in Boston, Chicago, Cleveland, Indianapolis, New York, Philadelphia, Pittsburgh, and Washington, D.C. The American Association included teams in Baltimore, Brooklyn, Cincinnati, Columbus, Kansas City, Louisville, Philadelphia, and St. Louis. The NL remained the stronger league, but the AA appeared to be permanently established. That appearance was deceiving.

After the 1889 season, the National League lured away from the Association its two strongest franchises, Brooklyn and Cincinnati, to replace the League's marginal clubs, Indianapolis and Washington. At the same time, the players again rebelled against the reserve clause by creating the Players League or Brotherhood.

The new circuit included some very able leaders, such as John Montgomery Ward and Charles Comiskey, but the odds against its success were too great. Both the National League and the American Association used minor league teams by including on the minors' rosters players that were reserved to major league patrons. This tactic not only sapped the pool of quality players, but also established what in effect were the first farm teams. The minor league teams involved were no longer independent businesses with control over their own rosters, but junior partners of a major league patron. This relationship, created under the pressure of a labor war, would be a primary source of controversy between the majors and minors in the twentieth century.

Rather than open major league baseball to competition, the major effect of the Players League's lone season was to restore the National League monopoly. The Brotherhood provided more competition than the American Association could handle, and after the 1891 season, the AA collapsed. As a challenger to the National League monopoly, the American Association had been far more successful than the Union Association or the Players League, but despite its accommodation through the National Agreement, it could not overcome the lingering desire of the National League owners to have exclusive control of the game.

At a time when the NL monopoly was under attack, the American Association provided the cover of competition. So long as no real competition for players ensued, the existence of the Association could be tolerated. When the players and their allies failed again in 1890, the pretext of competitive major leagues could safely be dropped.

While the major league charade played through the 1880s, other leagues had a chance to develop across the country without the predatory National League undermining the development of quality players and teams. In a sense, the lasting contribution of the American Association may have been as a shield that protected the fledgling circuits, which in time developed into important leagues in professional baseball.

DURING THE 1880s and 1890s, minor leagues came and went at a dizzying pace. A few survive to the present day, but most collapsed in futility. The International League, the oldest minor league, grew out of the Eastern League, which itself endured some tumultuous times. The ten-team League that had its first season in 1884 became a six-team circuit the following year and changed its name to the New York League, with clubs in Albany, Binghamton, Oswego, Rochester, Syracuse, and Utica.

In 1886 the New York League merged with an association of Canadian teams, and for the first time, the name International League was used for the eight-team circuit. Jersey City and Newark were added to the IL in 1887 after their association, the New Eastern League, folded. The ten-team format was too unwieldy, however, and in 1888 the League returned to an eight-team circuit with clubs in Hamilton, London, and Toronto, Ontario; and Albany, Buffalo, Rochester, Syracuse, and Troy, New York. Toledo and Detroit entered the League in 1889, replacing Albany and Troy.

Among the players whom the Society for American Baseball Research lists as minor league stars are several from this era in the International League.[5] Bud Fowler, for example, reappeared briefly with Binghamton in 1887 and hit .350 in thirty-four games before that franchise folded. Charles Columbus "Count" Campeau played for Detroit from 1888–90, in a career that extended from 1887–1905. Campeau played almost 2,000 games, primarily as an outfielder, and finished with a career batting average of .293. John Frisk, a pitcher before shifting to the outfield, started in the International League at Port Huron in 1898 and finished in the Northwestern League in 1915. Robert Gilks was a teammate of Bud Fowler on the 1887 Binghamton Bingos. Gilks's career ran from 1885 to 1909, during which he played in over 2,100 games, finishing with a .275 average and over 300 stolen bases.

LIKE THE AMERICAN Association, the International League suffered because of the Brotherhood war. The Players League claimed the Buffalo franchise, and Rochester, Syracuse, and Toledo jumped to the American Association. This raiding reflects not only the instability of organized baseball at the time but, more important reveals the major leagues' attitude of disdain toward the minors, which would recur whenever the majors felt threatened or saw opportunity.

The 1890 season was the low point in the history of the International League. For the only time, the circuit was unable to complete its season, with only six teams, Grand Rapids, Saginaw–Bay City, and Detroit in Michigan and Montreal, Toronto, and London in Canada. The eastern markets of the United States were abandoned to the warring majors.

Because the Brotherhood rebellion lasted for only one season, the International League was able to return to some old communities in 1891. Buffalo and Rochester were once again represented. The League changed its name back to the Eastern League in 1892, and it kept that name for the next twenty years.

The International League has always been important in the history of the minors because of its proximity to the major league markets, a setting that has been both a blessing and a curse. During the 1880s and 1890s, other leagues began to develop in more remote areas.

In the west, the California League and the California State League were organized in the mid-1880s. Each was a four-team league, and each established three teams in San Francisco. Other cities in these circuits were Sacramento and Oakland. This oversupply of teams in San Francisco was similar to the generous number of clubs in New York in the first years of professional baseball in the east.

The Pacific Coast League was not formed until 1903, but its roots were established with the California League. The PCL traditionally went its own way in organized baseball, and that attitude developed naturally in the isolated west. Bill Lange, an early star of California baseball, grew up in the Bay Area, and left a successful career with the Chicago Cubs to play in California. Lange was with Chicago from 1893–99, during which time he compiled a career average of .330 and stole 399 bases, certainly not the stats of an inferior player.

The Southern League, organized in 1885, was another of the unstable leagues of the time. It included teams at one point or another in the Carolinas, Alabama, Georgia, Tennessee, and Louisiana. Perhaps in that rural setting it was especially difficult to draw the crowds needed to make a franchise successful; and, since this was still a short time after the Civil War, the opportunity for leisure and recreation in Dixie was undoubtedly still limited.

The Texas League, which began operations in 1888 with clubs in Austin, Dallas, Fort Worth, Galveston, Houston, and San Antonio, also struggled with marginal franchises for several years. The ever-present Ted Sullivan appeared in 1895 to reorganize the League, and from that foundation it prospered in the twentieth century.

Minor league baseball would have its greatest impact in the midwest. The Northwestern League reorganized as the Western Association in 1888 and placed teams in Chicago, Des Moines, Kansas City, Milwaukee, Minneapolis, Omaha, St. Paul, and Sioux City. Five years later, this league again reorganized as the Western League, with clubs in Detroit, Grand Rapids, Indianapolis, Kansas City, Milwaukee, Minneapolis, Sioux City, and Toledo. The Western League was formed after the final turbulence of the major league wars that ended the Players League and the American Association. The National League had expanded to a twelve-team circuit, a bloated organization that had again been victorious in the organizational wars but was vulnerable to challenge.

The Western League proved to be the instrument that finally would break the National League monopoly. Under Ban Johnson's leadership, it improved the quality of its franchises and moved them into lucrative eastern markets, rejecting the NL's claim of being the only major league. After the Western League achieved major league status as the American League, the opportunity was opened for another important league in the midwest. That role was assumed after the turn of the century by the American Association.


MINOR LEAGUE BASEBALL in the late nineteenth century was a different game from that we have come to know. Organized baseball was so volatile during this period that it makes more sense to refer to non-League rather than minor league teams. Many excellent ball players performed for teams and leagues in an era that was too unstable to permit comparisons of the quality of the different leagues.

The National League serves as a useful point of reference simply because it is the oldest league in organized baseball, but being first did not necessarily make it best. And while it is reasonable to admire the administrative skills of Hulbert, Mills, and Spalding in stabilizing the business side of the sport, we can also be amazed at their persistent excesses that provoked opposition and triggered the very instability that the National League was so eager to prevent.

The most impressive feature of baseball in that era is the simple fact of how quickly its popularity spread across America after the Civil War. No part of the country failed to develop professional leagues with loyal followings. Even the most prominent teams of the northeast recognized the commercial value of barnstorming across country to take advantage of the game's appeal.

In light of the public's growing love for baseball, the organizational wars among the owners seem especially petty. In the skills of its players, the enthusiasm of its fans, and the determination of its executives, there was nothing minor about baseball in the smaller communities of America.

# TWO

# BREAKING THE MONOPOLY

THE MODERN ORGANIZATION of baseball may have developed under the glare of a greedy bartender. The story, perhaps apocryphal (but too good not to relate), is that, in 1893, Ban Johnson, a Cincinnati sportswriter, met with Charles Comiskey in a saloon that included an institution known as the Ten Minute Club. A variation on Happy Hour, each table had to order a round of drinks every ten minutes or the lagging customers would be asked to leave. At some point in the festivities, Johnson and Comiskey decided to resurrect the Western Association as the Western League. In ten years the National League monopoly would be broken by the Western League, but the minor leagues would become locked into an even more stifling structure of organized baseball.

According to a more prosaic history, the Western Association was reformed after the 1893 baseball season, a campaign in which it did not even compete. Comiskey was the player-manager of Cincinnati in the National League, and while on a scouting tour in the south, he met two former owners of Western Association clubs who were interested in reestablishing the League.

Comiskey recommended Johnson for the League presidency, and he was elected at November meetings in 1893. The new Western League comprised teams in Detroit, Grand Rapids, Indianapolis, Kansas City, Milwaukee, Minneapolis, Sioux City, and Toledo. Sioux City won the pennant in the inaugural 1894 season but drew only 42,000 fans for the year. Despite such disappointing attendance figures, all eight teams completed their seasons, and seven of the clubs turned a profit.

After that successful beginning, Johnson was prepared to return to journalism, but he decided to remain with the League after being goaded into believing that an old antagonist, John Brush, was plotting to remove him. Brush, the owner of the National League's Cincinnati franchise, had had a bitter relationship with Johnson for several years. Not only was Johnson unanimously reelected as president of the Western League, but he also persuaded Charles Comiskey to reject a new contract from Brush to continue with Cincinnati in favor of taking over the ownership of the struggling Sioux City franchise. Comiskey moved the club to St. Paul, where it became profitable immediately.

JOHN BRUSH IN certain respects evoked the values of baseball's earliest days. He tried to project the mystique of the gentlemen's clubs while also keeping a keen eye on the Cincinnati treasury. To him the sport was a profession, but the players, he thought, should be held to standards approaching amateurism both in compensation and comportment.

Brush took the lead in trying to impose Victorian standards on the players. David Voigt describes his effort in 1898 to impose the "Brush Resolution," "Goaded by Brush into puritanic fervor, the magnates endorsed the twenty-one point resolution, which would punish players with expulsion for such indiscretions as umpire-baiting and 'villainously filthy language.'"[1]

During the 1890s the National League owners fought fiercely among themselves. Most were sorely provoked by Andrew Freedman, the erratic owner of the New York Giants, and others feared that Brush's attempt to force Puritan standards on the players would trigger a disastrous lawsuit. Weak franchises battled stronger ones for a more equitable distribution of gate receipts. Schedules, salaries, Sunday baseball, and roster disputes were further grist for organizational battles.

Indeed, running the National League in the 1890s would have been a monumental challenge to the strongest executive. After the collapse of the Players League and the American Association, the National League was half again the size that Hulbert had insisted it should remain. The twelve franchises split into camps, with Baltimore, Brooklyn, Cincinnati, Cleveland, Louisville, and Washington, the struggling clubs, allied against powerful franchises in Boston, Chicago, New York, Philadelphia, Pittsburgh, and St. Louis.

The unwieldy size and the contentious owners were only two of the problems that an aspiring NL president would have faced. More troublesome still, the game had become a mess. As Bill James has noted, "A first baseman would grab the belt of the baserunner to hold him back a half-second after the ball was hit. Occasionally players tripped one another as they rounded the bases. Fights broke out from day to day. Players shoved umpires, spat on them, abused them in every manner short of assault. Fans hurled insults and beer bottles at the players of opposing teams."[2]

Enough people tired of that style of play that they stopped going to the park, complicating the owners' financial problems. One remedy for the clubs lay in an old device of that era, syndicate ownership. In a famous example, Baltimore owner Harry Von der Horst acquired a share of the Brooklyn franchise in exchange for Orioles manager Ned Hanlon, Wee Willie

Keeler, Hughie Jennings, Joe Kelley, and pitcher Jim Hughes, who had won twenty-three games for Baltimore in 1898, his rookie year. The revitalized Brooklyn Superbas then won the National League championship in 1899 and 1900.

Proponents of syndicate ownership saw it as a way to diffuse financial risks, similar to hedging a bet at the racetrack. When the syndicate included a major league club and one in the minors, a fledgling farm system was created that could aid player development. But one obvious drawback was that, as a lowly franchise improved, its best players could be transferred to a contender if one person had a controlling interest in both clubs.

This very practice of using one team to aid another was being exercised at the time by John Brush, who used the minor league draft both to improve his Cincinnati club and to create havoc within the Western League.

In his biography of Ban Johnson, Eugene Murdock describes the effects of the draft on Minneapolis, the champion of the Western League in 1896. Raided by the National League after the 1896 season, the club barely avoided last place in 1897. The finish was especially discouraging because the team had spent a substantial amount of money improving its ball park. The fans who had flocked to the park in 1896 to see a championship team stayed away the following year, turning Minneapolis into a marginal franchise.

Marcus Hayne, the Minneapolis president, objected to National League president Nicholas Young. Hayne correctly pointed out that such casual treatment of the minors would inevitably come back to haunt the major league teams. His point has been made many times in the history of organized baseball, but it is only appreciated by the majors when the adverse effects of their behavior are brought directly home.

Aggravating the problem, when the National League teams returned drafted players to the minors, they frequently sent them to competitors of their former clubs. The National Agreement did not require that drafted players be sent back to their original teams. The resulting chaotic effects on player development policies were a constant grievance of the minor league owners, and John Brush's abuse of the draft was particularly galling to Ban Johnson.

Brush owned the Indianapolis team in the Western League, as well as Cincinnati. He forged an exclusive agreement to bolster both his major and minor league clubs. Brush would send players from Cincinnati to Indianapolis for the sole purpose of defeating a rival in a critical series. After Indianapolis opened some breathing room, the Cincinnati players were moved back up.

Brush also used the draft to transfer players from one minor league team to Indianapolis after laundering them in Cincinnati. The practice caused the Western League to divide draft money equally throughout the circuit so that Brush's dealings with Indianapolis would provide at least some financial benefits to the other members of the Western League. The impact was minimal, and it failed to deter Brush.

Brush directly challenged the Western League in obvious attempts to strike at Johnson. He tried to get the National Board, baseball's governing body under the National Agreement, to undercut the Western League and reorganize it with Brush supporters. Johnson was able to defuse this plot.

Brush's provocations were good examples of the National League's misplaced arrogance. He was backing the Western League into a corner, thereby unwittingly aiding Johnson's long-term plan to break the National Agreement and challenge the National League monopoly.

Johnson bided his time, not only to improve the competitive base of his teams, but also to improve the quality of the game in the Western League. Johnson shared with Brush a revulsion at the brutal tactics and behavior of the National League players. Murdock reports that Johnson believed the college game exemplified what baseball should be. He also thought it was imperative to improve the status of the umpire: "My determination was to pattern baseball in this new league along the lines of scholastic contests, to make ability and brains and clean, honorable play not the swinging of clenched fists, coarse oaths, riots or assaults upon the umpires decide the issue."³ In that mission, Johnson was swimming against a strong current. As with hockey in our time, the owners appeared to favor fighting and rowdiness.

Johnson's efforts to improve the game in the Western League were hampered further by the paralysis of leadership in the National League. The owners' rivalries precluded any sensible strategy for improving the quality of baseball. Proposals to tame the rowdy behavior of the players were merely cynical power plays in an effort to control men whose pay was already stifled by the monopoly.

Other minor leagues were finding their place in the game, building new ball parks, developing loyal followings, and generating excitement over local stars; but the minors remained in a precarious position because of the power of the National League. Any glittering success by a minor league franchise would invariably draw the attention of the League. Unless the minor league had the kind of executive skills that Johnson displayed in his battles with Brush, the National League could be expected to press its advantage.

AS THE ORGANIZATIONAL battles approached their climax, the minors foreshadowed what baseball would offer America in the new century. The daring base running typified by Ty Cobb of the Detroit Tigers was displayed earlier by George Hogriever, who began his career with Hamilton of the Tri-State League in 1889. Hogriever played for a number of minor league teams over the next twenty-three years. In 1894, while with Sioux City of the Western League, Hogriever stole ninety-three bases in only 126 games. That was the team that won the championship in Ban Johnson's first year in the Western League. Hogriever's career then took a turn that aggravated Western League owners. Drafted by John Brush, Hogriever played sixty-nine games for Cincinnati in 1895 and then was sent down to Indianapolis, where he remained until his thirties. Hogriever established the minor league record for career stolen bases, with 948.

Bill Krieg was another great player of that era. His career ran from 1883 through 1901, primarily with teams in the Western Association. Krieg had played major league ball in the Union Association, the American Association, and the National League, but his highest average in those leagues was .255 for Washington in 1886. That was only his third year in professional baseball, and he soon developed into a consistently good hitter. Krieg would lead his league in hitting three times. In 1895 with Rockford of the Western Association, he had an outstanding season, leading the League with 237 hits, fourteen triples, eleven home runs, and a .452 batting average. Krieg remained with Rockford, won another batting title in 1895, and then moved to Brockton of the New England League. He ended his career with Terre Haute in the Three-I League in 1901, finishing with a career average of .335.

Ernest "Kid" Mohler was a left-handed second baseman who overcame that handicap and a meager .264 career batting average to play from 1890 to 1914. Mohler supplied some offense with 776 stolen bases for fourteen teams from London, Ontario, to San Francisco. Edward "Deacon" Van Buren was another reliable minor leaguer of that period. From 1895 to 1914, he compiled a .272 batting average during a career that, like Mohler's, migrated steadily west.

More successful was a first baseman named Percival Wheritt Werden. At six foot, two inches, and 210 pounds, Perry Werden was one of the first great power hitters of the minor leagues. His best year was 1895 for Minneapolis of the Western League, when he hit forty-five home runs and batted .428, both marks leading the League. To go with his power, Werden also stole 350 bases during his eighteen-year career, although a weight problem slowed him in his final years.

Werden's career suggests how uncertain a ball player's fortunes could be. He began his career with the Union Association in 1884 as a pitcher and outfielder, compiling a 12–1 record on the mound with a .237 batting average. After that league folded, Werden did not return to the majors until 1888, when he joined Washington for three games at the end of the season. In ten at-bats, Werden got three hits with two RBIs, but the next season found him at Toledo of the International Association, where he led the League with a .394 batting average.

The following year, 1890, Werden was with Toledo of the American Association, where he hit .295 with a league-leading twenty triples. He moved to Baltimore for the AA's final year and hit .290. Werden was picked up by St. Louis in the National League, and he dropped to .258 in 1892 before rebounding to .276 with a league-leading twenty-nine triples in 1893.

Despite those numbers, Werden was dropped from St. Louis and moved to Minneapolis, where he posted his best stats. In 1897 he was back in the majors with Louisville, one of the players from that great Minneapolis club that was raided by the major league draft. A .302 batting average was not enough to keep him in the big league. Back at Minneapolis he missed the 1898 season with a broken leg but hit .346 for the Millers in 1899. Minneapolis was part of the American League's first season in 1900, and Werden batted .315 while leading the league with eight home runs and thirty-nine doubles.

In 1901 the Minneapolis franchise moved to Chicago and became the White Sox, but Werden was with St. Paul of the new Western League. His final seasons were spent in the American Association, the Southern League, the Northern League, and finally the Cotton State League, where he played for Hattiesburg in 1905 and Vicksburg in 1906. One unsuccessful pinch-hit appearance for Indianapolis in the American Association ended Werden's career in 1908. He finished with a .341 minor league batting average and a respectable .282 major league mark.

The odyssey of Perry Werden raises some interesting questions about professional baseball in the 1890s. Why couldn't he stick with a major league team despite decent numbers in the majors and excellent marks in the minors?

Perhaps a significant gap in the quality of major and minor

league play had opened and an appropriate division in organized ball had developed. We might also speculate that Werden ran afoul of some of the behavioral codes of the major league owners. Equally plausible, Werden may have preferred life in the Western League. Under Johnson's leadership, it had the best reputation of that era, and though the pay was probably marginally better in the majors, other factors may have tilted Werden's preferences toward the minors.

But the best answer appears to be that the question itself is not a good one. Inevitably, when considering an outstanding minor league player, one asks why he did not play longer in the majors. Some players appeared in the majors briefly, then enjoyed brilliant minor league careers. Others never had a chance at all, while still others might have played well in the majors for a significant period before moving down to the minors. Baseball historians of that period stress that the concept of a player "moving down to the minors" is misplaced.[4] The leagues were not so far apart in salary and playing conditions that the major league game was compellingly attractive.

The important point about players like Perry Werden is not where they played but that they did play. They helped to spread baseball's appeal all over America. They entertained thousands of fans who never had a chance to see a "major league" game, and they undoubtedly inspired youngsters to chance careers in baseball. Few players have left more important legacies than that.

Another outstanding player in the Western League at that time was Daniel "Bud" Lally, who was a teammate of Werden's on the Minneapolis teams of 1895–97. Lally went to St. Louis during the 1897 season, further decimating the Millers. He hit .279 in eighty-seven National League games and then was returned to Columbus, one of the Millers' competitors in the Western League. Lally played all over the country in a career that extended from 1887 to 1905. He broke in with Haverhill of the New England League and later played in Toronto, Memphis, Atlanta, Butte, and other towns. His career batting average was .308, suggesting that even a quality player could expect little stability in his life. By personal choice or the fortunes of the game, ball players of that era were on the move, frequently away from the big time that remained confined to the northeastern section of the country.

IN ADDITION TO those players who never really cracked the majors, some of the game's immortals were perfecting their craft in the 1890s in the minors, out of the spotlight. A. D. Suehsdorf traced Honus Wagner's first year in professional ball.[5] Wagner began with Steubenville, Ohio, of the Inter-State League, but that team moved to Akron after seven games. The franchise collapsed after another five games, and Wagner was signed by Mansfield. Teams that had been scheduled for a week against Mansfield went bust, and that loss of revenue forced Mansfield itself to fold for the season. In June Wagner moved to the Adrian Demons of the Michigan State League. Two of his mates were George Wilson and Vasco Graham, black players who had been signed from Bud Fowler's Page Fence Giants. A month later, Wagner left for the Warren Wonders in Pennsylvania, a franchise in the Iron and Oil League. Allegations were made that racial tension contributed to Wagner's departure from the Demons, but those charges are not confirmed. Wagner finished the season with Warren. He compiled a batting average for that year of approximately .360, but his erratic fielding hardly suggested the grace with which he would dominate the shortstop position for the Pittsburgh Pirates.

The following year, Wagner played for Ed Barrow in Paterson of the Atlantic League. In 1897 Louisville of the National League acquired Wagner, complicating the life of an aspiring third baseman named Tommy Leach. As Leach told the story, he was playing for Auburn of the New York State League in 1898 and was told by the owner that he would be sold to either Washington or Louisville of the National League. Given the choice, Leach asked where he would be most likely to get a chance to play regularly. He was told to avoid Washington because they had a gifted third baseman named Wagner. While sitting on the bench at Louisville, Leach had the chance to watch his team's regular third baseman make a spectacular play. He asked who the player was and was informed that it was Wagner, the best third baseman in the League. Leach assumed he had been given erroneous information about Wagner's location until he discovered that the Wagner at Washington was Honus's brother Al.[6]

Leach's confusion is still experienced by baseball historians today. Suehsdorf meticulously records the problems with developing accurate histories of that period. Not only did Wagner have a brother who played with him on the Steubensville/ Akron team, but Honus himself was referred to as "Will." By the end of the season, he was known as "John," which gives a researcher a reasonable chance of identifying him. More difficult is the condition of statistical information. Box scores are not always available, especially for teams that would begin full of spring hope and then founder financially by Independence Day. Some box scores cannot be obtained because local newspapers did not publish on holidays. These limitations must temper any judgment about why a player like Perry Werden did not stay in the National League. It simply is not possible to apply a statistical evaluation to players of that era with the same confidence one would have today.

BY THE CLOSE of the nineteenth century, Ban Johnson had attracted some of the best executive talent in baseball to his Western League. He recruited Connie Mack to manage the Milwaukee club and with that one move improved the quality of the league dramatically. Mack's stature as a gentleman and strategist remains unrivaled. Donald Honig tells of a confrontation between Mack and umpire Bill McGowan after a close play at third base:

"That man looked safe to me, Mr. McGowan," said Mack.

"No, Mr. Mack," said Mr. McGowan, "he was out."
Feeling the patriarch's keen blue eyes contemplating
his judgment, the umpire felt constrained to add, "I
wouldn't lie to you, Mr. Mack."

"No, you wouldn't, Mr. McGowan," said Mr. Mack.
"Thank you."[7]

Along with Mack, Johnson secured the assistance of John
McGraw, Charles Comiskey, and Clark Griffith. Comiskey and
Griffith had been leaders of the Brotherhood movement, and
they, along with Mack, would launch a raid on National
League rosters that would shatter the salary restrictions of the
1890s. It is ironic that as owners, Mack, Comiskey, and Griffith
were among the tightest with their payrolls.

THE SERIES OF organizational gambits that established the
business structure of baseball in the twentieth century began
with some adjustments by the National League. The twelve-
team format that the League had employed in the 1890s was
trimmed back to eight teams in 1900. Baltimore, Cleveland,
Louisville, and Washington were abandoned. The League was
now the size that William Hulbert had favored, but still no one
was able to reconcile the contention among the owners. Freedman eventually left the Giants, but John Brush became the
team's new owner. Brush and other supporters of Freedman
remained locked in turmoil with the other League owners.

Ban Johnson made two adjustments in his own league. In
1899 the Western League had teams in Detroit, Grand Rapids,
Kansas City, Milwaukee, Minneapolis, St. Paul, and Toledo. A
five-year charter for the Western League was set to expire, and
Johnson used the occasion to reconstitute the League. For the
1900 season, the Western was rechristened the American
League, with teams in Buffalo, Chicago, Cleveland, Detroit, Indianapolis, Milwaukee, and Minneapolis.

The new title did not change the fact that the American League was a minor circuit still bound by the National Agreement, including submission to a draft by National League franchises. If there was any doubt that the American League was considered a poor relation, it should have been dispelled by the treatment given Charles Comiskey when he moved his St. Paul franchise to Chicago in 1900.

Comiskey was permitted to relocate so long as his team played on the South Side near the malodorous stockyards. The White Sox were subject to a special draft by the Cubs, and the American League team was not allowed to use the name "Chicago" before "White Sox." The conditions, but not the implied status, were accepted.

The National League owners tried to counter Johnson's maneuvers through an old device, the re-creation of the American Association to undermine the new threat to their monopoly. But this time they were too weak and divided to respond effectively. Spurred by the possible revival of the AA, Johnson made his move in 1901.

Conceivably, the American League could have remained in the midwest anticipating the westward expansion of the country. Instead, every original Western League city was abandoned. The new American League sites were Baltimore, Boston, Chicago, Cleveland, Detroit, Milwaukee, Philadelphia, and Washington. In 1902 the Milwaukee franchise moved to St. Louis, and one year later the Baltimore Orioles became the New York entry that the American League needed. The alignment of American League clubs for the next fifty years was set.

The new league might have been a great opportunity for the players because Johnson initially agreed that the reserve clause should be illegal. He opposed the breaking of contracts in mid-season, but he believed that once the season ended a contract expired and a player could consider competing offers. This willingness to accommodate some of the players' demands helped the American League to attract some of the NL's top players. But once the American League achieved its objective of parity with the National League, Johnson accepted the re-

serve clause rather than radically change the game's labor relations.

Johnson apparently preferred to establish the American
League with the blessing of the National League owners. He
requested an appearance before them in their winter meetings
of 1900 but was rudely dismissed. Coupled with the NL's
abusive treatment of its players, the conditions pointed to another labor war.

Most public attention at this time was focused on the luring
of star National League players such as Napoleon Lajoie and
Cy Young to the American League, but the pending battle for
talent had serious implications for the minor leagues as well.
The ten-year National Agreement was due to expire in 1901.
The American League did not consider the Agreement binding, since they claimed equal status with the National League.
The Nationals announced their abrogation of the pact in September 1901. The minors feared the effects on their clubs of a
war between the major league rivals, and they responded by
meeting to form a central governing body, the National Association of Professional Baseball Leagues.

*The Sporting News* blasted the National League for abandoning the National Agreement, describing the move as "a
foolhardy step and asinine departure from the regular."[8] The
new alliance among the minor leagues was expected to challenge the abuse of power that had characterized the National
League for so long. Baseball's bible anticipated that when a
new charter was drafted for organized baseball, the minors
would play an important part in writing the document.

While the minor leagues were threatened by the National
and American leagues, the competition for players between
the AL and NL focused primarily on the American League's
signing of players who had finished seasons with National
League clubs. Lajoie was the most dramatic case, and when he
transferred from the Philadelphia Phillies to the Philadelphia
Athletics, lawsuits were filed to prevent his playing in Pennsylvania. When the Phillies prevailed in court, Johnson persuaded
Connie Mack to trade Lajoie to Cleveland, beyond the court's
jurisdiction.

With all of the strife, it was only a matter of time before the pressure of a free labor market would unify the owners. In January 1903 representatives of the two major leagues met and concluded a truce that resolved player disputes, set up a structure to govern the game, and created the World Series. The agreement that ended the competition between the two leagues preserved the reserve clause, and banned farm systems but permitted unlimited drafting of minor league players and prevented other characteristics of a competitive market from intruding on the new order.

Ban Johnson's assault on the National League had provided the breath of life to a staggering organization. His two objections to the National League of the 1890s appear to have been to the brutality of the game itself and the inefficiency of its management. Johnson reversed both of those liabilities. The success of the American League preserved the essential qualities of organized baseball but subordinated the minor leagues to the commercial interests of the major league owners.

THE RUMBLINGS FROM the Western League alerted many observers to the pending attack on the National League monopoly. The expectation that Johnson's strategy would include an invasion of eastern markets opened the doors for another league to represent the midwest.

When Ban Johnson revived the Western League in 1894, he did so by abandoning traditional midwestern cities, specifically Omaha, St. Joseph, Lincoln, and Des Moines. These cities combined with Rock Island–Moline, Peoria, Jacksonville, and Quincy in Illinois to form the Western Association. Des Moines came to dominate the circuit, although their nickname, the Prohibitionists was apparently as far from accurate a description of the players as possible. Whatever the state of their sobriety, Des Moines so dominated the 1896 race that league president Tom Hickey declared a split season. But that strategy failed to raise interest in the campaign, and even Des Moines had trouble drawing its own bored fans.

By 1899 the Western Association was a financial bust, but it was able to seize the new opportunities opened by Johnson's raid on the National League. The American League's move east left the midwest bereft of some quality franchises. To fill that void, Tom Hickey pursued his own ambitious dreams. In 1900, after the first eastward move of the American League, Hickey took the abandoned Western League name and applied it to clubs in Denver, Des Moines, Omaha, Pueblo, Sioux City, and St. Joseph.

When the American League made its final relocation, Hickey revealed his ultimate plan. He secured Kansas City and Milwaukee, bringing the Western League to eight teams. He then announced plans for a second high-level minor league in the midwest. Taking the name American Association, the new circuit would include teams in Columbus, Indianapolis, Kansas City, Louisville, Milwaukee, Minneapolis, St. Paul, and Toledo. The Western League would then be limited to Colorado Springs, Denver, Lincoln, Omaha, Sioux City, and St. Joseph.

Hickey was fiercely opposed in this scheme by Western League owners. Forced to choose between his leagues, he went with the American Association, and he put teams in Minneapolis, St. Paul, and Kansas City, important cities to the Western League. For several years the American Association operated as an outlaw league, meaning that it did not have the blessing of baseball's new organizational hierarchy. The territorial and player disputes were resolved before the start of the 1904 season, and the American Association became one of the premier minor leagues of the twentieth century.

BY THE START of the twentieth century, the organization of baseball had assumed some of its defining characteristics. First, through the reserve clause, the owners dominated the players. Competitive markets for players were limited to shaky upstarts such as the American Association of the 1880s and the Union League. The idea of an association like the Players League in the twentieth century was becoming inconceivable.

Territorial distribution of teams favored the most secure markets. The sixteen teams of the major leagues were located in just ten cities. Only Cincinnati, Cleveland, Detroit, Pittsburgh, and Washington had a single team. Boston, Chicago, Philadelphia, and St. Louis each had two clubs, and New York had three. Locating franchises in smaller cities with potential for growth was too risky for the owners.

The minors saw themselves as an integral part of the new organization, but they were not. The League Alliance, the abuse of the American Association, the farming during the Brotherhood rebellion, and the manipulation of the draft by John Brush all indicate how the National League owners scorned the minor leagues.

Ban Johnson's aspirations were limited to achieving equal status for the Western League. His challenge was not intended to upgrade the conditions for all the minors, so the National League monopoly was again expanded rather than broken. Once the Western League had completed its transformation, it forgot its roots.

# Three

# THE MINORS
# ORGANIZE

AT THE TURN of the century, minor league baseball received its official stamp of inferiority. This organizational stigma was part of the truce of 1903 that ended the free competition for players between the American and National Leagues; ironically, the minors themselves were a party to the agreement through their new governing body, the National Association of Professional Baseball Leagues. Professional leagues that had been independent combined to form an elaborate organization that created a hierarchy among the leagues and sacrificed independence for security. The association recognized the American and National Leagues as major leagues and divided its own circuits into Class A, B, C, and D.

Very little about this new pecking order reflected the quality of baseball in the minors; rather, the National Association agreed to it for business reasons, as John B. Foster revealed in

1926 in his book *A History of the National Association of Professional Base Ball Leagues.* The Association itself published this volume in honor of its twenty-fifth anniversary. Nothing quite tips the hand of baseball executives like their own accounts of the game's history, and Foster clarified the priorities of the Association at the time of its founding:

> Property rights in 1901 were not rights; players refused to abide by contracts that were deemed essentially sound; players who had been admirably treated by their employers openly sought bidders for their services and denied any claim upon them, even when it was evident that it was by the assistance of those upon whom they shamelessly turned their backs that they had been advanced in the profession of ball playing. All this the projectors of the National Association set out to readjust, and to rectify, and they did so. Their reward is in their present condition of perfected organization.[1]

The condition that Foster paternalistically condemned was the third of the so-called "baseball wars," an ominous description for the free labor markets that were created when maverick owners defied the reserve clause.

This battle between the American and National Leagues forced the minors to evaluate their place in professional baseball. According to Foster, "The minor leagues emerged from the situation of helpless abandonment into which they had been cast until at length they were in that position where they could assert their full right as party of the second part to any future legislation and allotment of base ball values."[2]

Foster invariably equated the owners' financial interests with baseball's moral foundation. "Base ball values" referred to monopoly, the reserve clause, and other policies that enhanced the owners' profits and control of the game. In time, an antitrust exemption and the financing of stadiums through public treasuries would be added to the list of "values," creating a curious system of ethics for these capitalists who ostensibly were so committed to free and private enterprise.

When the National League announced its abrogation of its agreement with the minors, Tom Hickey, the president of the new Western League, called for a meeting of all minor league presidents. Seven leagues replied, and a meeting was set for Chicago on September 5, 1901. Assembled with Hickey were Pat Powers, president of the Eastern League (the forerunner of the International League); Michael Sexton, president of the Three-I League (consisting of teams in Illinois, Indiana, and Iowa); John Farrell, president of the New York State League (later the Eastern League); W. H. Lucas, president of the Pacific Northwest League; William Meyer, Jr., president of the Western Association; and T. H. Murnane, president of the New England League. Statements of support were also received from the Southern Association, the California League, the North Carolina League, and the Connecticut League.

The representatives met for two days in Chicago, reconvening in New York the following month. On October 25, 1901, a new National Agreement was announced to govern the minors for ten years. Its provisions included the restoration of the reserve clause and the imposition of salary limits. A National Board of Arbitration was established to enforce discipline especially against any party who tampered with the reserve clause. The Agreement was later incorporated into the National and American Leagues' decision in 1903 to share the major league monopoly. At that time the minor league's National Association was recognized by the major leagues as their official subordinate, and the Association expressed its gratitude for being, as Foster put it, "the party of the second part."

Foster's account of the founding of the National Association could be dismissed as a relic of the Roaring Twenties if the Association had not published an update of its history in 1952. *The Story of Minor League Baseball*, written in part by Robert Finch, expanded Foster's version of events. Baseball's third free labor market was described not only as a "war" but as "a death struggle."

In this fifty-year history, Finch concluded that, "the most significant feature of these early days is the revelation, by all that they did, of the sense of obligation felt by the pioneers for the well-being of the game. . . ." The impression is very strong that the Founders of the National Association were, basically, lovers of the game of baseball rather than merely business men, and that they assumed the role of battlers for the right chiefly because they wanted the game to live and thrive in this country."[3]

These pieties express the orthodox view of American baseball that insists the sport is not really a business at all but a pastime provided to the public through the owners' generosity. Because the owners are not interested in money, players who apply pressure for higher salaries are spoiled ingrates. Worse yet the players' union is a radical threat to the goose that is laying this golden egg. Since baseball is not really a business, antitrust law need not apply, and communities should show the proper feudal spirit by building stadiums for their sports franchises.

This orthodox view is Babbitry at its finest, as the executives' own statements demonstrate. Finch's description of the first baseball war includes this description of the Union Association's attack on the reserve clause: "Experience had not yet taught baseball men that this clause was to become the cornerstone of professional baseball."[4] The reserve clause was indeed the cornerstone of professional baseball because the real game until the 1970s was the game of owners controlling players.

The organization of the minor leagues in 1901 presented an opportunity to break from the monopolistic practices that had governed the game as well as from the simpleminded rhetoric that masked such tactics. When the minor leagues formed their National Association in 1901, they might have stated clearly that they represented businesses, not pseudocharities, and that, in the tradition of American enterprise, they were prepared to assume risks and to outperform their competition.

They might have fought for autonomy or for equality with the American and National Leagues. They might have experimented with a freer labor market that would have permitted some serious competition among the teams. Instead, they meekly accepted a secondary role in the game, hiding behind the same mindless platitudes that the National League had mouthed for years. That decision was unfortunate because the minor league game had much more going for it than its representatives in the National Association were willing to recognize.

WHILE THE OWNERS and executives created a stifling organization for baseball, the game itself was thriving. From the remnants of Ban Johnson's Western League, the American Association became the dominant minor league of the midwest. In California the Pacific Coast League was organized in 1903, drawing together franchises that could be traced to the Civil War. The International League competed successfully in eastern markets close to major league cities. The southern leagues completed the national base of the minors, a foundation on which the major leagues would rely for players and ultimately for markets.

While many of the players and teams in these minor leagues were the match of some of their major league cohorts, baseball in the hinterlands certainly lacked the resources and comforts of the majors. Since many of the players were just starting professional careers, it was extremely difficult to tell which of them might become "the Franchise." Complicating that task were haphazard scouting systems and the uncertain communication between the field and home office.

The problems with scouting and signing star players were recounted in a delightful book, *Humor Among the Minors: True Tales from the Baseball Brush*, written in 1911 by Edward Ashenback, the manager of Syracuse in the New York State League. Ashenback describes getting his start in the minors in 1890 with the Canton, Ohio, franchise. The job was provided by a friend with connections to the Cincinnati club of the National League. At the end of Canton's season, Ashenback returned to Cincinnati, where his friend asked if he had seen any major league talent. Ashenback told of a player he had met in Canton when first looking for the team's hotel: "I well remember our arrival there. The players evidently did not like my companion's makeup, for loud was the laughter and irritating the jibes that were hurled our way. The laughter and jibes, however, ceased the instant my companion stepped on the field the next day." It turned out that his companion, Cy Young, could pitch a little. "With this information, [my friend] rushed to the Cincinnati management but they failed to act, and a few days after this incident my companion pitched his first game in major league circles, wearing a Cleveland uniform, against Anson's Chicago club, giving them a measly three hits."[5]

Ashenback later owned the Charleston franchise of the South Atlantic League, a Class-C circuit. The Augusta, Georgia, team had a player whom Ashenback wanted desperately. Augusta was owned by a Mr. Carter, who resisted Ashenback's offers until the coveted outfielder misplayed a line drive in the ninth inning, costing Augusta a game against Charleston. Angrily, Carter told Ashenback that he could have Ty Cobb; when he had calmed down, he still agreed to sell the Georgia Peach for twenty-five dollars. Ashenback gave Carter the check and was told to expect Cobb on Monday's train to Charleston. The train arrived but Cobb did not. The following day a letter arrived from Carter with the explanation. Cobb had been claimed by the Detroit Tigers, who had been given the right to any player on the Augusta team because the Tigers had lent the Georgia team one of their pitchers, Eddie Cicotte. Ashenback concluded by writing that he still had headaches whenever he thought of how close he had come to getting Ty Cobb for a pittance. One can imagine the postscript Ashenback might have written a few years later, after Cicotte was banished from baseball as one of the Black Sox.

Before his days in South Carolina, Ashenback had owned

the Hampton team of the Virginia League. Still trying to help his friends in Cincinnati, he told them of another terrific pitcher he had seen on the Norfolk team. Ashenback described the lad as "a big strapping stripling of a youngster. . . . Here, indeed was a diamond in the rough, showing by his every action on the field that he was a coming star."[6] But Cincinnati's management was just as obtuse about Christy Mathewson as they had been about Cy Young. They ignored Ashenback's reports, and the New York Giants finally secured the great pitcher.

The tactics used in getting Matty to the big leagues show how the minors were treated at that time. The Giants took Mathewson from Norfolk with a promise to pay the club $2,000 if Mathewson stuck with New York. Subsequently Cincinnati drafted Mathewson from Norfolk and sent the standard compensation of $100. Cincinnati then traded Mathewson to New York for Amos Rusie, an aging star. New York got Mathewson in exchange for Rusie, Cincinnati got Rusie for $100, and Norfolk got the short end of the deal.

Norfolk and the Virginia League battled the Giants for years over the scam. They finally went to court and were represented by John Montgomery Ward, the star player from the 1880s who had organized the players against the reserve clause and had become a lawyer after his retirement from baseball. The litigation was successful, and the $2,000 was finally paid to Norfolk; but the incident lingers as an example of the petty bullying that characterized much of the majors' treatment of the minor leagues.

THE CONDITIONS AT the ball parks were another part of the special charm of the minor league game. Alfred H. Spink, a founder of *The Sporting News*, related a story by Frank Isbell of the Chicago White Sox from Isbell's minor league days at St. Paul. Isbell was pitching in a game against Minneapolis in 1898. Two runs up in the bottom of the ninth, Isbell had two out but two runners on base. The teams were playing in a park that had been built for Sunday baseball when the game was prohibited within city limits. The field was smaller than desirable, and a tall fence had been constructed to prevent cheap home runs. Line drives bounced back into play and restricted the offense. Isbell recalled that "the next man at bat lined out a high fly. It struck the high center field fence about twelve feet from the ground and everybody was certain we had the game won. But we didn't. The ball struck the fence—and stayed there. It struck directly on the sharp end of a wire nail, and before we could get a step ladder and climb up after it the Minneapolis nine had its three runs in and the game was over."[7] Major league parks of the day were less than architectural marvels, but they apparently never speared a ball in play.

Disastrous grandstand fires had already encouraged the building of new major league stadiums of cement and steel, but the minor league franchises often could not afford such luxuries. Rocks were the least of the problems in some of these fields. Gopher holes and drought devastated many of the minors' facilities and decided the outcome of some of the games.

Ashenback recalled some of the parks he had seen in his tour of the minors. The "horse restaurant" in Rome, New York, was adjacent to the barns of a fairground. In Troy, New York, the ball park was on an island in the Hudson River with wooden platforms extending the outfield above the water. Parks were built beside slag heaps, cemeteries, and shanties.

Galveston, Texas, and Atlantic City, New Jersey, had parks on the beach, and players struggled in the heavy sand. Batters in Oswego, New York, found nearby Lake Ontario reflected the sun like a mirror. Appalachian ball parks incorporated mountain climbing for fans who had to reach parks atop mountain ranges. The rugged terrain was sometimes also part of the playing field, and Ashenback's praise of Nashville's right fielder may be the only case of a player being lauded for playing his position like "a Rocky Mountain goat."

The ball park in St. Paul had its own problems. It was known as "the Cigar Box" because of the imposing telegraph poles that surrounded the park. The dimensions were so small that right fielders were frequently charged with errors if they failed to throw batters out at first.

Johnstown, Pennsylvania, apparently concluded from its catastrophic flood that portability is a virtue. The playing field for its entry in the Tri-State League slid on rollers into barns when the game was concluded, and the grounds were then made available for the town's children.[8]

Aside from conditions on the field, these early stadiums were short on such amenities as clubhouses, so finding a place to change from street clothes to uniform and back could be a challenge. Ashenback tells of renting a house next to the park in Haverhill, Massachusetts, for the players to dress. After being thrown out of a game by the umpire, Ashenback returned to the dressing room, only to hear the landlady on the roof screaming at the umpire who had just thrown out the visiting catcher from the game as well, "arousing the ire of the worthy lady. In a minute I was out on the roof beside the worthy Celt, who tried so hard to protect her tenants, and before I knew it we were both coaching my club on. The crowd went wild, evidently appreciating the old Irish lady's sincerity in her efforts." The unfortunate umpire also used the house for his quarters. "He appeared in due time, but, out into the street went his clothes, the landlady wildly yelling that no 'thieving empire' could even take his hat off in her residence."[9] Ashenback received a five-dollar fine from the league president, encouraging him to find a more suitable place for his troops.

The park could also be a place for spectacular stunts. At a game in Dayton, Ohio, in the early 1890s, a hot-air balloon ascended over the ball park, and out jumped a young woman with a parachute. She landed on second base unscathed. The feat would be repeated (from an airplane) at Shea Stadium in the 1986 World Series, but in our more litigious age, the acrobat had some explaining to do before a New York judge.

◆ ◆ ◆

PARACHUTING WOMEN AND irate landladies were not the usual models for women at the ball park. Most teams tried to draw women to the normally male preserve in order to attract a more upscale crowd. Baseball needed a gentling effect. The game was equivalent to modern ice hockey, a crude and violent game only occasionally showing its potential for grace. With brutes dominating the playing field, it was not surprising that the stands were populated with drunks, pickpockets, gamblers, and thugs.

To counter that offensive and unprofitable trend, women were encouraged to come to the games. Steven Riess writes, "Female spectators were expected to enhance business by improving crowd behavior and by inducing their gentlemen friends to take them to ballgames. The custom of Ladies' Day was derived from a tradition of the amateur clubs of the late 1860s, when athletes invited their wives or sweethearts to the field on certain days."[10] Women could only take advantage of Ladies' Day when accompanied by a male escort, a practice that continued until World War I, just a few years before suffrage was granted.

Ladies' Day was used by suffragettes as an opportunity to promote their cause. They sponsored several baseball games, using the forum to generate support. "The first such affair," Riess notes, "was held on 25 July 1914, at a Newark ball game at which 2,000 suffragettes gathered to hear Ella Reeve Bloor deliver a feminist lecture. A game between an all-girls team and an all-boys team preceded the regular contest, and fans were swamped with literature."[11]

The success of these efforts at the minor league level was so good that they spread to major league parks. Legitimate scalping was used to raise money for the suffrage movement. Tickets were bought at a discount and resold at face value. Clubs were enthusiastic because the technique opened a new market for the game.

Ladies' Day itself was widely adopted in the minor leagues. "Women were admitted free every day in three cities [in the Southern Association], and in Atlanta and Nashville a one-dollar season pass entitled a female fan to a grandstand seat at twenty-five designated games. The system was so popular in Atlanta that nearly 1,000 women took advantage of it in 1908."[12]

The treatment of women at the games resembles the courtesies extended to abstemious fans at some of today's stadiums: "Club owners made special efforts to improve their facilities so that ladies would be comfortable and want to return. Security forces were bolstered and separate sections were often set aside for women and their gentlemen friends."[13] An obvious tension between enthusiastic fans from the working class and more sedate spectators from wealthier backgrounds had to be balanced at the ball park. Riess notes that photographs confirm that women tended to sit in box seats or grandstands, almost never in the bleachers where the working class would congregate.

HAD THE ROWDY style of 1890s baseball taken hold at the minor league level, the growth of the game in this century would have been seriously threatened. Instead, as minor league executives met in Chicago in 1901 to form the National Association, leagues all over the country were growing stronger. From the time of the American-National League truce in 1903 to the start of World War I in 1914, baseball thrived all over America.

During those years, the International League consisted of teams in Baltimore, Buffalo, Jersey City, Newark, Providence, Rochester, and Toronto. New stadium construction indicated the circuit's prosperity and the franchises' permanence. Well-known ballplayers who retired from major league competition continued to play in the minors, and the International League received its share of these veterans.

One of the best of these players was "Ironman" Joe McGinnity. The nickname actually referred to his off-season job in his father's iron foundry, but it fit his remarkable durability on the field as well, highlighted by the five times that he won both games of a doubleheader.

In a ten-year major league career, McGinnity won 247 games, and he retired with a career earned run average of 2.64. More remarkably, he was not through with baseball. At the age of thirty-seven, he left the Giants at the end of the 1908 season and crossed the Hudson River to pitch for the Newark Bears of the International League. He won twenty-nine games in the 1909 season, pitched 422 innings, and occasionally managed the club. He continued to pitch in the minors until 1925, when he finally retired from professional baseball at the age of fifty-four.

McGinnity's longevity was surpassed by "Orator" Jim O'Rourke, who as late as 1912 was making spot appearances at the age of sixty in the Connecticut League. This could be dismissed as a token gesture, but O'Rourke was a catcher, a position he played regularly even at the age of fifty-three. His incredible minor league career followed a major league stint that had lasted nineteen seasons and had been good enough to land O'Rourke in the Hall of Fame.

Fritz Maisel also enjoyed a long minor league career in the International League. He played from 1911–13 with Baltimore before a six-year career in the majors. He returned to Baltimore in 1919 and continued with that club until 1928. The third baseman set an International League record for runs scored with 1,379.

Edward Onslow was the International League's best example of a career minor leaguer. From 1913–29 he played seventeen seasons in the International League and set career records for that achievement as well as for games played (2,109), hits (2,445), and triples (128). During those years he had the proverbial "cups of coffee" in the majors, but he represents a type of player that for the most part no longer exists, one who has an extended career in the minors without a realistic hope of graduating to the big leagues.

Out west, the Pacific Coast League was organized in 1903, but it was leery of joining the National Association and was consequently labeled an "outlaw league." The geographic isolation and splendid climate produced an idyllic setting for baseball, with seasons of over 200 games extending from March to Thanksgiving. The PCL was reluctant to lose its status, which it considered equal to that of the National and American Leagues, circuits that were known in the west as the Eastern Leagues, but in 1904 it began its stormy membership in the National Association.

In its first season, the PCL fielded teams in Los Angeles, San Francisco, Oakland, Sacramento, Portland, and Seattle. Other communities that were intermittently part of the League included Tacoma, Hollywood, San Diego, Salt Lake City, Vernon, and Fresno. After the Pacific Coast League agreed to join organized baseball, its old rival, the California State League, assumed the role of an outlaw. By ignoring the reserve clause and paying higher salaries, an outlaw league could expect a coordinated attack from the established order, and the California State League was not disappointed.

The National Commission that governed the major leagues declared, in conjunction with the National Association, that players who had broken their contracts to join the outlaw league would be banned for life. Those who had failed to respect the reserve clause were given thirty days to comply, and other players were threatened with fines. For players such as Hal Chase, the threats were intimidating enough to force them back to organized baseball.

Probably the critical factor in ruining the California State League was the cooperation of the PCL with these edicts. If the two circuits had cooperated, they might have used their regional advantages to go their own way, since many players preferred the climate and life in the west, along with the longer season and higher pay.

The west offered the minors their best opportunity to challenge organized baseball. At critical points, the independence that had been asserted collapsed, and the California State League became another outlaw that was civilized. It settled for smaller markets in the great San Joaquin Valley of central California, while the PCL secured the more lucrative communities along the coast. Today the California State League operates as one of the Class-A leagues in the low minors.

In a kind of West Coast parallel of Joe McGinnity, George Van Haltren returned to the minors in 1904 after seventeen years in the majors, playing six years with Seattle and Oakland before retiring from the game. "Ping" Bodie and Harry Heilmann were stars in Los Angeles before their major league careers began. Heilmann was one of the first superstars to come out of the western game. He played with Cobb and Sam Crawford in the Detroit outfield, batted .342 for his career in the majors, and was inducted into the Hall of Fame in 1952. If the organizational moxie had been there in the early 1900s, a major league on the West Coast could have accommodated such local talent as the DiMaggio and Waner brothers, Tony Lazzeri, and other immortals.

The extra-long seasons of the Pacific Coast League called for especially durable pitchers. Jim Whelan of San Francisco is estimated to have started between fifty and sixty games each year from 1901–5. His teammate Cack Henley beat Jimmy Wiggs of Oakland in the longest shutout game in organized ball, winning 1–0 in twenty-four innings on June 8, 1909, in a game that took just over three-and-a-half hours to play. To the north in Seattle, Rube Vickers pitched a record sixty-four games in 1906, compiling a record of 39–20 while striking out 409.

Many of the PCL records are distorted because of the 200-game seasons. They cannot be directly compared with the results from other minor leagues or the majors, but they do attest to the incredible athletes who played in the west, who were up to the task of plying their trade from March through November.

In the midwest, the American Association was providing memorable players and teams of its own. The Minneapolis Millers of 1910–11 are regarded by Bill James as the best minor league team of this era. The Millers included Rube Waddell, another ex–major leaguer who continued playing in the minors. Sam Leever and Nick Altrock were other pitchers on the team who had already concluded fine major league careers.

The best regular on the Millers was Gavvy Cravath, an outfielder who was between major league assignments. Cravath had started his career in the Pacific Coast League before joining the Boston Red Sox in 1908. Unable to cut it with Boston, he was traded to the White Sox and then the Senators before being sent to Minneapolis. With the Millers in 1911, Cravath hit .363 with twenty-nine home runs and thirty-three stolen bases. He had the most home runs in organized baseball that year. Cravath returned to the majors in 1912 with the Phillies. He became one of the top power hitters of the dead ball era, winning five home run titles in seven years from 1913 through 1919. In 1915 he helped the Phillies capture one of their rare pennants.

The season in the American Association was not so long as that of the Pacific Coast League, but the Association also had its share of iron-armed pitchers. Louis "Bull" Durham of Indianapolis pitched and won both games of five doubleheaders in 1908. U. S. Grant "Stoney" McGlynn of Milwaukee threw 446 innings in 1909 along with fourteen shutouts.

Another great minor league at the time the National Association was founded was the Southern Association. Teams were established in Birmingham, Chattanooga, Little Rock, Memphis, Nashville, New Orleans, Shreveport, and Selma (soon relocated to Atlanta). The Southern Association was the highest-ranking circuit in the south. Perhaps no other part of the country was as blanketed with professional teams.

The 1905 season revealed some of the hazards of playing southern ball. The New Orleans Pelicans were forced to play the second half of its season on the road because of a yellow fever epidemic at home. They were still able to run up a record of 84–45 to win the league championship.

Baseball is sometimes thought of as a rural southern game

that moves at a languid pace compared to other major sports. But that notion does not explain a game in Atlanta on September 19, 1910 between the Crackers and Mobile. In an experiment to speed up the play, Mobile prevailed 2–1 in a game that took thirty-two minutes, a record that still stands. In another game that day, Chattanooga at Nashville required a more leisurely forty-two minutes. Blessedly, the experiment was dropped.

During these years, southern fans were treated to the play of Tris Speaker, who played for Little Rock and won the league batting title in 1908. "Shoeless Joe" Jackson took the crown for New Orleans in 1910 before moving up to Cleveland at the end of the season. Jackson, of course, became one of the greatest hitters of his time, but his career was ruined by his involvement in the 1919 Black Sox scandal. In 1916 a teammate of Jackson's on that later Chicago team, Dickie Kerr, led the Southern Association with twenty-four wins. Kerr's reputation kept the gamblers from even asking for his cooperation in throwing the 1919 World Series.

The outstanding pitching performance in the Southern Association occurred in 1906 when Glenn Liebhardt of Memphis completed forty-five of forty-six starts and won thirty-five games, including nine of the ten he started in five doubleheaders.

WITH CLUBS DEVELOPING all over the country and talented young men discovering the game in greater numbers, any number of possibilities existed for the game's development in the twentieth century. Local heroes engaging in local rivalries that lead to a national championship seem like a natural model, but with few exceptions such drama was rejected in favor of a financially safer route. On the face of it, the most talented players gravitated to the major leagues because of the lure of keener competition and higher salaries. Class-A minor leagues were supposed to be better than Class B and so forth, but this organization was as much the cause of a disparity of talent as its natural reflection.

The first Class-A leagues included the Eastern League (the forerunner of the International League) and the Southern Association. These leagues were permitted higher numbers of players on their rosters, higher salary limits, and the right to draft players from teams in lower classifications.

The Pacific Coast League received Class-A status when it joined the National Association, but as an inducement to give up its independence, the major leagues exempted the PCL from the majors' draft. The American Association also began outside the National Association, but it too was brought in and given a Class-A assignment. By 1906 five leagues made up the elite of the minor leagues: the Eastern League, the Western League, the American Association, the Southern Association, and the Pacific Coast League.

Tensions between the larger minor leagues and the more numerous low minors strained the National Association almost from the start. In 1907 the American Association and the Eastern League tried to create a new classification but were voted down by the other minors. The following year, they tried to drop the Western and Southern Leagues to a lower classification but were again unsuccessful. In frustration, the two dominant minors tried to withdraw from the National Association. They were placated in 1909 by being raised, along with the Pacific Coast League, to a new Class-AA status. The significance of the new category was that it forced the majors to pay higher sums for players drafted from the AA teams, and it protected the other Class-A leagues from the possibility of being dropped to Class-B status if the census of 1910 showed that their population bases no longer met the criteria necessary for the Class-A category.

A new National Agreement in 1911 ratified the Class-AA status in the minors and the accompanying draft and option provisions. A kind of peace had been established that secured the principal goals of baseball's ruling class. The reserve clause had been preserved, and professional baseball had been organized under the control of the major leagues' national commission and the minor leagues' National Association.

The game's new structure included some benefits for the players. Irresponsible owners who went out of business while owing salaries to their players were now less common, although the financial base of the low minors was always precarious. The transactions among the various franchises that made up the game were now more orderly, with an established procedure for settling disputes. Above all, however, monopoly prevailed. More teams now shared in that monopoly; but the greater numbers only required more elaborate agreements to restrain competition, and those agreements were inevitably reached once the ostensible competitors realized the money to be made through cooperation.

This baseball peace that had been created in 1903 was directly challenged in 1914 by the Federal League, a circuit that had operated outside of organized baseball in 1913 without threatening the policies that the majors and minors held dear. With stronger financing, the Federal League began the 1914 season with teams in Baltimore, Brooklyn, Buffalo, Chicago, Cincinnati, Indianapolis, Pittsburgh, and St. Louis. The new league did not try to raid players who had signed with other teams, but they did refuse to honor the reserve clause and bid for players who had met their obligations to teams in organized ball.

The most serious aspect of the Federal League threat was that it offered an alternative to the established leagues and could thus be used by players such as Ty Cobb and Walter Johnson for bargaining leverage. This competitive feature was precisely what the owners and executives had worked so hard to prevent, and the dramatically higher salaries that were paid by the majors in 1914 and 1915 confirmed the worst fears of the owners.

The Federal League compounded its heresy by offering a reasonable labor relations package. Players were automatically entitled to 5 percent pay increases each year, and after ten years of play in the Federal League, players became free agents and could bargain outside of the reserve clause.

This new league also provided new stadiums, including Wrigley Field in Chicago, perhaps the Federal League's most endearing vestige. The Baltimore franchise built a ball park across the street from the stadium used by Jack Dunn's Baltimore Orioles, and the new league even competed on the same day in the same town as some of the established ball clubs.

Organized baseball reacted predictably with threats of blacklists and other monopolistic practices. The Federal League filed an antitrust suit, charging organized baseball with restraint of trade under the Sherman Act. Other suits followed by all parties, each seeking to keep players from jumping to the opposition.

Although the Federal League was struggling to become a third major league, it had its greatest effect on the minors. Harold Seymour writes that the Federals hired a total of 264 players, of whom 18 broke major league contracts and 25 broke minor league agreements. The reserve clause was ignored by 63 major leaguers and 115 minor league players. The balance of Federal rosters consisted of retired ball players or those with no previous experience.

The Federal League is best seen as a freshly created high minor league that lacked the preparation and resources of Ban Johnson's Western League when it successfully joined the major league ranks. The Federals did succeed in shaking things up during its brief existence, and the greatest turbulence affected the minor leagues' best team.

Jack Dunn's Baltimore Orioles, with Babe Ruth starring on the mound, took such a commanding lead in the International League race of 1914 that fans stopped going to the park and went to see the "major league" alternative across the street, thus forcing Dunn to sell players.

Despite selling Babe Ruth, Ernie Shore, and others, Dunn felt compelled to move his franchise to Richmond after the 1914 season. The shift invaded territory of the Virginia League,

Ed Ashenback's old stomping ground, and an indemnity had to be paid that further aggravated Dunn's financial problems.

Repercussions from the Federal League were felt even in the low minors because they had a more difficult time selling their players to teams in higher circuits. In spite of these problems, the minors continued to support the status quo ante with their usual mix of idealistic rhetoric and pragmatic calculation. John Foster recorded the oath of allegiance passed at the National Association's annual meeting in Omaha during November of 1914:

> Whereas, The practice of encouraging and inciting certain ball players to disregard their obligations to Organized Base Ball has raised a doubt in the minds of the public as to the honesty and integrity of ball players as a class; and
>
> Whereas, Certain newspapers have made a studied effort to create the impression that there is dissatisfaction and disloyalty in the ranks of the National Association of Professional Base Ball Leagues; therefore, be it
>
> Resolved, That we, the representatives of Organized Base Ball in the minor leagues, at this first session of our fourteenth annual meeting, most emphatically and unequivocally reaffirm our allegiance to Organized Base Ball as the ideal condition for the future prospects of the great national game.[14]

The resolution is a classic of its kind. The players' pursuit of their best interest purportedly compromises their moral character. The media are knocked for reporting discontent among the inner circles, and we are reminded lastly that this strange business is actually "the great national game."

Foster was more candid in a section that preceded his presentation of the resolution of allegiance. He acknowledged that a delegate at the Omaha convention proposed that the National Association break ties with the American and National leagues and form an alliance with the Federal League. Foster dismissed the proposal, commenting, "This, of course, would have been perfectly futile as a remedy toward good, because the situation did not warrant such action and the major leagues would have been able to do far more mischief to the National Association than the Federal League already had done, had the National Association aligned itself with an outlaw organization."[15]

In the end, the National Association remained loyal to the majors because they could have created even more problems than the Federal League was causing. Foster describes this loyalty as "the best act of its character in National Association history;"[16] however sincere the delegates at Omaha were, they were reaching their decisions under duress.

The majors held their ground against the Federals in 1915, although Connie Mack dismantled his great Philadelphia A's team rather than meet their salary demands. The brunt of the Federal challenge again fell on the minor leagues. The Newark Bears of the International League had to move to Harrisburg after the Federals' 1914 pennant winner, Indianapolis, moved to Newark.

Competition again proved too much for the majors, and after the 1915 season negotiations began between the Federal League and the American and National Leagues to negotiate an end to the free market. The resulting agreement required the Federal League to halt its effort to become a third major league, but it did allow the Federal owners in Chicago and St. Louis to take over the Cubs and Browns. The majors paid an indemnity to the other Federal owners and allowed them to try to sell their players on an open market. As had happened before, the threats of a blacklist proved to be hot air when the major league monopoly prevailed.

An important effect of the settlement was to leave the Federals' Baltimore franchise in the lurch. The city and its "major league" team were treated shabbily by the game's power brokers. Consequently, the Baltimore Federals reinstituted the antitrust suit that had been dropped by the league as part of the settlement with the majors. To finance the litigation, the Federal park in Baltimore was sold to Jack Dunn, enabling the International League to reclaim its old territory. The lawsuit proved to be pivotal in baseball's history: in its review, the U.S. Supreme Court found this peculiar business to be exempt from antitrust law.

Having recovered from one "war," baseball now faced the real thing. The Great War had savaged Europe from August 1914, and the United States finally entered the fray in February 1917. The major leagues were able to struggle through the next two seasons, but the minors took a beating. Only twenty minor leagues began the 1917 season, and only a dozen were able to finish. The following year was even more bleak, as only nine leagues fielded teams on opening day, and the International League was the only minor league circuit to finish that season.

Their financial problems caused some minor league officials to rethink their attachment to organized baseball. The major league draft and option policies were the specific concerns since many minor league teams had to rebuild after the disastrous effects of World War I. The major leagues were deaf to the minors' problems, and a confrontation brewed.

In January 1919 the minors issued an ultimatum that would have limited the major league draft to Class-A teams and increased the compensation to those franchises to $7,500. John Foster contended that the National Association had fallen into the hands of its "radical element," and compared to the sometimes timid leadership of the past, he was right.

The majors rejected the ultimatum, and for the first time since professional baseball organized, no National Agreement governed the game. The majors themselves were in the midst of serious organization changes. The three-member National Commission had been increasingly ineffective in providing leadership, and calls for restructuring dominated the annual meetings.

The organizational reforms came swiftly after the news broke in 1920 of the crooked World Series of 1919. The Black Sox scandal frightened the game's magnates, who could expect the public to lose confidence in a game that was not on the level. To restore that confidence, Judge Kenesaw Mountain Landis was hired as baseball's first commissioner in November 1920. Landis had presided over the Federal League's antitrust suit, and, though he had a reputation as a trust buster, he had made it clear to the Federals from the outset of the trial that he saw baseball and its monopoly in a friendly light.

Landis was also a strong supporter of independent minor leagues. He maintained that the minors were an equally legitimate part of the game, though they were confined to smaller communities. The commissioner's reputation for integrity put some moral force behind the financial interests of minor league owners such as Jack Dunn, who also appreciated the importance of independent minor league franchises.

Despite this fresh opportunity to assert themselves independently, the minors rushed back to the protection of the majors. The low minors found abuse from the high minors even more aggravating than abuse from the majors, and the Pacific Coast League had already enjoyed the benefits of draft exemption, so it had little to gain by seeing the National Agreement come to an end. The American Association and International League were less enthused about forging a new tie with the majors, but pressure was building in the minors to restore a National Agreement.

The American and National Leagues were less receptive. Part of the reason for their indifference was their need to recover from the Black Sox scandal, but the Baltimore Federal League suit also played a part. With the case in appeals, the last thing some of the major league magnates wanted was a comprehensive pact controlling all of organized baseball. The appearance of some independence for the minors served a purpose.

In January 1921, shortly after Landis's election, a new National Agreement was reached that compromised the differences between the majors and minors. The key provision allowed any minor league to exempt itself from the draft if in turn it declined to draft players from lower minor leagues. While some option rights were retained, the freedom to sell players to higher circuits at a market price (limited, as ever, by the effects of the reserve clause) was an important gain for the minors. The leagues that chose draft exemption included the three AA leagues—the PCL, the International League, and the American Association—as well as the Class-AA Western Association and the Class-B Three-I League.

The draft reform, of course, cut two ways. The teams in the exempt leagues had the chance to make a lot of money by selling their best players for far more than the $5,000 draft compensation to AA clubs stipulated in the National Agreement. In that way the new agreement helped to secure the minor leagues' financial base as independent suppliers of talent to the majors.

The effects on minor league players were less beneficial. Not only were quality players held back on Class-AA teams because no major league franchise was willing to pay more than a draft price for them, but the AA teams themselves were often unwilling to pay market price for players in lower circuits. For that reason, Landis, the champion of the minors, continued to press for a universal draft.

WITH THE NATIONAL Agreement of 1921 in place, a new era in professional baseball began. The period dating from 1876 had seen this enormously popular game develop into a major business with the usual organization issues of any industry. Unlike other American businesses, however, baseball continued to hold a romantic place in the culture and, more important, in the law. The resolution of disputes among franchises, players, and leagues turned primarily on the power of the participants, who masked their interests in pious rhetoric.

This period saw the minor leagues grow in numbers and popularity and shrink in significance. They began the twentieth century simply as other professional leagues, fully capable of pursuing an independent course with all the ensuing risks and promises. They chose instead to settle for the security of being junior partners in an elaborate organization that stood above all else for the preservation of privilege.

The Federal League, the Pacific Coast League, and Jack Dunn's success in Baltimore are some of the factors that suggest major league ball could have encompassed more teams and cities than the American and National Leagues represented. The National Association could have provided the leadership for that early expansion, but it chose the safer course.

Even in 1920, the minors were still in a healthy position. They were free from the National Agreement that contractually subordinated them to the majors, and a sympathetic figure would soon become the first commissioner. The minors again passed up this opportunity to assert their independence because of a dread of competition. The minor league magnates preferred nominal inferiority rather than the risks of independence.

The second era of minor league baseball continued to include minor league franchises that seem to have been better than some major league clubs. New chances to end the artificial hierarchy of organized baseball appeared, and eventually a serious effort would be made to do just that. At the same time, the majors became far more adept at controlling minor league teams, but they remained as obtuse as ever in their dealings with their junior partners.

### Part Two

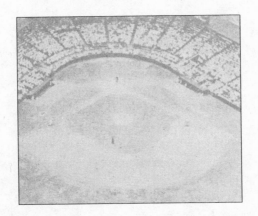

# THE MINORS'
# GOLDEN AGE

*F*ROM 1920 TO 1950, *baseball was dominated by the New York Yankees of Babe Ruth and Joe DiMaggio. Not only did the Yankees sustain their excellence throughout that period, but New York was also the center for the great writers who defined the game for the rest of the country. Other teams and players were given bit parts in the high drama that was played out in the Bronx every summer.*

*As the game settled under the Yankee dynasty, the organization of baseball underwent turmoil. The Black Sox scandal brought down a crumbling governing structure. The minor's draft exemption gave them a new shot at independence and equality with the majors. Great teams began developing beyond the focus of the New York media. For a time anything was possible in the game's business structure.*

*The minors weathered the Great Depression and World War II to reach a peak of popularity. Never before or since have so many people followed so many clubs. While the minor league game was enjoying its most exciting era, the business of baseball slowly imposed its familiar order.*

*Through the development of farm systems, major league clubs assumed control of the minors even as the minor league game achieved unprecedented prosperity. The minors' club officials and league executives had outpaced the majors in finding creative ways to promote baseball during tough economic times, but ultimately nothing counted so much as perpetuating the majors' domination.*

*This era displayed most clearly the two purposes of minor league baseball. Never has the game been so successful in the smaller communities of the country, and never were the pressures greater to force the minors under the control of the American and National Leagues. The beauty of baseball for its own sake vied with the majors' interest in player development.*

*As great minor league teams emerged and more teams were established in America's hamlets, baseball ended this era ready for the showdown between independent minor leagues and the power-hungry majors.*

# · Four ·

# THE BALTIMORE ORIOLES

AT THE TIME the major leagues were reeling from the Black Sox scandal, the minors fielded one of the best teams in the history of organized baseball. Jack Dunn's Baltimore Orioles won seven consecutive pennants from 1919 through 1925. Bill James describes them as "the greatest minor league team of all time." More important, the Orioles were probably better than a number of major league clubs.

The significance of this reputation is that Dunn's team was an independent franchise, run for its own purposes and not those of a major league patron. The Orioles epitomized what the minors could have been: self-sustaining franchises operating in smaller markets.

Jack Dunn was part of a tradition of former players who became club owners. Like Charles Comiskey, Clark Griffith, and Connie Mack, he was among the great players of the nineteenth century who followed the Horatio Alger trail from player to owner.

Dunn had played major league ball for several teams from 1897–1904. He was both a pitcher and an outfielder in the majors, and in 1905 he became the player-manager of the Providence Clamdiggers of the International League.

Dunn moved to Baltimore for the 1907 season, and he guided the Orioles to a pennant in 1908. This franchise replaced the old Baltimore Orioles of the National League that had been the best team in baseball in the 1890s. The old Orioles had first been gutted through wholesale trading of their best players to the Brooklyn Dodgers; then the franchise itself was shifted to New York in 1903 to give the American League representation in the country's biggest city. Baltimore was left with a minor league team to continue the tradition of baseball in that town. Dunn restored glory to Baltimore by building teams around great pitching. With a brilliant eye for talent, Dunn found Merle "Doc" Adkins among the medical students at Johns Hopkins. Adkins had twenty-victory seasons for the Orioles on three occasions; other twenty-game winners on that team included Lefty Russell and Rube Vickers.

In 1914 Dunn worked the other side of the tracks from Johns Hopkins, signing George Ruth, one of the incorrigibles at St. Mary's, a Catholic reform school. In contrast to the mediocre scouting that Ashenback encountered, Dunn showed persistence and thoroughness in being able to find such a player in such an obscure place.

The Orioles won their first pennant for Dunn in 1908, when "Doc" Adkins won twenty-nine games. Another of Dunn's great pitchers was Rube Vickers, who won twenty-five while losing twenty-four in 1910. The next year, Vickers led the league with thirty-two wins and 369 innings pitched. Vickers had been one of the players exchanged between Dunn and Connie Mack when Mack, apparently pushed to exasperation by Rube's antics, gave up a gifted pitcher.

Dunn's eye for talent was matched by a fierce determination to win, insistence on discipline, and generous rewards for the players who met his standards. At the Orioles' training camp in 1914, Dunn gave a lecture on the importance of gentlemanly conduct. His lesson was challenged by several of his charges, who tethered a horse to the desk in the lobby of the hotel where the Orioles were staying. When Dunn became aware that the horse had done what horses will do, he screamed his determination to fire the players responsible. Paternal devotion saved the culprits, who included Babe Ruth and Jack Dunn, Jr.

Ruth was making his debut that spring, not only in professional baseball but also in polite society. Until a month before spring training, the Babe had been enrolled, or perhaps incarcerated, at St. Mary's Industrial School. The Xavieran Brothers who ran the school had taken George Ruth off the hands of his parents, who were neither able nor especially willing to raise him. The Brothers provided Ruth with attention that he needed, discipline that never took, and an opportunity to play baseball that would make him one of the most famous people in American history.

The details of how Ruth was discovered by Jack Dunn were neglected by contemporaries, who preferred mythology to history. What remains clear is that Dunn was aware that schools in Baltimore were a rich source of players who might be developed then sold at a profit to major league clubs. Ruth was one of a number of youngsters from Baltimore schools whom Dunn signed. The most compelling aspect of Ruth's discovery by Dunn is its reinforcement of two cherished ideas—the extent of opportunity in America, and the wholesome outlet of sport for troubled youth.

For our purposes, another lesson should be stressed. Jack Dunn was a very serious businessman who made his living from the sport of baseball and who profited by extending opportunity to talented young men. Dunn was no wealthy sportsman pursuing a hobby; nor was he an idle figurehead who awaited profits while subordinates did the work. He knew the business of baseball as a player, manager, and owner. He knew what was required to be successful, including the risks that had to be assumed. Unlike other minor league owners who were content to be wards of the majors, Dunn trusted his own abilities and work ethic.

Dunn's experience with Ruth strengthened that self-reliance. Having signed Ruth to a $600 contract for the 1914 season, Dunn arrived in Fayetteville a few days after an intrasquad game in which, for the first time, Ruth had astonished a crowd with his power. He had hit a home run that surpassed a legendary shot by Jim Thorpe several years before. Dunn was pleased but apparently not surprised by the report.

Later in the spring, Ruth pitched a complete-game victory over the Philadelphia Athletics. A rematch in Baltimore was a disappointment: Ruth was hammered by the Athletics. Given another chance against major league competition, Ruth faced the Brooklyn Dodgers in a Sunday game that had to be played at a racetrack outside the city limits because of a local ordinance against baseball on Sunday. Ruth beat the Dodgers 10–6 and made a great impression with his hitting. As Robert Creamer relates the story, Ruth was robbed in his first at-bat by Dodger right fielder Casey Stengel, who ran down a long drive to right and made a great catch. Stengel was chastised by manager Wilbert Robinson for playing Ruth too shallow. As a lark, Stengel moved back thirty feet for Ruth's next at-bat and yelled sarcastically to the center fielder to ask if he thought Robinson would think he was deep enough. The answer was immediate. As Stengel remembered, "My God, if he doesn't hit one a mile. I was young and I could run. I could fly. Believe me, I could fly. I could go and catch a ball pretty good. But this one—this one was over my head. We lost the game. The kid beats us pitching and he beats us batting. That's when I first saw Ruth. I would say I was impressed."[1]

By this time, George Ruth had become the Babe, specifically Dunnie's Babe. In fact, Jack Dunn had assumed legal guardianship for Ruth until his twenty-first birthday. The assignment was hardly frivolous. The street kid with the awesome gifts was completely outmatched by the world. On his first train ride, he followed the advice of his teammates to rest his arm in the clothes sling in his sleeping berth. With his first paycheck, he bought himself a bicycle. A short time later, he was prepared to buy his first woman.

In Creamer's account, the Babe was discovered one night by teammate George Twombly sitting on the curb outside the Forrest Hotel in New York City where the Orioles stayed when playing Newark or Jersey City:

"What are you doing?" Twombly asked.

"I'm waiting for a girl."

"What girl?"

"I don't know," Ruth said, looking toward Broadway. "I'm just waiting. The boys at the reform school said if you're in New York and you want a woman, all you have to do is wait for a streetwalker to come along."

Twombly stared, undone by this lecherous innocence.

"You better get in the hotel," he said. "You better not let Dunnie catch you out here waiting for a streetwalker."[2]

The Babe in time learned the ways of the world and in turn taught the world a few lessons of his own.

Ruth's first professional season coincided with the first campaign of the Federal League, and despite the Babe's accomplishments, the Orioles were no match in popularity for the Federals' Baltimore Terrapins. The major league label that the Terrapins claimed made them a bigger attraction in Baltimore even though the Orioles were undoubtedly a better team.

On the Terrapins' Opening Day, the Orioles were playing the New York Giants across the street from the Terrapins' park. Dunn's team could attract only 1,500 fans while the Federals drew over 30,000, including the various pooh-bahs of Maryland.

In his pitching debut, Ruth shut out the Buffalo Bisons, who featured Joe McCarthy, later to be Ruth's last Yankee manager. Only 200 seats were filled, while the Terrapins were drawing over 20,000. This trend continued, to the devastation of the Orioles.

Despite the hard times, Dunn raised Ruth's salary twice in 1914. The Orioles' owner appealed to the National Commission to abolish the draft so that the Orioles could compete against the Federal League more effectively. Dunn was joined in his petition by Ed Barrow, the president of the International League. Barrow himself was pursuing major league status for the IL. Both requests were denied, and the episode proved to be just one more example of major league indifference to the struggles of the minors.

Dunn turned to his fellow owners in the International League. He asked permission to move the Orioles to Richmond, Virginia. Because an indemnity was required for such a move, permission was denied.

Boxed in and facing financial ruin, Dunn saw no choice but to sell his star players. Ruth went to the Boston Red Sox along with Ernie Shore and Ben Egan for something like $25,000. Other players were sold to the Yankees, Cincinnati, and other major league clubs, until the Orioles, who had been leading the International League, were devastated and fell precipitously from contention.

The most galling moment for Dunn must have come in September 1914, when Babe Ruth returned to Baltimore in the uniform of the Providence Clamdiggers, an affiliate of the Red Sox. The Babe pitched Providence to a victory over the Orioles, and he hit a home run to boot.

The Orioles had begun the 1914 campaign with Babe Ruth and an impressive supporting cast, and the season ended in shambles. The Federal League makes a convenient excuse for Dunn's financial woes, but the major league monopoly was a very powerful accessory. The objective of organized baseball seems to have been to protect the major league privilege of monopoly. The minors were left to fend for themselves, as the majors would not even suspend the draft to protect Dunn's Baltimore franchise.

Even with the money raised from selling his best players, Dunn, for the moment, was whipped in Baltimore. In 1915 he received belated permission to move his franchise to Richmond, where it struggled through that season. Dunn sold the club the following year, after the Federal League's collapse. He then purchased the Jersey City franchise and moved it back to Baltimore, where it played in the Federal League's Terrapin Park.

Dunn rebuilt the new Orioles into a contender. Their great star was Jack Bentley, who played his first year for Dunn in 1916. Bentley had played three years for the Washington Senators with unimpressive numbers, yet he would become known as "the Babe Ruth of the International League." Bentley was outstanding both as a hitter and pitcher. He compiled a 7–3 pitching record with a 2.12 ERA and a .243 batting average in 1916; the following year he batted .342 while pitching only one inning.

Bentley was joined on the 1916 Orioles by Chick Fewster, who enjoyed an eleven-year major league career, and Bill Lamar, who batted .310 in nine major league seasons. In 1917 the Orioles pitching staff added Herb Thormahlen, who won twenty-five games, and Jim "Rube" Parnham, who added twenty-two wins in 1918. Parnham proved to be a great pitcher for Dunn, who was less disturbed by Rube's antics than Connie Mack had been when Parnham was with Philadelphia. In eight campaigns with Baltimore, Parnham won 139 games despite missing the 1921 and 1925 seasons.

In 1918 the International League was the only minor league circuit to finish its season. The Orioles played without Jack Bentley, who was in the military. Ralph Worrell was another of Jack Dunn's discoveries who showed brilliant promise in his rookie year. Still a teenager, Worrell won twenty-five games for the Orioles in 1918 but, tragically, died after the season in the worldwide flu epidemic that was such a catastrophic postscript to World War I.

The first year of the Orioles' dynasty was 1919. Parnham won twenty-eight games, and a teammate, rookie Harry Frank, had a 24–6 record. Only one of the Orioles' regulars failed to hit .300 that year, and the team had a terrific contingent of fielders.

This first of seven consecutive pennant winners reflected Dunn's persistence in overcoming the problems of the Federal League; World War I; the shifts to Richmond, Jersey City, and back to Baltimore; and the indifference of the major leagues. In a league of teams that were independent franchises, Dunn had no peer. He repeatedly discovered talent in Baltimore from sandlots to reform schools to colleges. Few other baseball executives worked as hard or as successfully as Dunn. As long as the International League rejected the major league draft, Dunn would likely be the paramount power in the League.

The 1920 team is arguably the finest minor league club ever assembled. It won 110 games, for a winning percentage of .719, yet that was barely good enough to capture the pennant. The Orioles had to win their final 25 games to hold off the Toronto Maple Leafs, who took 24 of their last 26 games to finish two-and-a-half games back.

Johnny Ogden was the ace of the Orioles' staff that year. Dunn picked him up from Rochester after the 1919 season, and he responded with a 27–9 record. Harry Frank won twenty-five games in his sophomore season, and Jack Bentley added sixteen wins in relief. Bentley's hitting was remarkable: twenty home runs, a league-leading 161 RBIs, and a .371 batting average. Merwin Jacobson led the International League for Baltimore with a .404 batting average.

All of these players would be eclipsed by a left-handed pitcher who would become Jack Dunn's vindication for the loss of Babe Ruth. Lefty Grove had been born in the coal country of Lonaconing, Maryland, on March 6, 1900. After an eighth-grade education and a few years of shoveling coal, Grove left to work on the railroad. His pitching talent landed him a job with Martinsburg in the Blue Ridge League in 1920. Little time elapsed before Jack Dunn was on his trail. For $3,500, Lefty Grove joined the Orioles, where he went 12–2 in his first year with Baltimore.

By this time, Dunn had assembled one of the finest teams in

organized baseball at any level. Major league teams were after Bentley, Grove, and Ogden, but without the coercion of the draft, they had to deal with Dunn as an equal. The fact is that few of the major league executives were Dunn's equal, and he refused to capitulate to their demands.

Dunn had a chance to display the quality of his team at the end of the 1920 season, when the New York Yankees came down for an exhibition. It was another return for Babe Ruth, who was rewriting baseball strategy with a fifty-four-home-run season. Other ex-Orioles on that Yankee team included Fewster, Thormahlen, Bob Shawkey, and Ernie Shore. The Orioles beat the Yanks 1–0 and went on to defeat St. Paul of the American Association in the Junior World Series.

The 1921 season was expanded to 168 games. Dunn had found yet another college star for his pitching staff in Tommy Thomas, a minor member of Buffalo's pitching staff in 1920 who won twenty-four games for the Orioles in his first season with Baltimore. Dunn not only could find talented players, but he also knew how to develop them. Grove edged Thomas with twenty-five wins, and Johnny Ogden led the International League with a record of 31–8.

The outstanding individual performance on the Orioles that year was unquestionably that of Jack Bentley, who set a record for the International League with a batting average of .412. He added twenty-four home runs among 246 hits. This tremendous production was only part of Bentley's contribution. He also posted a 12–1 record as a relief pitcher.

This team, which had won its final twenty-five games to capture the pennant narrowly in 1921, went on another win streak in 1922 to run away with the season. In the middle of May, the Orioles started a twenty-seven-game winning streak that broke the race open. They concluded the season with a record 119 wins and a pennant-winning margin of twenty games.

The Orioles stumbled in the Junior World Series, losing to Joe McCarthy's Louisville Colonels. Despite the Colonels' upset, no one could dispute that the Orioles were the finest minor league team of that era, perhaps one of the best in organized baseball at any level. In David Chrisman's history of the International League, he concludes, "It is conceivable that these two teams [the New York Giants and Yankees, the pennant winners of 1921] were superior to Dunn's 1921 Orioles. But it is difficult to support the theory that any of the other major league teams of that era were."[3]

Certainly the major leagues were becoming impatient with so much talent beyond the reach of their draft. Branch Rickey was about to begin the full development of the minor leagues as farm systems for the majors, and a resource as rich as Jack Dunn's Orioles would be an irresistible attraction for major league teams looking to improve themselves.

While Dunn came under pressure from the majors, he had also begun to irritate other franchises in the International League. Chrisman makes a persuasive case that other clubs in that league were quite good. To see Baltimore take pennant after pennant was beginning to rankle. Some franchises saw closer ties to the majors as a means to overcome Dunn's superior talent and energy.

Dunn himself remained unaffected by these concerns. He rejected offers for Jack Bentley after the 1921 season because he did not think he was offered a fair price. Bentley, whose frustration had apparently grown along with his production, resented being kept in the minors, but in 1922 he posted a .350 batting average with twenty-two home runs and 128 RBIs. Bentley also enjoyed another outstanding pitching season, going 13–2.

Baltimore took its fourth straight pennant, winning 115 games for a ten-game margin over runner-up Rochester. Pitching again was the hallmark of the team: Ogden was 24–10, Grove went 18–8, and Thomas was 18–9. Harry Frank had recovered from arm trouble to win twenty-two games, and Rube Parnham returned after a year's absence, going 16–10.

After that year, Dunn got his fair price for Jack Bentley. The New York Giants paid $72,500 for Bentley, who remained the Babe Ruth only of the International League. As a major leaguer, Bentley was a modestly successful pitcher with the Giants. He was 13–8 in 1923, 16–5 in 1924, and 11–9 the following year, but his best ERA was 3.78.

Bill James notes that Bentley hit .427 in 1923, but that was based on only eighty-nine at-bats. John McGraw, who had played with Dunn on the old Orioles of the National League, had resented not getting a chance to buy Babe Ruth when Dunn sold the Babe in 1914. McGraw may have seen a chance to recoup that loss with the acquisition of Jack Bentley, but Bentley was never played full-time at first base. He was a pitcher who occasionally hit. The conversion that had turned Ruth from a great pitcher to the greatest power hitter was never attempted with Bentley.

The 1923 Orioles had to overcome not only Bentley's departure, but the death of Jack Dunn's son, a loss from which Dunn never fully recovered. On top of those distractions, the habit of winning had induced some complacency, which showed up in postseason play. The Orioles had dropped a series to a Class-A team after the 1922 season. But the talent on the team was deep enough to overcome apathy and grief. The Orioles won a record fifth consecutive pennant with a record of 111–53. Jimmy Walsh, replacing Bentley at first base, hit .333 with fifteen home runs and 134 RBIs. Dick Porter, in his second year with Baltimore, was developing into a star outfielder, hitting .316 with eighteen home runs and 111 RBIs.

In a deal with Rochester in midseason, Dunn picked up Clarence Pitt. As Chrisman describes it, "In those days, even when he wasn't trying, Dunn couldn't help but fall into success. Apparently, he had picked up the journeyman Pitt as defensive outfield help and wound up possessing the 1923 batting champion."[4] Pitt hit .35738 to take the crown from Marty Archdeacon of Rochester, who hit .35736.

The pitching maintained its customary brilliance. Lefty Grove was 27–10 and set league records in innings pitched with 303 and strikeouts with 330. Johnny Ogden added a 17–12 record, and Tommy Thomas was 15–12. Harry Frank's career ended with arm trouble, but he managed a 9–2 record in his final season.

The star of the show was an incredible performance by Rube Parnham. He set a record by winning thirty-three games, including his last twenty in a row, still a minor league record. But nothing was ever simple with Rube. He took off the last week of the season for a vacation. Returning on the final day of the campaign, he pitched and won both ends of a doubleheader. Rube was obviously a left-hander trapped in a right-hander's body.

Parnham's antics reveal another quality of Jack Dunn. When Rube was with Connie Mack, he pitched with limited success and was dealt to Baltimore before his potential could be developed. Mack was apparently unable to deal with Parnham's unusual personality, and he gladly passed him to Baltimore. Jack Dunn could not have been happy about Parnham's behavior, but he was able to get the most from Rube without letting the team's discipline deteriorate. After Parnham bolted the team with a week to go in the season, it would have been understandable if Dunn had suspended him. By having him pitch both games of a doubleheader, Dunn showed an impressive capacity for imaginative leadership. Neither leniency nor toughness seems always to be the right approach. Dunn had a gift for knowing the response required for each situation.

The 1924 Baltimore contingent needed further adjustments. Max Bishop, the Orioles' second baseman, had been sold to Connie Mack for $25,000 as part of Dunn's continuing efforts to recover financially from the disastrous days of the Federal League and the below-market sale of Babe Ruth. Bishop was replaced at second by Dick Porter, who took the International League batting title, hitting .364, with twenty-three home runs and 125 RBIs.

Fritz Maisel had become a fixture at third base. Maisel had played for the Orioles from 1911–13. He moved to the Yankees for four seasons and spent one year with the St. Louis Browns before returning to Baltimore in 1919. He hit consistently above .300 for the Orioles and was one of the few players who played on all of Dunn's consecutive pennant winners.

Merwin Jacobson was another of the Oriole regulars. He hit

a league-leading .404 in 1920, and he batted well over .300 in his other seasons with Baltimore. In addition to adding some power to the lineup, he was an outstanding defensive player.

Lefty Grove was the ace of the staff in 1924 with a record of 26–6. (This would be his final year in Baltimore, as Dunn would finally get a fair price for him, and the majors would get perhaps the best pitcher in the game's history.) Ogden had a 19–6 record, and Tommy Thomas was 16–11. Cliff Jackson, Ed Tomlin, and George "Moose" Earnshaw were new pitchers who won sixteen, eleven, and seven games respectively.

Baltimore won 117 games, winning the pennant by nineteen games over Toronto. This sixth consecutive title pushed Dunn's relations with baseball to the breaking point. The majors were irritated by their inability to obtain star players easily, and other teams in the International League were frustrated by the six years of Baltimore dominance. Dunn's reply, as quoted by Chrisman, was straight to the point: "Let the rest of the league build themselves up to the level of success enjoyed by the Orioles—rather than try to tear us down to their level. I offer a direct challenge to the other teams in the league to attain the same level of proficiency enjoyed these many years by the Baltimore franchise."[5]

Dunn enjoyed a unique place in organized baseball in those years. He declined to leave Baltimore for a major league post, rebuffed schemes to dismantle the Orioles, and repelled calls for a return to a draft for the International League. He achieved what everyone else wanted: consistent excellence. He saw nothing inferior about success in Baltimore, considering it as enjoyable as victories in Boston, New York, or Philadelphia. He felt no compulsion to submit to the demands of major league magnates, who felt entitled to feast off Dunn's efforts by drafting star players for tens of thousands of dollars below fair market prices. Nor was Dunn swayed by the jealous ambition of competitors in the International League, who worked neither so hard nor so well. Jack Dunn was a rare man—successful, content, but always eager to improve.

Dunn's motivation was not simply an obsession with winning. As the owner of the Orioles, he was aware of financial realities and opportunities. The greatest opportunity in 1924 was the option of selling Lefty Grove to a major league team. In five years with Dunn, Grove had a record of 109–36. He was a paramount strikeout artist and had been ready for the major leagues for several years. All Dunn had been waiting for was the right price. For the chance to have Lefty Grove, Connie Mack abandoned his tightfisted policies and paid the unprecedented sum of $100,600. This exceeded the amount the Yankees had paid for Babe Ruth, and it was in fact the largest fee ever paid for any player up to that time.

Even after parting with Grove, who had become a kind of foster son to Dunn, the Orioles managed to claim their seventh consecutive pennant in 1925. The pitching staff might actually have improved, as Tommy Thomas posted a 32–12 record along with Odgen's 28–11 and Earnshaw's 29–11 marks. A revamped offense hit .300 at every position but catcher and supplied the expected timely hitting. The Orioles won 105 games to take the pennant by four games. Even the players had grown weary of their success. The fans were also bored, and everyone may have tired of Dunn's sustained demands for excellence. Dunn raised more money by selling Tommy Thomas to the White Sox, but he also planned moves to strengthen the Orioles for the 1926 season.

Finally in 1926 the spell broke. The Toronto Maple Leafs beat the Orioles by eight games, even though Baltimore won 101 games. The second-place finish was disappointing for Dunn, and it would be his last competitive season. Despite his efforts to overhaul the club, the Orioles collapsed to sixth place in 1927 and fifth in 1928.

Whether Dunn could have rebounded to compete successfully against the rising powers of the International League is uncertain. In late October 1928, while enjoying a field meet for his beloved hunting dogs, Jack Dunn died of a heart attack. From his desperate circumstances just a dozen years before, Dunn had accumulated an estate worth over a million dollars.

*The Sporting News* printed a list of twenty player sales that enriched Dunn by over $400,000. A fair price for Babe Ruth would certainly have boosted the total to more than half a million. The money is a crude indication of Dunn's success, but it does demonstrate that his principles of self-reliance, planning, and hard work were profitable.

Branch Rickey was among the most vocal of those who maintained that minor league teams could not survive without the patronage of a major league sponsor. The farm systems would indeed prove to dominate and eventually monopolize the minor league game, but Dunn's Orioles should be appreciated for showing that a successful independent minor league franchise is more than a pipe dream. To make a team prosperous in a smaller market may take more work, but Dunn proved that smaller cities and towns could be more than affiliates of the great urban centers. More remarkably, Dunn's success came in the middle of the major league's most populous markets. Just up the road from Clark Griffith's Washington Senators with Walter Johnson, just south of Connie Mack's Philadelphia Athletics, not far from the three teams in New York, Dunn thrived by doing his job better than anyone else.

Some of his players may have wished to move on to the big leagues, but Dunn eased their restlessness by treating them to the best hotels and in some cases to better pay than they would have received with a major league team. In his negotiations with major league executives, he was fierce, but his objective was simply to receive a fair price for his players.

In baseball's organizational mythology, the instruments that the major leagues have used to dominate the minors are always characterized as indispensable. The draft, the option, and the reserve clause formed an unholy alliance that sustained major league franchises that may have been less productive or entertaining than some minor league teams. Jack Dunn proved that, freed from the draft and option clauses, minor league teams could do just fine. The success of the Orioles was hardly inevitable. Under less capable leadership, they might have struggled in mediocrity, as indeed they did for many years after Dunn's death. Their great string of pennant winners was a direct result of Dunn's talent and his energy. Owners who have looked for an easier, safer, or cheaper way to operate a ball club have had an interest in stifling that kind of independence and fostering the bogus mythology of organized baseball instead.


EXAMINING DUNN'S ORIOLES in isolation makes them seem quite impressive, but one can properly wonder about the competition they were thrashing each year. To put Baltimore in perspective requires a look at those who challenged them.

In one context, the invincible Orioles seemed to have been a bit weak. The Junior World Series featured Baltimore's champions from 1920 through 1925, and the results were mixed. In the best-of-nine series, the Orioles won titles in 1920, defeating St. Paul 5–1; in 1922, beating St. Paul again, 5–2; and in 1925, with a 5–3 triumph over Louisville. In the other three years, the Orioles were whipped, by Louisville, 5–3 in 1921; Kansas City, 5–4 in 1923; and St. Paul, 5–4 in 1924.

The excuse given for Baltimore's postseason collapses was that the team was overconfident and complacent, a plausible explanation but not an obvious one. The failure to dominate the postseason play raises some questions about the Orioles and their competition in the International League, but the format of such a series was too limited to allow comparisons between Baltimore and other minor league pennant winners. Extended play against the best teams in the other minors would have been interesting, but such speculation remains part of that wonderful hypothetical world of baseball.

Did the Orioles attain such dominance in the IL because other teams in the league simply collapsed? Perhaps Baltimore was like the big fish in the little pond, facing even bigger fish when they reached the Junior World Series. Just how good was the Orioles' competition? The short answer is that many of the teams were quite good indeed. SABR's *Minor League Baseball Stars* is a good source for locating outstanding players, and among those mentioned who played the seven-team circuit of the International League during this period (which, in addition to Baltimore, consisted of teams in Buffalo, Jersey City, Newark, Reading, Rochester, and Toronto during most of this era) is David Alexander, who played first base for Toronto in 1927 and 1928. The Oriole dynasty had already passed by then, but Alexander's record reflects the quality of play in that circuit. He hit .338 with twelve home runs in 1927 before a spectacular season in 1928 that launched his major league career, when he led the league with a .380 average and was the IL's top slugger with thirty-one home runs.

Maurice Archdeacon played for Rochester in the early 1920s, batting .325, .321, and .357 before joining the White Sox. Archdeacon led the International League in hits, runs, and stolen bases. Albert Head joined Rochester in 1924, the year after Archdeacon had left for Chicago. Head caught for eight seasons in the International League with Rochester, Jersey City, and Montreal. He hit over .300 five times while he consistently caught well over 100 games a season. Head was a tough out: while in the Southern Association, Head struck out only three times in 468 at-bats in 1933 and only once in 402 trips to the plate in 1935.

Hiram Carlyle spent the 1925 and 1926 seasons with Toronto, hitting well over .300 both years. His time in the International League was limited, but he enjoyed a fifteen-year career in the minors, with a lifetime batting average of .314.

Frank Gilhooley moved to the International League after four seasons in the American League. Gilhooley was a fine hitter who led the IL with 230 hits while with Reading in 1922. In sixteen minor league seasons, he hit only seventeen home runs, but his career average was .323.

Mickey Heath was a first baseman who hit .335 for Toronto in 1926. He finished with a .298 average in a career of more than 2,000 minor league games. Herman Layne spent the 1924–26 seasons with Toronto, batting .341, .345, and .350.

George Whiteman holds the record for most games played in the minor leagues with 3,282. He passed through the International League several times in his twenty-five-year career, including a two-year stint with Toronto in 1919 and 1920.

"Rabbit" Whitman played for almost every IL team except Baltimore from 1923–33. His career batting average was .324, and like Albert Head, he was a difficult batter to strike out. He fanned three times in 514 at-bats in 1925 and three times in 575 at-bats in 1928. In two other years he struck out only five times, with 561 and 628 at-bats.

David Chrisman's annual reviews of the Orioles' pennant runs include some appraisal of the competition. In 1919 George "High-pockets" Kelly batted .356 for Rochester and led the league with fifteen home runs. That performance earned him a call from the New York Giants, where he began a sixteen-year major league career that culminated in election to the Hall of Fame. Chrisman's review of the International League in 1919 also mentions star pitchers, including Ed Rommel at Newark and Bill Hubbell, Bill Hersche, and Paul Justin at Toronto. Manuel Cueto and Bill Lamar were hard-hitting outfielders at Rochester. A number of quality catchers also appeared in the league in 1919: Steve O'Neil, Gus Sandberg, Joe Cobb, and Ben Egan.

In 1920 Toronto had a terribly frustrating season. Despite winning twenty-four of their last twenty-six, their total of 108 wins left them two games back of the Orioles. Red Shea anchored Toronto's staff with a 27–7 record, while Jack Ryan and Lore Bader each posted 19–9 records.

Akron had joined the league, and it had three prominent home run hitters, including the legendary Jim Thorpe, who hit sixteen homers, as did Pete Shields. Jimmy Walsh added fifteen home runs to the powerful attack. Joe Finneran led the Akron staff with a 20–11 record, one of five twenty-game winners in the International League that year.

Jack Bentley's great 1921 season eclipsed some impressive play around the league. Fred Merkle, down from the Giants, hit .340 for Rochester. Bob Fothergill hit .338 with twelve home runs while playing left field for Rochester. His teammate, Maurice Archdeacon, hit .325 that year, and Homer Summa led the club with thirteen homers. John Wisner won twenty-two games and Sherrif John Blake notched twenty-one as Rochester totaled 100 victories that season.

In 1922 Merkle led the league with 130 RBIs. Though he hit only seven home runs, his average of .347 was highly productive. Fothergill won the batting title for Rochester with a .383 average, and Cliff Brady and Tom Connelly both hit over .300 with over ninety runs driven in.

The Toronto Maple Leafs were a powerful hitting team that season. Al Wingo clubbed a record thirty-four home runs, and rookie Joe Kelly hit twenty-one. Andy Anderson and Ed Onslow added more punch to the order, each batting in more than 100 runs and hitting over .300.

Sunny Jim Bottomley, one of the first stars to emerge from Rickey's farm system, hit .348 with fourteen homers and ninety-four RBIs. Bottomley would be elected to the Hall of Fame in 1974. Bill Kelley at Buffalo and Jim Holt at Jersey City were other outstanding hitters in the International League.

In 1923 Merkle continued his fine minor league career. In Rochester he was removed from the New Yorkers, who remembered him only for his failure to touch second base against the Cubs in a decisive play in the 1906 pennant race. He drove in 166 runs while batting .344 with nineteen home runs. John Wisner led an impressive pitching staff with a record of 26–15, but the Colts again were no match for Dunn's Orioles.

Toronto again had an impressive offense, but its lack of pitching precluded a run at Baltimore. Buffalo was assembling an impressive challenger, but they were several years away from contending with Dunn. Newark and Syracuse also had elements of quality, but no team could match Baltimore's balance nor the domination of their pitching.

The 1925 season offered more impressive numbers from the contingent of bridesmaids. Bill Kelley of Buffalo began a string of three consecutive seasons in which he led the International League in runs batted in, an unmatched achievement. Andy Anderson, who had come over from Toronto, hit twenty-three homers and led the club with a .335 average.

Merkle had another outstanding season for Rochester. He broke his old club record with twenty-two home runs, drove in 138, and batted .350. Wisner posted an 18–13 record, second-best on the staff to Walter Beall's 25–8.

The final year of Baltimore's run, 1926, anticipated the emergence of new powers in the International League. Toronto finally began to match Dunn's pitching staff. Myles Thomas led the club with a record of 28–8, while Walt Stewart went 21–12. Sam Gibson added another nineteen wins, while George Smith won seventeen games and Claude Satterfield added another thirteen. Charlie Gehringer provided much of the offense while polishing his skills for a Hall of Fame career with Detroit. Joe Kelly led the league with twenty-nine home runs. Frank Gilhooley and Roy Carlyle rounded out the Toronto outfield.

Buffalo's pitching collapsed that year, taking the Bisons out of the race. Among the array of stars in the International League in 1926 was Moe Berg of Reading. Berg would play fifteen years in the majors, compiling a modest .243 batting average but with a reputation as one of the brightest players in the history of the game. The old saw about Moe, a Princeton graduate, was that he could speak twelve languages but could not hit in any of them.

Toronto ended Dunn's string of pennants in 1926 with a pitching staff that Carl Hubbell could not crack. This team won 109 games with an offense that was short on power but produced a lot of runs with timely hitting.

Rochester, Buffalo, and Syracuse were among the cities in the League that rejoiced at Baltimore's downfall and looked forward to making runs at the flag themselves. Bill Kelley moved up to the majors in 1927 but never again matched his three great campaigns in the minors. Al Head combined with Del Bisonette to power the Rochester offense. Dan Clark led Syracuse with a club record thirty-one home runs, driving in 110 runs with a .364 average.

Dunn's final two years with Baltimore were utterly frustrating. The club fell to sixth place, as their pitching thinned to a reliance on one or two hurlers. The offense became similarly unproductive, and the Orioles assumed the position of its former pursuers. The Birds had a few bright spots but not enough depth to challenge the new powers of the league.

THIS REVIEW OF the International League in the era of Baltimore's dominance is necessarily limited. Numbers alone do not offer conclusive evidence of the level of performance, and the presence of a handful of Hall of Famers does not prove much about the rest of the League. In addition to such immortals as Grove and Hubbell, the International League during this period had some of the finest players in the history of the minors.

More critical than the quality of Dunn's competition is the record that one talented man produced with a minor league franchise when he was protected from the predatory major league clubs.

Dunn's Orioles were part of a rare group that was insulated from the raids that even Spalding had decried almost fifty years earlier. If not for the debilitating effects of the Federal League war and the lack of support from either the majors or the rest of the International League, Dunn might have been able to change organized baseball radically.

If Dunn could have retained Babe Ruth, imagine the team that Dunn would have had in the 1920s. His Orioles are thought to have been better than many of the major league clubs of the day. With Ruth on board, they might have been one of the best of any day.

But, instead of being the inspiration for future minor league teams, Dunn's Orioles remain an example of what might have been. The draft exemption was the vital foundation of Baltimore's success, and pressure was building to restore the draft at all levels of the game. The National Agreement of 1923 expired in 1927, and both the low minors and the major leagues were eager to eliminate the draft exempt option that had benefited the high minors. For four years, organized baseball operated without a national agreement, but the minors were also without the militant leadership that had guided them after World War I. In 1931 a new agreement restored the draft, eliminating the possibility of another team duplicating Dunn's performance in Baltimore. Other great minor league teams would develop, but none would have the independence of the Orioles. In the future, the quality of a minor league team would be determined to a great extent by the decisions of its major league patron.

# Five

# RICKEY AND THE FARMS

THE MAJOR LEAGUE clubs were in a frustrating position in the 1920s. Baseball was more popular than ever, thanks to the grand heroics of Babe Ruth; but for the first time in the history of the professional game, the access to cheap talent had been cut off. Intimidation of the high minors had been futile, and so the big leagues tried a new strategy: they would bypass the nettlesome issue of the draft by buying minor league clubs outright and squelching their independence.

The consummate practitioner of this farm system strategy was Branch Rickey. Not even Connie Mack left so significant an impact on the game through so many eras. Having created the farm system in the 1920s, Rickey integrated baseball with Jackie Robinson in the 1940s, and he provoked the expansion of the major leagues in the 1960s. But if Rickey was a Moses who led black players into organized baseball, he was also a

Pharaoh who developed the bonds that held the minor leagues in their subordinate state.

Born in 1881 in rural Ohio, Rickey grew up with unshakable moral convictions that he openly displayed, to the chagrin or annoyance of many opponents. He received a college education at Ohio Wesleyan and a law degree from the University of Michigan. In addition to this excellent education and ethical foundation, Rickey developed a love for sports, especially baseball. He played briefly and poorly for the Browns and the Yankees, but his obvious talent was in the front office. His experience with the college game left him with the same impression that Ban Johnson had had, that college baseball was a model of what the professional game should be.

Whether resisting a player's demand for a pay raise or lobbying for racial justice, Rickey's style was as impressive as the point he was making. In the oratorical tradition of William Jennings Bryan, Rickey would argue, importune, and cajole with unlimited energy and moral certainty. His bushy eyebrows, bow ties, and ever-present cigar were props that completed the picture of a larger-than-life character who could occasionally be tiresome but never boring.

More the flamboyant entrepreneur than the adaptable organization man, Rickey faced one persistent problem throughout his long career in baseball. He never had the complete freedom and security to run a franchise just as he wished. He always worked for or with men who eventually grew weary of one too many battles and forced Rickey out. In that respect, he followed a very different path from Jack Dunn's. As sole owner and manager at Baltimore, Dunn could make his own decisions without concern for the reaction of a superior or a partner. Perhaps that was the reason Dunn declined offers of positions with major league clubs.

The first of Rickey's employers was Robert Lee Hedges, who owned the St. Louis Browns. Murray Polner, a Rickey biographer, writes that Hedges was impressed by Rickey's personal qualities: his refusal to play on Sundays, his rise from childhood poverty, and his abstinence from liquor.[1] Hedges himself was one of the ambitious club owners brought into the game by Ban Johnson. Under Hedges's leadership, the Browns soon played in a new facility, Sportsman's Park, a stadium with adequate security to permit the promotion of Ladies' Day.

Rickey began as one of Hedges's players, though not an especially memorable one. In 1912 Rickey was hired to scout for the Browns because of his eye for talent, developed in his days as a college coach. Soon he was brought in to manage the Browns, but he never was able to bring home even a .500 team during his tenure from 1913–15.

The Browns' mediocrity was relieved in 1915 when Rickey lured George Sisler away from Pittsburgh with some sharp moves that led the National Commission to nullify a contract that young Sisler had signed with the Pirates without his parents' consent. Rickey's maneuvering was one of the first indications that his moral scruples would not preclude resourceful and stubborn tactics to benefit his own interests. Many of his rivals found hypocrisy in Rickey's love for both the Bible and a negotiating advantage, but Rickey was never troubled by conflict between his two passions.

Sisler proved to be one of the greatest players in the history of the game. His fifteen-year career included a lifetime batting average of .340. Twice he hit over .400, and he was a splendid fielder. Despite these gifts, Sisler was unable to turn the Browns around. After his rookie year, Robert Hedges, weary of the Browns' mediocrity and the financial distress of the Federal League war, sold the club to Philip Ball.

The change was disastrous for Rickey, who had commanded such respect from fellow teetotaler Hedges. Ball was a different sort. Upon meeting Rickey for the first time, he announced, "So you're the goddamned prohibitionist."[2] The new owner's abrasive manner was a terrible burden to Rickey, a young man with a growing family, who needed a good job during hard times. As far as possible, he tried to placate Ball.

After one season, Rickey was able to escape across town to the St. Louis Cardinals, where he had been offered the club presidency. It took a lawsuit for him to leave the Browns, because Ban Johnson hated to see talent escape the American League, and Ball held a grudge about Rickey's leaving for many years. Still a relative novice in the game, Rickey had already earned the animosity of the Pirates and the Browns before he settled into a long run with the Cardinals.

St. Louis's National League entry was another casualty of the combination of the Federal League and World War I. Rickey was the president of a bankrupt franchise. The financial plight had the advantage of leaving Rickey without a boss. He had a free hand in his first few years before a young automobile dealer, Sam Breadon, obtained a 72 percent interest in the club in exchange for an $18,000 loan.

Breadon also assumed the club presidency, demoting Rickey to vice-president. But the loss in status did not bring a loss of responsibility: Rickey continued to run the front office while managing the Cardinals for over six years, beginning in 1919. As a field manager, Rickey had limited success. His best results with the Cardinals were third-place finishes in 1921 and 1922. He also had a curiously ambivalent attitude about managing. When Rickey was not protesting that he did not want the job, he was complaining that Breadon was taking his protests seriously.

The neater fit for Rickey was as a general manager. Two qualities are evident in his many years in that position for several teams. First, he was as tightfisted as they came in player negotiations. He held his first jobs during such difficult times that an ability to stretch every nickel was important. This frugality was legendary by the time Rickey held his last job, with Pittsburgh in the 1950s. He cut Ralph Kiner's salary by over 20 percent in 1953 despite Kiner's leading the National League in home runs for the seventh consecutive year. As the only star on the lowly Pirates was told, "Son, we could have finished last without you."[3]

The second ability in which Rickey was unsurpassed was his skill in assessing baseball talent. His experience as a college coach, the need to get the most from limited financial resources, and his scientific approach to the game combined to give him an eye for skills that others had missed. He also knew where to look for this talent. Hedges had first hired him to scout the midwest and Pacific coast; Rickey also maintained his contacts with college coaches for players who could make the move from campus to the big leagues.

The specific event that triggered Rickey's plan for a farm system may have been the Cardinals' acquisition of a minor league pitcher, Jesse Haines. The purchase price of $10,000 had caused Breadon to hesitate and Rickey to start thinking of other ways of moving players to St. Louis. (Their gamble paid off as Haines pitched in the big leagues for nineteen years and was later inducted into the Hall of Fame.)

The National Agreement of 1921 that had precluded the use of the draft permitted another opening for the advancement of players, allowing minor league teams to be owned by major league clubs. This was a variation of syndicate ownership, which had been banned; with some refining, it solved the problem of supplying quality players at a low cost.

Robert Hedges had attempted to develop a small farm system for the Browns in 1913 when he financed the purchase of a local franchise in Alabama with the stipulation that the Cardinals could buy any player from that team for the price of $10,000. The informal agreement collapsed after one season.

The flaw in these understandings between major league and minor league teams was their informality. The infusion of some cash led some major league owners to think that they had exclusive rights to players from the subsidized club. (An exception was the tie between Jack Dunn and Connie Mack. Their relationship seems to have been based on the confidence each had in the other's baseball judgment. If either thought this mutual respect would translate into charity, he was quickly disabused of the idea.)

Rickey apparently was confident that financial gain would not override a gentlemen's understanding when he first invested Breadon's money in minor league franchises. A purchase of half ownership in the Syracuse franchise of the International League led Rickey to think that the Cardinals had a lock on the Stars' players. When Rickey tried to secure Jim Bottomley in 1921, Syracuse owner E. C. Landgraf balked. He explained that Bottomley had attracted so much attention from other major league clubs that he was considering selling the first baseman to the highest bidder. Rickey pressed his case with Landgraf and successfully obtained Bottomley, who justified Rickey's judgment by having a Hall of Fame career.

Polner's account of the Bottomley case concludes with the opinion that Landgraf's price for his star player was the Cardinals' purchase of his half of the Syracuse ownership. Breadon was happy to oblige, and Rickey realized the final adjustment in syndicate ownership. No agreement, handshake, or understanding could substitute for controlling ownership of a minor league franchise. Only formal legal and financial power could ensure the personnel moves that otherwise would fly in the face of market forces.

UNDER RICKEY'S LEADERSHIP the Cardinals began scouting entire minor league teams as other clubs scouted individual ballplayers. By 1928 St. Louis had seven farm teams, from the low minors to Class AA, and were beginning to reap the benefits of this new strategy, as evidenced by their World Series championship in 1926. By the end of the decade, they were challenging John McGraw's Giants as the dominant team in the National League.

The farm system was financially profitable as well. Ira Irving described the returns from the Cardinals' Texas League entry, the Houston Buffaloes: "The Texas League champs gave up several of their stars to major league clubs for handsome prices. The Cardinals received Hallahan, Littlejohn, Selph, and Jonnard. The Detroit Tigers of the American League handed over to the Cardinals $35,000 cash for shortstop Heinie Schuble and pitcher Frank Barnes. Both cost the Cardinals practically nothing, being developed at the farms."[4]

Players that the Cardinals could not use themselves, such as

Schuble and Barnes, were still valuable as sources of income when sold to other clubs. In effect, the Cardinals' farm system supplied players to the majors while bypassing the draft and its restrictions. The players went to St. Louis cheaply, and to other major league teams at market value, with the money going to the St. Louis treasury. One account cited by Murray Polner claims that from 1922 to 1942 the Cardinals made over $2 million in player sales to other major league franchises.

The new flow of revenue enabled Rickey to set up tryout camps all over the country. He used reliable scouts to recruit players that other clubs were unable to find. Rickey developed an organization that accomplished on a large scale the task at which he had excelled: finding gifted ball players in out-of-the-way places.

The similarities and contrasts with Jack Dunn are again worth noting. Both Rickey and Dunn were talented and tireless scouts who found great players at the very beginning of their careers. If these players were not needed in Baltimore or St. Louis, they were sold to other teams at a market price. When Dunn exercised his skills, he antagonized both major league and minor league executives, who thought he was upsetting the status quo. Rickey made his enemies over the years, but, given his major league position, none of them challenged the propriety of his tough bargaining.

The St. Louis farm system began in 1920 with part owner-ship of the Houston Buffaloes of the Texas League and a work-ing arrangement with Fort Smith, Arkansas, in the Western League, a Class-C circuit. The purchase of Syracuse, a fran-chise that was moved to Rochester in 1928, gave Rickey control throughout the minor league system. Players could be placed at levels appropriate to their skills, and then the best of them could be advanced to the Cardinals when the time was right or sold to another club if St. Louis enjoyed a surplus.

The system grew relentlessly. In 1940 thirty-two minor league teams belonged to the Cardinals, who had working agreements with another eight clubs. Over 600 players were in the pipeline to St. Louis, inspiring one of Rickey's innumerable maxims, "Out of quantity comes quality."

The Gashouse Gang of the 1930s was one of the best teams in major league history, and it was the ultimate product of Rickey's farm system. One of its stars was Pepper Martin, who labored in the minors for seven years before making his major league debut in 1931 at the advanced age of twenty-seven. When Martin was ready, he replaced Taylor Douthit, who had been one of the first players to advance to the Cardinals from Syracuse.

Martin played for thirteen years in the majors before returning to the minors as a manager. He had been a fine ball player at St. Louis, appreciated as much for his honest, unpretentious manner as his play. Pepper Martin stories were a staple in the coverage of the Gashouse Gang. Red Smith recalled one from Martin's days as a minor league manager:

As leader in Miami, he was suspended for reasoning with an umpire while clutching that dignitary firmly by the throat. This was a crime too heinous for the league president. The case went up to the baseball commissioner, Happy Chandler.

Confident that there must be some mitigating circumstances, Chandler adopted a conciliatory tone. "Tell me, Pepper, what were you thinking when you had that man by the throat?"

"I was thinking," Pepper said, "that I'd choke the son of a bitch to death."[5]

Joe "Ducky" Medwick was another star of the Cardinals of the 1930s. An even better ball player than Pepper Martin, Medwick had his best year in 1937, when he led the National League in home runs with thirty-one, batting with a .374 average, and RBIs with 154. He ended a seventeen-year career in 1948 with a .324 lifetime batting average, and twenty years later he was inducted into the Hall of Fame. Medwick was a great example of the effectiveness of the Cardinals' farm system. When he broke into the majors at the end of the 1932 season, he replaced another Hall of Famer, Chick Hafey, who was the reigning batting champion of the National League. Hafey had had the temerity to press Rickey for more money; for his trouble, Rickey traded him to last-place Cincinnati. When Pepper Martin had replaced Taylor Douthit, the Cardinals also saved some money in Martin's salary, but the move was dictated more by Martin's superior ability.

The treatment of Hafey was more cavalier, and it was possible because Medwick had hit .354 in the Texas League and was ready to join the Cardinals. Rickey had a steady supply of talented players constantly challenging the established veterans. This pressure enhanced Rickey's and Breadon's control over the players and helped them deal with the likes of Frankie Frisch, Leo Durocher, and Rogers Hornsby.

Hornsby was traded to the Giants in 1927 for Frisch because the Rajah had tangled with Breadon. Durocher was dealt to Brooklyn when he could no longer get along with Frisch. That quarrel would not have been sufficient by itself to force Leo's departure, but the farm system had again done its job by producing Marty Marion, who would shortly become a fixture at shortstop for the Cardinals.

During Rickey's years with St. Louis, the Cards won pennants in 1926, 1928, 1930, 1931, 1934, and 1942, winning the World Series in 1926, 1934, and 1942. The team sparked interest amidst the gloom of the Great Depression. For most of the Cardinals' reign, they had the stage to themselves. Babe Ruth was in his waning years, and no competitor could command the press coverage that the Gashouse Gang generated. Both the achievements and the headlines masked an important fact about the St. Louis franchise: the players were assets managed for the financial interests of Sam Breadon.

Murray Polner recorded some of the player sales that helped Breadon through the hard times of the 1930s. Johnny Mize earned more than $50,000 for Breadon. Bob Worthington and

Charlie Wilson each netted $60,000. Don Padgett was worth $35,000.

Most remarkable was the Chicago Cubs' payment of $185,000 for a pitcher at the tail end of his career, a player whose name, age, and place of birth were beyond the certain knowledge of anyone in the game. Dizzy Dean came up to the Cardinals at the end of the 1930 season, a campaign that began for him in St. Joseph, Missouri, where he had a 17–8 record. In August he was promoted to Houston and went 8–2 for the Buffaloes before joining St. Louis. He had the chance to pitch one game after the Cardinals had clinched the pennant, beating Pittsburgh 3–1 in a five-hitter.

Making the most of his major league record of 1–0, Diz appeared in Branch Rickey's office that December to make sure that "Branch" (Dean was ever the egalitarian) appreciated the talent that had come his way. As Red Smith records the scene, Rickey stumbled from his office after two hours of a classic Dean performance looking utterly beleaguered. "'Do you know what that—that busher said to me?' Rickey said. 'He told me, "Mr. Rickey, I'll put more people in your park than anybody since Babe Ruth." That—that country jake! Judas priest, if there were one more like him in baseball, I'd get out of the game.'"[6]

Rickey received a respite when Dean was sent back to Houston early in the 1931 season. Although he missed the month of April, Dizzy surpassed every pitcher in the minor leagues in wins (twenty-six), strikeouts (303), and ERA (1.53). He completed twenty-eight of his thirty-two starts, with nine relief appearances. After that performance he was back in Rickey's life for seven years, during which he won 134 games, including thirty in 1934, the last time that has been done in the National League.

Dean's remarkable career prematurely ended after a line drive in the 1937 All-Star game fractured his toe. He tried to come back too soon from the injury and hurt his arm—an ailment from which he never recovered. After winning 134 games with the Cards, he managed just 16 more wins in the next three seasons with the Chicago Cubs.

In 1947, at the age of thirty-something, he tried a comeback with the St. Louis Browns but was shelled in the first inning of his only start. With his pitching skills gone, Dizzy's personality saved him. He became a baseball announcer for network television, where his own version of the king's English left an entire generation thinking that the past tense of "slide" is "slud."

Why did Phil Wrigley pay so much money for Dean, a pitcher with a bad arm? Rickey himself advised Wrigley that Dean would not be the pitcher he had been. Polner concludes that Wrigley "went along with the deal, explaining—or so rumors had it—that Dean would sell a lot of chewing gum for him, good arm or not."[7] That explanation would fit with the kind of exhibitionism that kept Babe Ruth in the game until he became a spectacle as a coach of the Brooklyn Dodgers. Even the best players in the days of the reserve clause received a fraction of what they would have made today, so baseball included a kind of sideshow where sentimental fans enriched both aging stars and unsentimental owners.

BY THE LATE 1930s, baseball was dominated by the New York Yankees, who had followed Rickey's example by building a farm system that established dynasties not only in the Bronx but also in their Newark team of the International League. With the Cardinals holding sway in the National League, the prospect of a couple of major league franchises advancing several levels above their competitors began to trouble some of baseball's magnates.

One of those most concerned was the commissioner, Kenesaw Mountain Landis. For flamboyance, moral certitude, and bushiness of eyebrow, Landis was Rickey's match. Their relationship was not a good one. Landis had little use for Rickey, and Rickey found in Landis another powerful man whom he could not directly challenge. Landis was thoroughly opposed to the development of farm systems, primarily because he believed they compromised the integrity of the minor league game. Since the Cardinals' farm system began at the very time of Landis's installation as commissioner, a collision over this issue was inevitable.

SYRACUSE WAS THE last stop in Rickey's farm system before a player joined St. Louis. The Stars were one of the teams that chased Jack Dunn's Orioles in the early 1920s, and although the club was weak in pitching, it had one of the great players of the International League, Sunny Jim Bottomley, who sparkled at first base in 1922, hitting .348 with fourteen home runs and ninety-four RBIs. If Bottomley had played for Jack Dunn, he would certainly have been kept in the International League until a major league team was willing to pay the kind of money Dunn felt he was worth. As it was, Bottomley was in a Cardinal uniform by the end of the season. He played for St. Louis for ten years, and he added another six seasons with other teams. This Hall of Fame player could have done a lot for baseball in Syracuse, either through his own performance or through the money that he would have brought in a sale on the open market. But, in the farm system, Syracuse was little more than a colonial outpost whose purpose was to serve the interests of the Cardinals.

For several years, the Stars had a splendid double-play combination with Tommy Thevenow at short and Gard Gislason at second. Wattie Holm was a fine outfielder for a Syracuse team that struggled with mediocre pitching. By 1926 the Stars were on their way to becoming a power in the International League. Dan Clark set a club record for home runs with thirty-one in 1926, a year in which he also hit .364 and drove in 110 runs. The first baseman, Frank Hurst, added 129 RBIs, with eighteen home runs and a .331 average. Pepper Martin had joined the team at second base. Gus Mancuso hit .372 as a catcher in 1927 before being called up to the Cardinals. Howie Williamson, Harry Layne, and Homer Peel were the outfielders who left little if any mark in the majors but hit well over .300 for Syracuse.

The Stars' pitching was catching up to the team's offense. In 1927 Bill Hallahan and Syd Johnson were wrapping things up with Syracuse before moving to St. Louis to begin major league careers in which each would win over 100 games. Some capable relief pitching left Syracuse fans eagerly awaiting the 1928 season.

Their expectations were rewarded when the team captured its first pennant since 1897. Unfortunately for Syracuse, their team was now located in Rochester.

The decision to move the Stars was made by Rickey in St. Louis in the spring of 1928. The inducement was a modern ball park adjacent to an affluent neighborhood in Rochester. The stadium in Syracuse was a deteriorating wooden facility that could not compare with the new park in Rochester. On the face of it, the franchise shift was an especially cynical move. If the Stars needed a new stadium, why didn't the Cardinals build them one? Isn't that what the paternal relationship between the clubs would suggest?

By moving to a park in Rochester that others had financed, Rickey and Breadon showed how little regard the major league patron could have for the minor league town. It was one thing to move a Bottomley or a Martin to the Cardinals when their potential became evident, but the move of the entire franchise left Syracuse without any team during the years 1928–34. Surely they deserved better treatment than that. Especially galling to Syracuse was the emergence of Rochester as the new dynasty of the International League. Rickey himself had renamed the club the Red Wings to emphasize (in case anyone had missed it) the team's connection to the Cardinals, and the Wings won four consecutive pennants, from 1928 through 1931.

Jim "Ripper" Collins began a stint with Rochester by hitting .375 while filling in at first base. Second baseman "Specs" Toporcer and shortstop Charlie Gelbert combined with Joe "Poison" Brown at third to establish the all-time record for double plays in organized baseball, an incredible 246. Boyce Morrow had come over from Syracuse to handle the catching, and he was assisted by Hank Gowdy, who had ended a seventeen-year career in the majors.

The first pennant in 1928 was a bit tainted, since the difference between the Red Wings and the Buffalo Bisons was one rained-out game that was not replayed. Other clubs also were in the thick of the pennant race until the final month of the season, and the International League showed promise of great vitality after so many years of dominance at the hands of Baltimore.

Jack Dunn's tragic death in 1928 virtually ensured that the Orioles would not resume their dominance of the League. That season was more of a watershed than could have been known at the time. As David Chrisman puts it, "If Baltimore's decline was clearly etched in the minds of International League fans, the more abstruse rise of the Red Wings was not."[8]

From the narrow margin of the 1928 championship, Rochester moved on to win the 1929 and 1930 pennants more comfortably. The Cardinals were now settled at enough positions that some stability on the field allowed Rochester to enjoy Toporcer, Collins, and Martin for several years. Collins batted .315 in 1929 with thirty-eight home runs and 134 RBIs. The following year he hit .376 with forty home runs and a league record 180 runs batted in. In Pepper Martin's last year with Rochester, he hit twenty home runs with 114 runs batted in while hitting .363. Paul Derringer won twenty-three games for the Red Wings, giving them a rare pitching performance to match their great hitters and fielders.

The one curious aspect of the Rochester team was its managing. In maneuvering that anticipated the Yankees of the Steinbrenner era, Rickey shuttled managers between St. Louis and Rochester. The Cardinals began the season with Bill McKechnie at the helm, the man who had guided St. Louis to a pennant in 1928. Midway through the season, Rickey sent McKechnie to Rochester to switch places with Billy Southworth, who had also been a pennant winner with the Red Wings the previous year.

Southworth, a former major league outfielder who ended his

career with the Cardinals, was thought to be a brilliant strategist. After his half season with the Cardinals, he returned to Rochester, where he guided the Wings to their next pennants. He would not return to major league managing until 1940, when he rejoined the Cardinals and led them to three pennants in six years.

Despite McKechnie's success, he was replaced in St. Louis by Gabby Street. McKechnie made it back to the majors in 1930 with the Boston Braves. He moved to Cincinnati in 1938 where he enjoyed more success. He retired in 1946 after twenty-five years as a major league manager, and in 1962 he was inducted into the Hall of Fame.

OTHER MAJOR LEAGUE franchises, especially the Yankees, were beginning to recognize the benefits of Rickey's farm system to the Cardinals, and they were preparing to follow the same strategy. Jack Dunn had found his course more difficult in his last couple of years, and after his death no one emerged to challenge the concept of a farm system with an independent franchise.

Chrisman's summary of this period of the International League emphasizes the different qualities of the dynasties in Baltimore and Rochester:

> . . . Dunn's primary aim was always to win—and provide the citizens of Baltimore with the very best baseball teams that money and organization could attain. And once success was assured, Dunn sought to hold on to his stars for as long as the law (or financial solvency) would allow. It was always Dunn's announced intention to win for Baltimore and not to prepare his players (necessarily) to star for someone else on the major league level. Thus, his entire philosophy was predicated upon establishing Baltimore (not St. Louis or Philadelphia) as the best baseball town in America.

On the other hand, after the St. Louis Cardinals decided to move their Syracuse franchise to Rochester, that city's baseball team had but one objective and that was to develop and train the future stars of Rickey's major league club. If they could win the International League pennant in the process, then so much the better.[9]

Chrisman also points out that Dunn's players remained with Baltimore far longer than Rochester's did. Specs Toporcer, the only Red Wing to play on all four pennant winners, was joined only by Jim "Ripper" Collins in the International League Hall of Fame.

By resisting the major league draft and paying his players as well as they would have been paid in the majors, Dunn kept stars who were often content to remain in Baltimore despite the alleged lure of the major leagues. By the end of the Oriole dynasty, twelve of their players had been voted into the International League Hall of Fame along with Dunn himself.

The transfer of power in the International League in the 1920s from Baltimore to Rochester symbolized the transition in the minor leagues from what they could have been to what they became. Dunn's approach was risky and in certain respects limited because it required a minor league club to be run by someone as talented and committed as Dunn himself. The emergence of the farm system also relied on Rickey's executive talents and energy, but the rewards were more apparent as the risk was diminished. More important, the rewards were greatest for the major league franchises, which could not have missed the obvious superiority of this method over trading with the likes of Jack Dunn. At the same time, the minor leagues were assured of the financial security of a major league patron, thereby eliminating the risk of operating independently. Only Dunn seems to have relished the challenge of that risk.

Jake Ruppert, owner of the New York Yankees, had become aware of Rickey's use of Rochester for the benefit of St. Louis. He set about to duplicate the practice with the Newark Bears.

The combination of powerful farm systems in St. Louis and New York promised to challenge other franchises in ways that could not be ignored.


FARM SYSTEMS WERE especially obnoxious to Commissioner Landis, who objected to them on the grounds that the benefits of local ownership were lost, that players with major league talent could be held back and even hidden in the minors, and that only the wealthiest major league clubs would be able to afford to carry a chain of minor league franchises.

Rickey's experience with the Cardinals seemed to belie Landis's last concern. The St. Louis farm system was begun precisely because the Cardinals were a bankrupt organization with no other way to secure the players they needed. Buying minor league clubs was a somewhat risky and unprecedented investment, but it was the only investment the Cardinals could afford in the early 1920s.

On the other hand, the transfer of the Syracuse Stars to Rochester showed that community loyalty counted for nothing when the local franchise was run by a major league club in a distant metropolis. More common than moving an entire ball club was the practice of bringing a player up to the majors even when he was needed in a minor league pennant race. Under Rickey's system, where the overriding purpose of the minors was to serve the major league patron, fans in smaller New York and Texas communities were told to take comfort in the fact that their loss was St. Louis's gain.

The inevitable showdown between Rickey and Landis occurred over the issue of whether players were being unduly restrained in advancing to the major leagues. This issue was central to Landis's understanding of how the labor market should operate. He frequently alluded to "the free market in players," but that is surely not what he meant.

In principle, Landis seemed committed to the elimination of any barriers that kept quality players from the big leagues. In practice, that seemed to mean that minor league clubs should be independently owned and operated but their players should be bound by the reserve clause and their entire rosters open to a major league draft. With this stance Landis managed to oppose both Jack Dunn and Branch Rickey.

The success of the St. Louis farm system was eliminating the independent course that Dunn exemplified, and Landis proposed to rein in the farms themselves. Technically, Landis was in a tough position. The National Agreement of 1903 had banned gentlemen's agreements between major and minor league teams, the informal farm system that preceded Rickey's scheme. Only in 1913 was the formal ownership of minor league clubs by major league teams outlawed, but that prohibition was ignored during the chaotic days of the Federal League and World War I.

Formal ownership was permitted under the National Agreement of 1921, but Landis's opposition was threatening enough that Rickey acquired minor league teams in as unobtrusive a way as possible. By the winter meetings of 1929, open war between the Cardinals and the commissioner was imminent.

As Murray Polner relates the fight, Landis initiated things by condemning the St. Louis farm system and announcing his intention to destroy it:

> Breadon exploded with indignation and said he had five statements from minor league clubs favoring the system. To Landis, he shrieked, "You've gone out of your way to hurt my business." The Judge's response was that he and Rickey were the troublemakers. He accused them of robbing small-town America of its precious heritage of independent minor league baseball. "You are both guilty of raping the minors," he told Breadon, who shook with rage at the charge.[10]

Rickey remained circumspect where Landis was concerned. Breadon, as a club owner, had the freedom to challenge the commissioner directly. Rickey, though committed to the wisdom of the farm system, needed to steer a course between Breadon and Landis, but that ultimately proved impossible.

Landis held Rickey in contempt. Polner writes that Landis referred to Rickey as "that hypocritical preacher" and "that Protestant bastard [who's] always masquerading with a minister's robe."[11] Since both Rickey and Landis vested their business arguments with moral certitude, their disagreements easily escalated to religious wars with all of the ugliness that such conflicts involve.

In 1931 Landis tangled with Phil Ball in federal court over Herschel Bennett, a player in the Browns' farm system who claimed that he was being unfairly prevented from getting a chance to play in the majors. Landis's order to Ball to put Bennett on the Browns' roster or release him was challenged by Ball as an infringement of his property rights. Judge Walter Lindley upheld Landis's order, but Landis then lost the larger battle.

Lindley sustained the legality of the farm system, providing players were treated fairly within its organization. After this ruling, Landis changed his strategy to focus on the operation of player movements within the farm systems, and the Cardinals became a favorite target of his interest.

By 1938 the Cardinals farm system had become massive. Not only were individual teams tied to St. Louis, but in violation of league rules, entire leagues were under Rickey's control. The Nebraska State League was one Class-D circuit whose every team was a subsidiary of the Cardinals. This caricature of a farm system finally broke the integrity of the minor leagues that were so controlled.

The argument could be made that the taking of the occasional star to help in a major league pennant race was a small price for a community to pay in exchange for a solid financial foundation beneath its local team. The moving of an entire franchise was a sufficiently rare event that it had not become a serious problem for the majors. But the control of several

teams in one league removed all pretense about the competitiveness of those circuits.

Rickey is one of the most revered and respected figures in
the history of organized baseball. His brilliant work in bringing
Jackie Robinson into the game has been justly praised as perhaps the moral apex of the game's history. His development of
farm systems has also been praised for the resulting economic
returns and the great Cardinal teams that were so built, but by
the late 1930s, the farm system had failed any reasonable moral
test.

Landis had directed his associate, Leslie O'Connor, to inves-
tigate the elaborate operations in the Cardinals' low minor
leagues. During spring training in 1938, Landis summoned
Rickey for another defense of the Cardinals' behavior. In what
became known as the Cedar Rapids case, the commissioner
charged that an agreement that St. Louis had with Springfield
of the Three-I League violated essential principles of a competitive game. Springfield had agreed to let Rickey buy any one of
its players for $2,500 at the same time that the Cardinals oper-
ated Danville in the same league.

In a famous exchange, Rickey admitted that "it was in the
agreement" that Springfield's opportunities to improve its
team to compete against Danville and other teams had been
seriously limited. Referring to that restriction, Landis asked,
"That is in this [the agreement with Springfield], isn't it?"

Rickey: "Yes, that is in there."

Landis: "Big as a house isn't it?"

Rickey: "It is not big as a house."

Landis: "I think it is as big as the universe. This is just as
important in the Three-I League as it would be in the National
or American Leagues."[12]

Rickey left this meeting confident that once again he had
stayed within bounds, but he was quickly disabused. Landis
declared seventy-four players in the Cardinals farm system to
be free agents. He also fined several of the minor league clubs
that had cooperated with the Cardinals' scheme. Although
Landis had freed players before, the scale of this release was
unprecedented.

As sweeping as this measure was, it barely slowed the Cardinals' accumulation of players. Two years after Landis's ruling, the Cardinals had ownership of thirty-two clubs and working agreements with another eight. Over 600 ball players remained in the Cardinal organization, so the loss of seventy-four was a blow but not a fatal one.

For Rickey, the long-term effects of Landis's move may have been more serious. Breadon rushed to his defense when the decision was first announced, but the relationship between the two became strained, perhaps as a result of this episode. Polner cites a writer, J. Roy Stockton, who attended a meeting between Rickey and Breadon and said that the Cardinals' owner was embarrassed about the disclosures and furious with Rickey for the entire incident.

For years Breadon had deferred to Rickey's superior judgment about baseball, but their relationship was becoming more difficult. Breadon chafed at Rickey's receipt of 10 percent on all player sales, and Rickey, in turn, resented Breadon's salary cutting and other economies. His association with Breadon had certainly been better than that with Phil Ball, but once again the problems of working with a forceful owner surfaced.

After the World Series in 1942, Branch Rickey resigned from the Cardinals. The final rift with Breadon was Rickey's objection to a brewery sponsoring the broadcast of Cardinal games. More important, Breadon believed that he could run the club as well as Rickey had, and the Cardinals' owner had also tired of the battles with Rickey.

EVEN MORE THAN the Gashouse Gang, the legacy of Branch Rickey in St. Louis was the farm system. When he began with the Cardinals, the minor leagues were freed from the draft, and indeed they had no formal association with the major leagues. The possibility of independent minors was theoretically greater than it had ever been, and Jack Dunn in Baltimore was demonstrating how that theory could be practiced.

In a few years, Rickey had reversed all of that. Through prudent investment in a few minor league clubs, the supply of cheap talent to the major leagues was restored. The supply was so bountiful that the sale of unneeded players to other teams allowed St. Louis to move quickly from being a marginal franchise to one of the most prosperous. By receiving a percentage of these sales, Rickey enriched himself, but he remained an employee subject to Breadon's wishes.

The financial success of the farm systems was so compelling that other clubs copied the idea. Landis's freeing of the Cardinals' farm players and an even more sweeping release of minor leaguers in the Detroit Tigers' farm system in 1940 could not hinder the growing major league dominance over the minors.

Ironically, Rickey the moralist created the most serious problem with farm systems. The Cardinals' ownership of several clubs in the same league was such a blatant violation of competitive integrity that any rhetorical concern about the benefits of farm systems for the minors was obviously a hollow claim.

Rickey had made no pretense that Rochester and his other minor league teams were operated primarily for the benefit of the St. Louis Cardinals. The Cedar Rapids case showed that the value of the minors as competitive teams in smaller communities had been cynically abandoned in the rush to collect future major leaguers. Like the recent collusion of the major league owners in shunning free agency, this front office corruption may be less repugnant than the Black Sox scandal, but it may be no less serious a threat to the integrity of baseball.

# ◆ Six ◆

# THE AMERICAN ASSOCIATION

FOR FIFTY YEARS, the midwestern American Association prospered in the high minors, until the major leagues decided that raiding players was such a good idea that raiding markets would be even better.

From 1902 to 1952, the circuit of Columbus, Indianapolis, Kansas City, Louisville, Milwaukee, Minneapolis, St. Paul, and Toledo was a model of stability. In 1952 the Braves moved from Boston to Milwaukee, and the eventual collapse of the American Association was under way. In time, Kansas City, Minneapolis, and St. Paul would also be grabbed, and from 1963 through 1968, deprived of its major markets, the Association ceased to exist.

The destruction of the American Association was part of a pattern in which the major leagues undermined or simply took the important markets of the minor leagues, but the fate of this

particular circuit was perhaps the cruelest step in a dreary process. Farm systems changed the character of the International
League, and the Pacific Coast League fell from being a near
major league to simply another colonial outpost; but of the
high minor leagues, only the American Association collapsed
entirely.

LIKE THE PCL and the International League, the American
Association might have prospered with independent teams. At
one point or another, the Association included the great Yankee managers Miller Huggins, Joe McCarthy, Casey Stengel,
and Ralph Houk. Walter Alston, Charlie Dressen, and Burt
Shotton guided Dodger teams to eleven pennants from 1947
through 1974 after apprenticeships in the Association. Leo Durocher led pennant winners for the Dodgers and Giants. Fred
Haney won titles for the Milwaukee Braves in 1957 and 1958,
and Charlie Grimm brought the last pennant to the Chicago
Cubs in 1945. These outstanding managers were part of a pool
that the American Association enjoyed during its final decades.

THE BALL PARKS of the American Association were another
asset that added to the special quality of baseball in the midwest. The most remarkable facility was Nicollet Park in Minneapolis. From 1896 through 1955, players tried to adjust to
dimensions that ran from 279 feet in right field to 435 in center
to 328 in left. The park included a mirror image of Fenway
Park, with its monster in right field. After Joe Hauser crushed
sixty-nine home runs in 1933, a thirty-foot fence was built in
right field with another fifteen feet of screen atop.
   The peculiarities of Nicollet Park added to the rivalry between the Millers and the St. Paul Saints. The teams played
home-and-home doubleheaders on holidays, with a morning
game in one town followed by a trip across the Mississippi for

the afternoon contest in the other. The setting for this spirited rivalry lasted until the mid-1950s, when Nicollet Park was demolished in 1955, just a few weeks after the Millers captured the Junior World Series championship. Lexington Park in St. Paul was torn down in the following year.

The loss of these ball parks anticipated the loss of the rivalry itself. When the Washington Senators moved from the nation's capital in 1961, they replaced both the Millers and the Saints from the Twin Cities while taking over the Millers' Metropolitan Stadium.

Borchert Field in Milwaukee was another ancient marvel of the American Association. The park was built in 1888 and used until 1953, when the Braves arrived from Boston, occupied County Stadium, and displaced the Brewers in the process. Borchert Field proves that not all old parks were charming. Few seats afforded a decent vantage of the field, and fierce storms occasionally blew parts of the edifice onto neighboring homes.

Under the reign of Bill Veeck, who owned the Milwaukee Brewers during the early 1940s, Borchert Field gave the Brewers an unprecedented home field advantage. Veeck liked to mingle with the fans during a game, and he was often asked why the park had a short right field when the team had no left-handed power. Veeck introduced a remedy by means of a sixty-foot wire fence that cut down the power of the opponents.

Never lacking in imagination, Veeck realized he was on to something. When he improved his own club's hitting the following year, he concluded that some modifications were needed at the ball park. "Calling upon my Lewis Institute training, I designed a system for sliding the wire fence back and forth along the top of the wall by means of a hydraulic motor. When the visiting team had more left handed power than we did, the fence would stay up. Otherwise, we would reel it back into the foul line."[1]

As outrageous as it was to adjust the field on a game-to-game basis, Veeck was just getting started. "From there it was only a short hop to the ultimate refinement. In the best of all possible parks, the fence would be up for the opposition and down for us. We could do this without any trouble at all—and we did do it—by reeling the fence in and out between innings. That is, we did it once. They passed a rule against it the next day."[2]

The demise of Borchert Field was no great loss to Milwaukee, but the associated—and pointless—loss of the Brewers was. The Braves, it turned out, were simply visiting Milwaukee. They moved to Atlanta in 1966, as if Milwaukee itself were responsible for the fading skills of some of the stars of the pennant-winning teams of the late 1950s.

Major league baseball returned to Milwaukee in 1970 when the Seattle Pilots, in their second year of existence, became the new Milwaukee Brewers. Milwaukee now enjoys a team that is locally owned by people who plan to replace County Stadium with a privately financed open-air baseball stadium with a grass field. This is a just reward for a city that has suffered so much in the past from the whims of major league ownership.

MORE THAN ITS managers and ball parks, the American Association's prominence relied on its players. Among the most memorable was Joe Hauser, who set home run records for his hometown of Minneapolis. Hauser began in the minors with Providence of the Eastern League in 1918. The following year he led that league in home runs with six.

His success propelled him to Milwaukee of the American Association. In two years with the Brewers, Hauser was converted to a first baseman in an effort to make use of his powerful bat. Hauser became an immensely popular player in his hometown. The German-American fans dubbed him "Unser Choe," our Joe. He developed sufficiently to attract the interest of Connie Mack, who had passed on Hauser several years before when the lad was trying to make it as a pitcher. After the 1921 season, Mack acquired Hauser for $25,000 and four players.

Hauser proved to be a fine major league first baseman. In his first three years, he hit .323, .307, and .288. That dropoff in average in 1924 was more than made up for by the twenty-seven home runs he hit that year. With several years of experience, Hauser, at the age of twenty-five, seemed to be ready for an outstanding career.

In the first month of the 1925 season, Hauser fractured his kneecap on a routine play at first. A comeback in 1926 was unsuccessful, and the following year he was sent to Kansas City of the American Association, where he rebounded with a league-leading twenty-two home runs.

Back with the Athletics in 1928, Hauser's major league career was shortened by two of the game's immortals. Ty Cobb, perhaps resentful that Hauser was hitting better than the Georgia Peach in his last season, offered to "help" Hauser with his hitting. By the time Cobb's advice had been resisted, taken, and its effects undone, Jimmy Foxx had arrived to secure first base for Connie Mack.

In 1929 Hauser had a brief stay with Cleveland before being sent back to Milwaukee. The next season he was in Baltimore, where he belted sixty-three home runs, a minor league record and a new mark for organized ball. Another injury halved his home run output in 1931, and Baltimore let him escape back to the American Association.

The Minneapolis Millers were the beneficiaries of Hauser's greatest production. He hit forty-nine home runs in 1932, with 129 runs driven in despite missing the final month of the season. Unser Choe enjoyed one of the greatest offensive seasons of any player in the history of organized baseball in 1933. He hit an astounding sixty-nine home runs with 182 runs batted in and an average of .332.

Hauser remains the only professional ball player to hit more than sixty home runs in two seasons. His record sixty-nine homers was tied by Bob Crues in 1948 in the West Texas–New Mexico League, and it was surpassed when Joe Bauman hit seventy-two in 1954 for Roswell of the Longhorn League. Incredibly, Bauman never batted in the major leagues. Crues and

Bauman worked their magic in the low minors, while Hauser's Minneapolis team was one notch below the majors.

The dimensions of Nicollet Park may appear to taint Hauser's record, but he had a response for people who tried to demean his achievement. Hauser recalled some heckling he received during a speech in Milwaukee, "Some wiseacre in the audience yells out that wasn't such a great feat in Minneapolis because of the bandbox of a ball park they had there. I called back to him, 'When I was hitting, they were all bandboxes.'"[3]

Hauser also noted that the thirty-foot screen compensated for the short porch. A few routine flies might have become home runs, but some screaming line drives might also have been reduced to singles. If further support is needed for Hauser, the sixty-three home runs in Baltimore demonstrate that this was no Punch-and-Judy hitter converted into a slugger by a freak ball park.

An article about Hauser by Eugene Murdock in the *Baseball Research Journal* adds to Unser Choe's legend with the story of two games in Kansas City at the start of the 1934 season. In a stadium with a right field 375 feet from home, Hauser hit a total of five home runs in his first two games of the season, a record for that ball park.

The 1934 season was another mixed year for Hauser. He batted .348 with thirty-three home runs and eighty-eight RBIs, but he suffered another disastrous injury. This time he broke his left kneecap, making him without question the greatest home run hitter to have broken both kneecaps in a career. His numbers tailed off in his remaining seasons, but Murdock's summary of Hauser's years in Minneapolis is on the mark: "In those five great years (1930–34), although missing nearly a full season, he had belted out 245 homers (an average of 49 per year) and driven in 672 runs (an average of 134 per year)."[4]

Another great hitter in the American Association was Antonio Bordetski, better known as "Bunny" Brief. Most of Brief's career was spent with Kansas City, but he played 183 games in the majors for the St. Louis Browns, the White Sox, and the Pirates. In 1921 he led the American Association with

forty-two home runs and 191 RBIs. His batting average was
.361, and he also led the AA in doubles with fifty-one and runs
scored with 166.

Brief's performance that season was consistent with the shift
to more aggressive offenses that relied on the home run and
the big inning, but it remains curious that he never again was
called back to the majors after his short stay with Pittsburgh in
1917. He continued to lead the Association in home runs and
RBIs on three other occasions, and his mark of 1,776 runs
scored ranks eighth on the list of career leaders in the minor
leagues. Within the American Association, Brief is the career
leader in home runs with 276, RBIs with 1,451, hits with 2,196,
runs with 1,342, and doubles with 458. Many players with less
impressive credentials have been given more of a chance at the
big leagues.

Players who had great seasons in the American Association
included Nick Cullop, who hit thirty-seven doubles, twenty-
two triples, and twenty-eight home runs for Columbus in 1933.
Jay Kirke had 282 hits in 1921 for Louisville. Rudy York earned
a promotion to the Detroit Tigers with an outstanding season
in 1936, when he added twenty-five doubles and twenty-one
triples to thirty-seven home runs.

A more puzzling case is that of DeWitt LeBourveau, who
set a career batting average of .360 for the American Association. "Bevo" played over 1,500 games in the minors over a
span of seventeen years from 1918–34. He played fewer than
300 games in the majors during that time for the Phillies and
the Athletics. His career batting average in the majors was a
respectable .275, but he never secured a place in the big
leagues.

Bevo's time with Connie Mack's A's reflects the sometimes
strange life of the career minor leaguer. In 1929 Bevo had a cup
of coffee in Philadelphia, appearing in twelve games, in which
he got five hits in his sixteen at-bats for a .313 average. Sent
down to Toledo in 1930, he led the league with a .380 average,
drove in 100 runs, and stole thirty-six bases, yet he never appeared in the majors again. By this time, Bevo was no kid. He

was in his mid-thirties and could not have been expected to enjoy a long career anywhere. But in 1931 he batted .375 for Toledo, and one has to wonder if he could have helped the dismal Browns, Reds, or White Sox of that era.

Spence Harris was another Minneapolis Miller during ten years of a career that stretched from 1921 through 1948. He established career records in the minors for runs, hits, doubles, and total bases. Harris is also included among SABR's fifteen all-time all-stars.

THE AMERICAN ASSOCIATION launched Bill Veeck's career as an owner and promoter. The consummate hustler, Veeck bought the Milwaukee Brewers using his perennial financial strategy: "$500 down and the rest when you catch me." The Brewers were a terrible club that could not have drawn fans to a decent ball park, let alone Borchert Field.

Veeck's plan for turning the franchise around emphasized promotions to boost the gate over the short run while steadily gathering better players. In the early years, Veeck awarded door prizes to fans, including a dozen lobsters, six live squabs, a 200-pound block of ice, and six ladders. Few people would have gone to a game in the hopes of winning such honors, but many went for the fun of watching the winner manage the prize through a nine-inning game. When World War II broke out, Veeck scheduled a Rosie the Riveter morning game, for which women factory workers who arrived in their welding gear were admitted free and served breakfast by tuxedo-clad ushers.

Veeck's style rankled other American Association owners, which bothered him not at all. Believing that his club was at a disadvantage when visiting Columbus because of a high mound and poor lighting, Veeck had the Brewers play wearing miners' hats while the coaches waved lanterns.

Understandably, other teams were enraged when the Brewers flooded their infield to hamper quicker opponents or when the ground crew delayed the start of a game by four or five hours to get more favorable lighting conditions. In Veeck's mind, any rule could be bent or broken if it helped the Brewers. The league could rein him in if it chose, but self-discipline would not limit his mischief.

Baseball has had its share of win-at-all-costs types, and their inability to handle defeat is a nuisance, even to fans. Veeck did not belong to that group, however: his antics were governed by a childlike love of fun. He believed an integral part of the game was tweaking the opposition and, especially, deflating the pompous.

Veeck had a special affection for his wayward players. He intervened with judges and offended bartenders to try to salvage the lives and careers of some of his charges who had drinking problems. When one of his players shot himself in the foot and had an allergic reaction to the medicine he received at the hospital, Veeck spent the night dabbing oatmeal on the man's blisters—the curious but prescribed treatment.

By the time Veeck entered the Marines for service in the Pacific, the Brewers had become a force in the American Association. They finished first from 1943 through 1945, although they were never able to win the Shaughnessy playoffs. Veeck returned from the war with a terrible wound that would eventually cost him his leg, and for personal reasons he was ready to give up his ownership of the Brewers. In his memoirs Veeck wrote:

Milwaukee was the great time of my life. What can you say about a city after you have said that? Milwaukee was my proving grounds. It was the place where I tried out all of my ideas, the good and the bad, without the terrible pressure to succeed that comes with a major-league franchise. Milwaukee was all fun, even when I was running around from loan company to loan company. It was all light, all laughter.

I sold, not because I wanted a capital-gains deal or

because I wanted to move on to the major leagues. I would have been content to remain in Milwaukee for the rest of my life.[5]

Veeck's first marriage had been strained by his peripatetic style of running the Brewers, and he left baseball in an unsuccessful attempt to patch things up.

Veeck later returned to the game, owning several major league teams over his career, and the nature of his ownership was always the same. He owned marginal franchises that he turned around through incredible promotions. The midget in St. Louis, the exploding scoreboard in Comiskey Park, and the showers in the bleachers of Wrigley Field are part of Veeck's legacy; so is the low-key integration of the American League with Larry Doby of the Cleveland Indians.

Always out of tune with the other owners, he was treated as a nuisance who turned baseball into a burlesque. His peers were happy to see him go, and they worked very hard to block his return. Such hostility was simply a setup for Veeck, who delighted in finding a scheme to buy another ball club and run it just for the fun of it.

Veeck's ownership of the Brewers makes some interesting points about minor league baseball in the 1940s. From a fan's perspective, he was perhaps the ideal owner, but one can understand how he would drive his colleagues to distraction. As an independent minor league owner, Veeck could have indulged his promotions to his heart's content. Veeck would have embodied the ideal of minor league baseball as a game for smaller towns, a business that reveled in the diversity of American communities. Somewhere a perfect match would have been found between Bill Veeck and his kind of fans. Winning would be important, but not so important as having fun on your own terms.

As it was, Veeck was not quite so free. He worked in the world of baseball as big business, on its way to corporate ownership. Being innovative would become less desirable than conforming would. Juggling creditors would become unseemly, while ownership based on tax write-offs and corporate marketing would become the norm.

For Veeck, the ball club was the means for enjoying life; for so many of his colleagues it would be the means to sell the products of their real businesses. For Veeck, the ball club was his commercial life; for so many other owners, the team would be a hobby, and one that they seemed to suffer rather than enjoy.

ANOTHER AMERICAN ASSOCIATION owner who left his mark on the game was Mike Kelley, who purchased the Minneapolis Millers in 1923. Kelley, born in Massachusetts in 1875, pursued a professional career in baseball despite scholarship offers from several Ivy League colleges. He initially hooked up with the Millers in 1906, managing the club after a few seasons with the St. Paul Saints.

Kelley was soon banished from the American Association when he made some intemperate remarks about the integrity of some umpires, contributing to a riot that cost the Millers a forfeited game. He was readmitted to the Association in 1908, and he returned to manage St. Paul through the 1923 season. In thirty years as a minor league manager, Kelley's teams won 2,390 games and six pennants, including four from 1919–23.

When he bought the Millers, he also became their manager from 1924 through 1931. The club's second-place finish in 1928 was the best they could do with Kelley at the helm. Donie Bush brought the team home a winner in 1932, the Millers' first pennant since 1915.

The 1932 season was Joe Hauser's first with the Millers. The club had a tremendous offense that averaged almost seven runs per game. The Millers played the Newark Bears in the Junior World Series, and in the fifth game one of the great umpiring disasters of organized baseball occurred. Newark had runners on first and third with two out in the ninth and the game tied 8–8. Johnny Neun, the Newark batter, hit a sinking liner to center field. Harry Rice appeared to make a diving catch to end the Newark threat, and the second and third base umpires so indicated.

Al Mamaux stormed from the Newark dugout. The Bears' manager argued that Rice had trapped the ball. The umpires conferred and reversed their decision, giving Newark the go-ahead run. Donie Bush then joined the melee, contending that the initial call had been the correct one. Incredibly, he convinced the umpires to reverse themselves again. After forty minutes of this pandemonium, the umpires changed their first decision a total of five times. Rather than continue the debate, Bush protested the decision when the sixth call went against the Millers. His petition was denied when the committee of appeal, composed of equal numbers from the American Association and the International League, split evenly. The Millers lost the series the next day when the Bears rallied for three runs in the ninth.

After a year in the major leagues, Donie Bush returned to manage the Millers to pennants in 1934 and 1935. In 1938 Ted Williams joined the Millers, the year before his great career with the Boston Red Sox began. At the time Williams was as nonchalant in the field as he was intense at the plate. Bush threatened to resign if Kelley did not fire the temperamental Williams, but Kelley reportedly replied, "We're going to miss you, Donie."

Williams's autobiography, *My Turn at Bat*, reveals that he was a lonely, insecure minor leaguer with tremendous ability. Frustrated one day after popping up a pitch he should have drilled, he punched out a water cooler, nearly ending his career. His fits of temper caused him to threaten to quit, but Bush summoned enough patience to save his star from himself.

Williams candidly wrote about the emotional burdens he carried in those days. Describing an occasion when Bush defused a threatened return home, Williams wrote: "The thing is, I was such a long time getting myself straightened out. A sharp liaison between the parent club and the minor league team would have picked this up right away and somebody at the top would have said, 'Listen, this kid is *going* somewhere. He's knocking the damn fences down. He's leading the league in everything. Let's not worry about his hitting, let's work on his fielding.'"[6]

A "sharp liaison" might have recognized that Williams's problems stemmed more from a tough childhood than from his glove. Some additional emotional seasoning in Minneapolis might have spared Williams some of the grief he later suffered with the press in Boston. He described that season in Minneapolis with some fondness: "I think any player will tell you that in the minor leagues you get a lot closer to the fans, that the fans take more of a family interest. There's fewer of them, to begin with, and you're younger and less reserved, so you talk to them more, even while you're on the field. I was always jawing with somebody in that little park in Minneapolis."[7]

Williams's recollections are similar to those of Bill Veeck. Life in the minors is in some ways more enjoyable because there is less pressure than in the majors. While Williams's intensity was very different from Veeck's frivolity, both in some ways were better suited to life in the minors, where following the beat of their own drummers was less threatening than it would prove to be in the majors.

Mike Kelley retained ownership of the Millers through World War II. He sold the club to the New York Giants, completing the transformation of the American Association to a league of farm clubs.

From the time that playoffs were introduced to the American Association in 1933, the Millers had qualified for postseason play eleven times through the 1950 season, including three times when they finished first during the regular season. They had never won the playoffs, but the 1951 season looked promising, as the Millers were led by a spectacular new center fielder, Willie Mays. In the middle of May, the Millers were 21–14, with Mays hitting .477 with eight home runs and thirty runs batted in.

Mays was the quintessential franchise player, but given the realities of a farm system, the franchise was located in New

York, not Minneapolis. Snatched from the Millers less than two months into the season, Mays became the National League's Rookie of the Year, helping the Giants to win their miraculous 1951 pennant. Bereft of their star, the Millers fell out of their race, failing even to qualify for the playoffs. The local reaction to the loss of Mays was noted by Stew Thornley in his book, *On to Nicollet:*

> Mays wasn't the first, but to that point he was the most significant, player to be plucked in mid-season by the parent Giants. Recalls of other Miller players followed, prompting *Minneapolis Tribune* columnist Dick Cullum to claim, "Baseball on the Triple-A farm is mere exhibition training and is not being conducted with an earnest effort to win games." On the same subject, Halsey Hall remarked, "Let [general manager] Rosy Ryan and [manager] Tommy Heath have the gold removed from their teeth and send it to the New York (Giants) front office. They'll get it sooner or later anyway."[8]

The frustration over losing Mays is certainly understandable, but it also points to the dilemma of farm system baseball. If Mays had been left with the Millers for a full season, he would have been just as great a player when he made it to the majors, and the Millers would have enjoyed a full season of his brilliance, just as they had enjoyed Ted Williams. But without Mays the Giants would never have caught the Dodgers in a torrid stretch drive, and Bobby Thomson would likely be a forgotten journeyman outfielder. The price of one of the most dramatic moments in baseball history may have been paid by the fans of the Minneapolis Millers.

The majors' ability and willingness to raid minor league rosters despite the effect on the farm team undoubtedly contributed to some cynicism about minor league pennant races.

Some of the eagerness of cities such as Milwaukee and Minneapolis to attract a major league franchise must have reflected frustration with the subservient status of the minors.

The Millers struggled back to the playoffs in 1952 and 1954, but they lost in the first round both years. In 1955, under manager Bill Rigney, the Millers had their greatest season since the glory days of Gavvy Cravath. They finished first in the regular season by eight games and then stormed through the playoffs, sweeping Denver and Omaha each in four straight.

For their first appearance in the Little World Series, the Millers faced the Rochester Red Wings of the International League. The Millers rallied to take the series in seven games. The finale was the first of several poignant farewells of the 1950s, as that game was the last played in Nicollet Park. The old facility had always been a curiosity in the minors, but it was totally unsuited to the major league game that Minneapolis hoped to attract. ✓

The Millers opened the 1956 season in what would become Metropolitan Stadium. In that and the following season, they reverted to form by making the playoffs but being knocked out in the first round. After the 1957 campaign, it was time for another goodbye.

When the Giants joined the Dodgers in moving to California, Minneapolis was one of the affected parties. Fans eager for major league ball had hoped that the Giants would move to Minneapolis, and Horace Stoneham, the Giants' owner, had in fact planned such a move. In the confused mythology about the movement of New York's National League teams, Walter O'Malley, the Dodgers' owner, is alleged to have lured Stoneham's Giants out of New York.[9] Not true—he lured them out of Minneapolis. The Giants had planned to leave New York regardless of what the Dodgers did. By raising the prospect of continuing their rivalry on the West Coast, O'Malley offered Stoneham a more attractive market for the Giants.

Not only did Minneapolis lose the Giants, but they then lost the Millers, whom the Giants transferred to Phoenix. The San Francisco Seals, a Boston Red Sox farm club that had been dislodged by the Giants, were then shifted to Minneapolis, where they assumed the Millers' name.

On the face of it, nothing was lost. Minneapolis was a Triple-A city in 1957, and they were still one in 1958. Not even the name of the team was changed. But beyond the surface, quite a bit had changed. The traditions of the franchise had been lost. The rivalry with the St. Paul Saints was now void of a heritage of struggle between the two best clubs in the American Association. A tradition of over fifty years was not transferred to the Arizona desert, nor was it conferred on Joe DiMaggio's old minor league club that had been uprooted from its home by the San Francisco Bay. If this relocation of major league franchises was progress, it came at a terrible price to the minor leagues.

The new Minneapolis Millers took the curse off this disruption by rising from a third-place finish to win the American Association playoffs in 1958. They then swept Montreal to give Minneapolis its second Junior World Series title.

The 1959 season ended in an even more dramatic way. The Millers again made it to the Junior World Series against a team beyond the borders of the United States. This series was far more exotic, as the Millers battled the Havana Sugar Canes. To complicate matters, the series was being played in the first year of the reign of Fidel Castro.

The first three games were scheduled for Minneapolis, where cold weather hampered the first two games and then caused the cancellation of the third. With five games scheduled for Havana, the Millers fell behind three games to one before rallying to knot the series at three games apiece. Though thoroughly distracted by the setting, the Millers led 2–0 in the eighth inning of the final game, but the Sugar Canes came back to tie the game in the eighth and then capture the series with a run in the bottom of the ninth.

Thornley quotes the recollection of Millers' pitcher Ted Bowsfield about those road games: "Nobody minded losing the game in that country and under those conditions. We were just happy to get out of town with our hides. During every game we could hear shots being fired, and we never knew what was going on."

Thornley continued, "Lefty Locklin remembered warming up before the seventh game when Castro made his entrance, passed the Minneapolis players in the bullpen, put his hand on his revolver and said, 'Tonight we win.'"[10]

Despite such ill manners, the International League tried to stay in Cuba for another season but was forced to move the Havana franchise to Jersey City in mid-July of 1960.

That year was also the last for minor league baseball in the Twin Cities. The Washington Senators received permission to move to Minnesota just as they were ready at last to become a respectable franchise. The long-suffering fans in the District of Columbia were compensated with an expansion club that floundered until 1972 when they moved to Texas, leaving the nation's capital without major league ball.

The demise of the Millers and the Saints, Thornley notes, was ignored by Minnesota fans, who were thrilled to be finally included in the majors. Since the 1950s, virtually any community has been willing to trash its minor league club for a major league franchise in its place, but that attitude developed within the perverse logic imposed by the majors themselves.

The expansion of the major league game into minor league markets has assumed that historic minor league traditions must inevitably be lost. Such is the case only if the expansion is totally under the control of the major league owners. Big-league baseball could also have come to these minor league cities through the upgrading of their existing franchises.

Many of the minor league parks were used for a few years until new facilities were built, and the use of the names Orioles, Padres, and Angels showed a willingness by some of the major league owners to capitalize on the heritage of another franchise. The growth of major league baseball would inevitably have meant some difficult adjustments for the minor leagues, but the price did not have to be as brutal as it was.

# · Seven ·

# THE NEWARK BEARS

W HILE KENESAW LANDIS and Branch Rickey battled over the soul of minor league baseball, other major league magnates had to decide which of the two Wagnerian figures to follow. Fear of Landis or respect for his position may have prevented a few clubs from developing farm systems, but the success of Rickey's Cardinals induced other organizations to secure formal control over minor league clubs so that player development could be more certain and, not incidentally, less expensive.

Of the clubs that followed the Cardinals' lead, none was more successful than the New York Yankees. The players that graduated to the Bronx between 1931 and 1964 were the core of a dynasty that won twenty-three pennants and seventeen world championships in those thirty-four years. The Yankee teams of the 1920s included many great players, but they will always be associated with Jack Dunn's ward. The championship teams of the later decades increasingly reflected the relentless perfection of the organization rather than the brilliance of one individual.

This pattern began under the ownership of Colonel Jacob Ruppert, who had purchased the Yankees in 1915 for less than half a million dollars. Ruppert had been joined in the venture by a partner, Colonel Tillinghast L'Hommedieu Huston. The two colonels had a falling out in 1923, and Ruppert bought Huston's interest to become sole owner.

Ruppert had made his fortune in his father's brewery and in real estate ventures. Although he toiled in menial jobs to learn the beer business, Ruppert became quite the flamboyant man about town. As described in Ronald Mayer's book about the Newark Bears, "He owned race horses, was a member of the Jockey Club, and exhibited his St. Bernards at the Westminster Kennel Club show in Madison Square Garden. He was a fastidious dresser, who changed his clothes several times a day, wore custom-made shoes, and had a valet. He collected jades, porcelains, and first editions."[1]

His military title had been bestowed after service in the New York National Guard on the governor's staff. He also served four terms in Congress, and he remained a bachelor throughout his life. Neither his wealth nor his privileged pursuits challenged him sufficiently, hence his interest in the Yankees.

Ruppert had the good sense to hire people who had forgotten more about baseball than he would ever know. Among the most prominent was Ed Barrow, the former president of the International League. Barrow had left his minor league post to become the manager of the Boston Red Sox. Barrow followed Babe Ruth to the Yankees after the 1920 season, and he was soon promoted to general manager.

Barrow's particular blessing—or curse—seemed to be his tie with Ruth. Much of the work in the Yankee front office of the 1920s revolved around efforts to control the perpetual adolescent who bridled under authority. Barrow, Ruppert, and manager Miller Huggins all had their rows with the Babe.

At the end of Ruth's time with the Yankees, Barrow made a move that would have a more enduring effect. He persuaded Ruppert during the minor league meetings of 1931 that the Yankees should hire George Weiss to develop a farm system for New York.

Weiss, thirty-seven years old at the time, had spent the previous two years as Jack Dunn's successor in Baltimore's front office. The knowledge that he gained there about the International League was added to his previous experience as a baseball promoter in New Haven, Connecticut.

While in New Haven, Weiss turned his high school baseball team into a semipro club after graduation. At Yale he ran another semipro team that became more popular than the local Eastern League franchise. Robert Obojski notes his promotional skills in taking advantage of Connecticut's ban on professional games on Sunday to benefit his own teams: "He imported a Chinese team, a 'bloomer girls' team, and a major league all-star team led by the great Ty Cobb (who would appear while his Detroit Tiger teammates were idle in either Boston or New York)."[2]

Weiss was so effective in countering organized baseball in New Haven that he was given the opportunity to buy New Haven's Eastern League franchise for $5,000. This offer followed unsuccessful attempts to undermine Weiss by intimidating major league players and clubs into not playing his club.

When Weiss bought the New Haven club, he became a part of organized baseball. In his new capacity, he met Ed Barrow under inauspicious circumstances. In 1920 Weiss booked the New York Yankees for an exhibition. When Babe Ruth failed to appear, Weiss refused to pay Barrow the Yankee's share of the receipts. Barrow was indignant, but Commissioner Landis ultimately upheld Weiss. Barrow did not hold a grudge, and years later, when the opening appeared in the Yankee organization, Barrow's man was Weiss.

Originally Weiss was hired to run the Newark team that Ruppert had purchased after the 1931 season. But Weiss, Ruppert, and Barrow planned Newark as one part of a Yankee

farm system that would eventually rival Branch Rickey's operation in St. Louis. They succeeded beyond all reasonable expectations, and most of that credit belonged to George Weiss.
Ruppert died in 1939; Barrow was out of baseball at the end of
World War II; but Weiss continued to run the Yankees until
1960. When Bill Mazeroski homered in the ninth inning of the
seventh game of the 1960 World Series, he not only brought
Pittsburgh a world championship, but he also ended two remarkable reigns in New York. In the clumsy reorganization
that followed, the Yankees "retired" George Weiss and Casey
Stengel.

Both men were up in years, but they were not through with
the game. Weiss was hired in 1962 to run the expansion New
York Mets, and he immediately hired Stengel as the field manager. The Mets were as inept on the field as the Yankees had
been brilliant, but Stengel and Weiss assembled a team that
beat the new-look Yankees in attendance, affection, and media
attention. They also managed to corral enough talent to build a
team that would win the World Series in 1969.

Weiss relied on Rickey's model for developing a chain of
minor league clubs from Class D to the high minors. Like the
Cardinal system, players were developed not only to be promoted to the Yankees, but to be sold to other major league
clubs. The scheme provided some stability to minor league
franchises and also ensured a flow of revenue to the Yankees.
Fifteen minor league teams belonged to the Yankees by the
mid-1930s under Weiss's direction.

FOR MINOR LEAGUE teams, whether to remain independent
or opt for a place in a major league farm system was just one of
several critical questions they confronted during the Great Depression.

The National Association of Professional Baseball Leagues
had been led by Mike Sexton since 1901, following the brief
reign of Pat Powers. The Association felt the need for new

leadership when the Depression led to the collapse of nine of the twenty-five minor leagues in the two years that followed the stock market crash of 1929.

During the minor league meetings in December 1932, William Bramham was elected to succeed Sexton. Bramham had been the president of the Piedmont League, and he had served for two years on a committee that had examined the organization and purpose of the National Association.

One of Bramham's first reforms was the introduction of the "deposit" rule. This measure required minor league club owners to put up two weeks' payroll to protect the players in the event of bankruptcy. The low minors were an especially turbulent part of organized baseball, and when local economies contracted, the local baseball team was often among the casualties. Bramham's "deposit rule" eased the worst effects of "shoestring operators," owners "who usually started out with little or no capital, staggered through until the Fourth of July double-header, pocketed the gate from that event and then folded up, leaving the town submerged in debts which resolved into territorial liens."[3]

With a more secure financial foundation in place, the number of leagues that competed in the Association in 1933 grew to fourteen, almost three times the number that had been expected. In 1934 that number increased to nineteen. The deposit rule proved to be an effective way to keep all but serious owners from fielding teams.

Bramham also faced challenges to territorial rights, a prohibition on locating a franchise within ten miles of another club. The ban was sustained by the Association.

The Texas and Southern Leagues were awarded Class A-1 status, closer to Double A than before but still a notch below the elite of the minors.

Throughout the 1930s, the number of minor leagues continued to grow despite the continued sad state of the national economy. By 1937 thirty-seven minor leagues were in operation under the authority of the National Association. The minor league convention of that year was able to find a dark lining to the silver cloud: "It was noted that in line with the numerical growth and expanding fan attendance at games, there was an inclination among clubs to revert to the old days of wild spending in a scramble to acquire a pennant."[4]

The admonition against "wild spending" reprised an issue that dated to the 1880s. The salary limits that still were imposed in the minors reflected a lack of confidence in the owners' abilities to run their clubs prudently. L. H. Addington, in the minors' official history, pointed to the culprits who risked financial ruin: "Despite repeated warnings from President Bramham, admonishing clubs not to go 'high hat' again, the trend was clear in the numerous suggested amendments calling for increased salary limits, increased player limits and other moves which pointed toward increased overhead operating expenses. Apparently, words of warning fell on many deaf ears, for there seldom was a year when there was not some effort to increase expenditures."[5]

In the 1880s the owners had circumvented their own salary caps by paying players for promotional gestures. In the 1890s strong league leadership was resisted because of the opportunity to make profits recklessly. From time to time in the history of organized baseball, players are chided for being overpaid or less skilled and committed than their predecessors. This complaint neatly skirts the fact that salaries are not only determined by the owners, but that to get the players they want, owners will evade the restrictions that they themselves have imposed.

THE VITALITY OF the National Association's leadership improved under Bramham, and the marketing of the game received a boost when the minors introduced night baseball. Games under the lights had been played as far back as 1880, just one year after Edison's invention of the incandescent lamp. These games were exhibitions, held every few years more for the purpose of marketing the lighting system than for drawing a new audience to baseball.

The Depression motivated baseball executives to consider new ways to attract fans to the park. At the minor league meetings of 1929, E. Lee Keyser, owner of the Des Moines club of the Western League, announced his intention to install lights at the Demons' park for the playing of night games in 1930. The news triggered skepticism and imitation. The Demons opened on the road in 1930, giving Independence, Kansas, of the Class-D Western Association the opportunity to host the first regular-season night game in organized baseball. But Keyser's leadership in this area was acknowledged by the presence of Commissioner Landis along with a crowd of 10,000 at Des Moines's first night game on May 2.

Keyser delivered an important innovation rather than a farce because of his commitment to quality. The banks of lights on six towers ninety feet in height were so effective that during World War II they were moved to illuminate a munitions plant. Other clubs were not so responsible. Addington wrote that "some of the lighting systems, hastily thrown up, were crude and produced undesirable shadows on the playing fields, but the public continued to evince an interest and the manufacturers of light plants were not long in improving their equipment."[6]

Undoubtedly some fans were drawn to the night games as a novelty, but they were also a greater convenience for those fortunate enough to have jobs. The major leagues held off until 1935 before Larry MacPhail introduced night baseball at Crosley Field in Cincinnati.

In 1933 Harry James O'Donnell was already praising Keyser and others for saving the minors with night ball. In an article entitled "Are the Minor League Skies Clearing?" O'Donnell credited night games for reversing the sharp decline in the minor leagues during the early years of the Depression. "Although the novelty of the nocturnal pastiming may have lost appeal in some cities that have had it now for a year or two, there is no denying that it rescued minor league ball from the very brink of annihilation. Its conceivers should be made knights of the garter and have bestowed upon them all the medals of valor that can be struck in the nation's foundries in a 40-hour week."[7]

Four years later, *Baseball Magazine* surveyed minor league presidents, who praised night baseball for stabilizing their leagues with needed revenues. Their opinions indicated that the night game was not just an emergency measure but a permanent fixture.

Addington concluded that "night ball, of course, was revolutionary in many ways. Certain rulings had to be changed. The lives of the players were turned upside down, with a necessitated change in their hours for meals and sleep. But few will argue that the inception of the night game did not save the Minors from financial disruption."[8] Addington might have mentioned that in addition to changes in dining and slumber, adjustments also had to be made for drinking and carousing. With so many nights occupied, the modern player was challenged to fit off-field pursuits into his schedule.

ANOTHER MARKETING INNOVATION was the introduction of league playoffs. The idea was Frank Shaughnessy's, a long-time player and executive in the minors. If an eight-team league had a runaway pennant winner, the trailing clubs had serious trouble drawing fans. Shaughnessy's solution was a postseason playoff in which the first-place team would play the fourth, the second would meet the third, and the winners would meet in a league championship series.

The plan was a great success in sustaining fan interest. Even second-division teams merited watching, since a late season spurt might propel one of them to a fourth-place finish and a playoff spot.

While there was no denying the impact of the playoffs on attendance, some were concerned about the impact on the integrity of the regular season. Addington wrote of the plan, "It was distasteful to some, including President Bramham, but the public had the answer, the fans seemed to like it and patronized it, and it is still in vogue."[9] For a business that was enduring hard times, it was impossible to reject any measure that attracted the public's money, but such urgency does not necessarily justify the action.

Shaughnessy took his idea from the playoffs in hockey. At the present time, an interminable season is played in the NHL to eliminate a handful of the worst teams from the playoffs. The situation in the NBA is only slightly better. Major league baseball itself flirted with an expanded playoff system during the strike-shortened 1981 season. The split-season concept, borrowed from several minor leagues, awarded a partial pennant to first-half and second-half winners, who then met in a playoff. The owners were adamant that they had no intention of introducing an elaborate playoff system, but if hard times return in the future, who knows?

Back in the 1930s, some teams complained that the pennant should go to the club with the best regular-season record, with the playoffs restricted to a postseason tournament with diminished championship qualities. These objections help to raise an important question: What should the purpose of the Shaughnessy playoffs be?

Their most obvious function is to increase fan interest in teams that are not in a pennant race. Another rationale might be the determination of the best team in the minors. If fan interest is their sole purpose, then professional wrestling between innings or "adult" movies on the scoreboard are also possible. The long-term interest of the game is better served by resisting carnival appeals, no matter how popular, and staying with contests that ultimately determine the best team in the game.

An ideal playoff system would have determined the best team in each classification by pitting the regular-season pennant winners in each appropriate league against one another. The champions of each classification could then have met to determine the best minor league team. This ideal system would, however, have sacrificed the regular-season revenues generated by the artificial interest in fourth-place finishes.

In the 1920s, a playoff between the Baltimore Orioles and the Fort Worth Panthers would have been a natural as each team ran its string of consecutive pennants. In the 1930s the Newark Bears and the Los Angeles Angels would have been a great match. If the majors had had the nerve, the best team to come out of the minor league playoff would have met the best of the National and American Leagues for a true champion of organized baseball. That challenge would normally have been settled in a rout, but from time to time the World Series winners would have been embarrassed by the champion of the supposedly inferior leagues.

Night baseball and the Shaughnessy playoffs were the keys to saving minor league baseball in the 1930s. The farm systems were also significant, but to credit the majors for saving the minor leagues goes too far. In O'Donnell's article on the recovery of the minors, he lists farming as one of several aids, all secondary to night baseball, that helped the minors: "Other serums injected into the very sick minors that have enabled them to continue on a stable basis and serve to illuminate the future, included: franchise shifting, holiday receipt pooling, major league ownership, classification raising and lowering, 'emergency teams,' sane salary limits and efficient governing of the leagues."[10]

Along with the playoffs and the deposit rule, these measures were for the most part innovations within the minors themselves. They suggest that the minors had enough executive talent to make their game profitable.

Bramham served as president of the National Association from 1932 through 1946. He revitalized its authority and helped to reverse the economic collapse of the minor leagues. In the process he also rigidly enforced rules that protected umpires. Like Ban Johnson, he deplored the rowdy brawls that demeaned the game.

The minor leagues would enjoy one more burst of prosperity after Bramham's departure. They would rebound from World

War II to a peak of popularity before the major league assault of the 1950s reduced them to peonage. The golden era of the 1930s and 1940s was not an inevitably successful period. The minor leagues had to react wisely to the upheavals of the Depression and the war. Their success in meeting those challenges was due more to their own efforts than to their adoption by major league patrons.

GEORGE WEISS'S ARRIVAL at Newark coincided with many of these developments in the minor league game, including Bramham's tenure with the National Association. The Rickey-Landis feud was building to a head, and the Yankees had made a bold decision to follow Rickey's example with their Newark club, with one distinction. Colonel Ruppert balanced the interests of his farm teams more evenly with those of the Yankees than Rickey did. The sole purpose of the Cardinals' minor league teams was to help St. Louis win pennants, but Ruppert professed an enthusiasm for the success of his minor league teams in their own leagues.

David Chrisman describes the Yankees' purpose for Newark: "Ruppert announced to the Newark fans that his 'sole interest' was to develop players for the parent Yankee organization and to give Newark 'the best team possible.'"[11] Ruppert's syntax is interesting. He combined into one "sole interest" the two goals over which Rickey and Landis had been battling.

Ruppert's commitment to the Yankees was evident, but he was also enamored with the minors, as suggested in Chrisman's observation that "Ruppert fell in love with Newark (and her fans) and was determined to field a representative minor league club there even at the risk of not always winning the American League pennant at the parent level."[12]

Ruppert's affection for Newark was fueled on Opening Day in 1932, the Bears' first game under the new regime. Against Toronto, the Bears entered the bottom of the ninth trailing 5–1. A grand slam tied the game, and the home team pulled out the victory in the tenth inning. The Yankee owner had stayed to the end along with 13,000 fans who braved subfreezing temperatures. After the game Ruppert declared, "I've had few happier days in my life. No World Series games the Yankees ever won gave me a greater thrill. And they call it minor league baseball. New York clubs would be lucky to draw as many people on such a day."[13]

Ruppert's aspirations for Newark and his other farm clubs depended on Weiss's ability to stock the Yankees with an abundance of talent so that the overflow filled the minor league rosters. Weiss succeeded because he had scouts who could locate the talent and because Ruppert and Barrow were willing to pay for these players when they were discovered.

In describing Weiss's strategy, Mayer writes, "Despite his baseball genius, it was physically impossible for Weiss to cover every campus and sandlot throughout the country, searching to find young raw talent with a major league future. . . . Dedicated men like Bill Essick, Gene McCann, Johnny Nee, and many more served as Weiss's arms and legs. This team of scouts was headed by none other than the super scout of them all, Paul Krichell, the former St. Louis Browns catcher with the slightly bowed frame."[14]

Krichell's reputation was made when he discovered Lou Gehrig at Columbia University. He also supervised scouts who were responsible for geographic regions. By working in small committees, each person's judgment was checked. Mayer relates the story of scout Bill Essick being sent to California to appraise Joe DiMaggio. Essick sent back an enthusiastic evaluation including an optimistic prognosis of a knee injury that DiMaggio had sustained. Barrow remained skeptical, but Weiss relied on Essick's first-hand observation. Weiss appealed to Ruppert himself, who gave the green light along with $25,000 to sign the Yankee Clipper. During the Yankees' extended reign over the American League, the organization was characterized by talented people in key positions who were trusted to do their jobs.

By the mid-1930s, George Weiss had built a farm system for

the Yankees that included fifteen teams from Class D to Double A. In 1938 Kansas City, champions of the American Association, defeated Newark four games to three in the Junior World Series. Both clubs were owned by the Yankees, a remarkable tribute to Weiss's success.

THE NEWARK BEARS remained part of the International League through the 1949 season. The team could not sustain the fans' interest after World War II, and the Yankees sold the Bears to the Chicago Cubs early in 1950. The Cubs then moved the franchise to Springfield, Massachusetts.

During the eighteen years that Newark was run by George Weiss, the Bears compiled a remarkable record. They finished first in the International League in 1932, 1933, 1934, 1937, 1938, 1941, and 1942. They made the League's playoffs an additional nine times, missing only in 1947 and 1949, and they won those playoffs in 1937, 1938, 1940, and 1945.

The 1937 Newark Bears are among the candidates for the greatest minor league team. They won 109 games during the regular season, capturing the International League pennant by twenty-five-and-a-half games over runner-up Montreal. Their longest losing streak during the campaign was two games, and that occurred only once. In the Shaughnessy playoffs, the Bears defeated Syracuse four games to none and then swept Baltimore in four games to establish total mastery of the League.

The Junior World Series was more interesting. The Bears played the Columbus Red Birds, one of the St. Louis Cardinals' top farm teams. Columbus took the first three games, all of which were played in Newark. The series shifted to Columbus, with the Birds needing only one game in their home park. They never got it. The Bears rebounded to take the final four games by scores of 8–1, 1–0, 10–1, and 10–4. As spectacular as this victory was, its recounting still allowed for some embellishment. Willie Klein, who covered the Bears for the *Newark Star-Ledger*, recalled the fourth game some years later to his son David:

The fourth game was a close affair. In the bottom of
the ninth inning Columbus had a one-to-nothing lead,
and the first two Bears made out. That left them one
out away from extinction.

Joe Gordon was the next batter, and when he left the
dugout he stopped and said something to Charlie Keller. We all saw him do it, we just didn't know what he
said.

Later, he told us. "I asked King Kong if he thought I
could hit a home run and tie the game. He said if I did,
he promised to hit another one and win it. I told him I
would, and if he didn't keep his end of the bargain, I'd
break a bat over his head. I laughed and he laughed.
That's how loose we were."

Hollywood scriptwriters would never believe it,
much less write something this unlikely. But Gordon
went up to the plate and hit a home run on the first
pitch.

And then Keller came to bat and swung at the first
pitch he saw.

From the second he hit it, we knew it was gone. It
was the longest home run he had ever hit. And on two
pitches, the Bears were back in the Series.[15]

In an account of the game by Ronald Mayer, the fourth game
was a very different contest. The Bears held a 2–1 lead through
the first five innings, then they scored four runs in the top of
the sixth, and added single runs in the seventh and the ninth.

At the risk of appearing pedantic, it is useful to make historical records clear, even though Klein's version makes for a better story. Part of the wonder of baseball is its oral tradition, in
which great moments are passed from one generation to the
next. That method of relating information will inevitably substitute drama for accuracy, so an occasional check of the facts is
important.

The Bears' comeback in the fourth game was a remarkable
performance even if less miraculous than Willie Klein's ac-

count. His tale reveals less about his memory than it does about the appeal of baseball. The games, especially in the minors, are important in that they give a community a sense of itself. By sharing crucial games, bonds are established throughout small towns all over America.

THE 1937 SEASON gave the Newark Bears a chance to dominate every phase of the game. They ran away during the regular season, decimated their closest league rivals in the Shaughnessy playoffs, and spotted Columbus an unprecedented advantage in the Little World Series before showing the character to rebound from certain defeat on the road.

That record encourages the opinion that the Bears of 1937 were the greatest minor league team ever. Their most famous player was second baseman Joe Gordon, who bided his time at Newark while Tony Lazzeri finished his career with the Yankees. Babe Dahlgren, who succeeded Lou Gehrig, covered third base for the Bears. Charlie Keller, an outfielder, led the International League in batting with a .353 average. Bob Seeds and Jim Gleeson were the other outfielders, and both enjoyed successful big-league careers. George McQuinn played first, and Nolen Richardson was the shortstop. Willard Hershberger was the Bears' catcher. He also began a successful career in the majors, but tragically took his own life at the age of twenty-nine. Of the seventeen nonpitchers on the 1937 Bears, sixteen played in the big leagues.

The pitching staff included only one twenty-game winner, Joe Beggs, who went 21–4. Atley Donald was 19–2 with a fourteen-game winning streak. Steve Sundra was 15–4 before appendicitis ended his season in September. Vito Tamulis had an 18–6 record. All of them had successful big-league careers, although none posted the spectacular numbers that could be found on other minor league staffs.

In the 1977 *Baseball Research Journal*, Randolph Linthurst made the point that the 1937 Bears were nearly matched by the

1932 and 1938 editions. In 1932 the Bears also won 109 games, but they lost to fourth-place Buffalo in the playoffs. The 1938 team won 104 games, took the Shaughnessy playoffs, but was upset by the Yankees' other Double-A team, Kansas City. The 4–3 loss in the Junior World Series cost the Bears of 1938 a shot at immortality.

The 1938 season did include an unforgettable performance by Bob Seeds. On May 6 in Buffalo, Seeds hit four home runs in four consecutive innings and added two singles for twelve RBIs. The next day he hit three more home runs. In the two games, he went nine for ten with seven home runs and seventeen runs batted in. Only Nig Clarke has surpassed that explosion.

Bill James disputes the claim that the 1937 Bears were the greatest minor league team ever; in fact, James contends they were not even the best minor league team of the 1930s. He holds out for the 1934 Los Angeles Angels on the grounds that the Pacific Coast League was superior to the International League.

James makes the important point that judging minor league talent on the basis of how players later performed in the big leagues is of very limited use. The Angels were a relatively independent franchise, and so they had fewer chances to get to the majors than eastern teams did. In that same vein, the geographic isolation of the West Coast restricted media coverage, so the PCL players were less well known. James argues quite reasonably that such factors, which minimized the reputation of the Angels, should in fact enhance it.

The Newark Bears fit somewhere between the Baltimore Orioles and the Rochester Red Wings in the pantheon of the International League. As an independent franchise, the Orioles were immune to losing their star players to a major league patron. But by the same token, they were unable to receive the help from the majors that Newark sometimes received from the Yankees.

Ruppert's philosophy included more room for his farm teams than Branch Rickey's did, so the Red Wings' championships were achieved despite some imposing obstacles. The Yankee farm teams might be thought of as a special case. The dynasty that had been established in the Bronx was unrivaled in the history of the major leagues, so the subsequent effects on the Yankees' minor league teams are also hard to compare with other great teams of the minors.

Moses Fleetwood Walker, one of
the black players of the
nineteenth century before the
color barrier. *(National Baseball
Library, Cooperstown, NY)*

Bud Fowler, another nineteenth century black player, with his Keokuk, Iowa,
teammates in 1885. *(National Baseball Library, Cooperstown, NY)*

TOP ROW L TO R
JERRY NOPS PITCHER JOE MCGINNITY PITCHER PAT CRISHAM CATCHER GEO MCCHANCE 1ST B HARRY HOWELL PITCHER FRANK KITSON PITCHER.
2ND ROW L TO R. DUCKY HOLMES L.F. BROADWAY ALEX SMITH CATCHER WALTER STEVE BRODIE C.F. JOHN J MCGRAW 3RD B & MGR.
WILBERT ROBINSON CATCHER & CAPT. FRANK CHICK HARRIS UTILITY INFIELD STEVE MCKENNA PITCHER.
FRONT ROW L TO R. DAVE FULTZ OUTFIELD GENE DEMONTREVILLE 2ND B. BILLY KEISTER S.S. (JIMMY SHECKARD R.F. ABSENT)

BALTIMORE ORIOLES
1899
JOHN J. McGRAW MGR

The 1899 Baltimore Orioles, perhaps the greatest minor league franchise.
*(National Baseball Library, Cooperstown, NY)*

Jack Bentley, "the Babe Ruth of the International League," and one of the stars of Jack Dunn's Baltimore Orioles. *(National Baseball Library, Cooperstown, NY)*

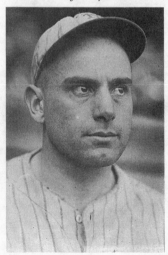

Buzz Arlett, the minors' best switch-hitter. He hit .341 for his career from 1918–1937. *(National Baseball Library, Cooperstown, NY)*

Ike Boone played from 1920–1936. He had the highest career batting average, .370, in minor league history. *(National Baseball Library, Cooperstown, NY)*

Ox Eckhardt hit .367 for his career from 1925–1940, but he played in only twenty-four major league games. *(National Baseball Library, Cooperstown, NY)*

Spencer Harris had 3,617 hits from 1921–1948, a minor league record. *(National Baseball Library, Cooperstown, NY)*

Jim "Ripper" Collins was one of the stars of Branch Rickey's St. Louis Cardinals farm system. *(Associated Press)*

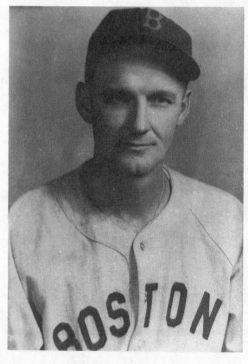

Frank Shellenback won 315 games in his career from 1917–1938, including 295 in the Pacific Coast League. *(National Baseball Library, Cooperstown, NY)*

Smead Jolley, a converted pitcher, hit .366 over his career from 1922–1941. *(United Press International)*

The DiMaggio brothers (from left to right), Vince, Joe, and Dom, back in their San Francisco Seals uniforms for a reunion game. *(Associated Press)*

Joe Hauser, "Unser Choe," twice hit over sixty home runs in the minors. *(National Baseball Library, Cooperstown, NY)*

Joe Bauman set the home run record for organized baseball with 72 for Roswell, New Mexico, in 1954.

Steve Bilko, a great power hitter in
the Pacific Coast League during the
1950s. (*National Baseball Library,
Cooperstown, NY*)

Ban Johnson, who broke the
National League monopoly by
founding the American League.
(*National Baseball Library,
Cooperstown, NY*)

Jack Dunn with Judge Kenesaw Mountain Landis and John McGraw.
*(National Baseball Library, Cooperstown, NY)*

A wistful Jack Dunn, owner of the Baltimore Orioles, watches Babe Ruth sign with the Red Sox in 1914, while Sox owner Ned Hanlon looks on. *(National Baseball Library, Cooperstown, NY)*

George Weiss (upper left), future architect of the New York Yankees farm system. *(National Baseball Library, Cooperstown, NY)*

Weiss (right) with Ed Barrow, Yankees general manager and former president of the International League. *(National Baseball Library, Cooperstown, NY)*

Branch Rickey, mastermind of the farm system for various major league teams. *(Associated Press)*

Frank Shaughnessy, International League president and designer of the minor league playoff system. *(National Baseball Library, Cooperstown, NY)*

Offermann Stadium, home of the Buffalo Bisons and site of the film *The Natural*. *(Marbury-Fitzgerald Air Photo)*

Pilot Field, the Bisons' new stadium and Buffalo's hope for a major league future. *(John L. De Pasquale Photo)*

Seabaugh catching Nashville Tenn 1908

Baseball in the South
in the early 1900s:
Sulphur Dell in
Nashville,
Tennessee, and Engel
Stadium in
Chattanooga,
Tennessee. *(National
Baseball Library,
Cooperstown, NY)*

Norton Street Stadium in Rochester, New York, home of the Red Wings.

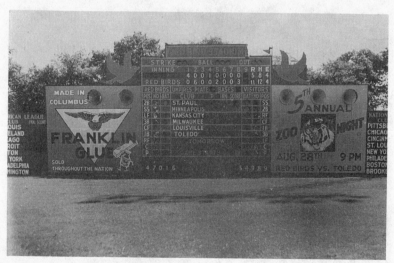

Red Bird Stadium in Columbus, Ohio.

Estadio El Cerro in Havana, Cuba, where the minors' World Series became caught up in the 1959 riots and the Cuban revolution. *(National Baseball Library, Cooperstown, NY)*

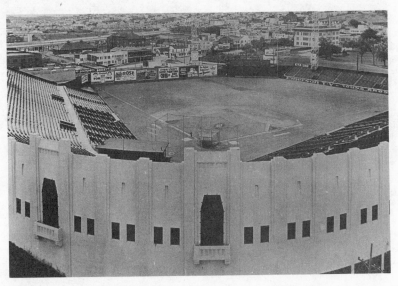

Ballparks in the West: Seal Stadium in San Francisco, California.

Left inset: Gilmore Field, home of the Hollywood Stars, Hollywood, California.

Right inset: Mission Stadium in San Antonio, Texas. *(National Baseball Library, Cooperstown, NY)*

Albuquerque Stadium, Albuquerque, New Mexico.

# Eight

# THE TEXAS LEAGUE

BASEBALL IN TEXAS has rarely failed to entertain. The Texas League has never been included in the high minors, but that does not lessen the importance of the game in Texas. With more than 100 teams in organized ball, Texas has had greater participation than any other state. Away from the glitter of baseball in mass media centers, it is easier here to see what the game can mean to smaller communities in America.

The Texas League was established in 1888, and it endured the turmoil of other leagues during that era. "Honest John" McCloskey was one of those gifted organizers who recognized the growing popularity of baseball and capitalized on it. McCloskey had played in Texas while barnstorming, and he organized a meeting for mid-December of 1887 to establish a new league in the Lone Star State.

The circuit comprised six teams: Austin, Dallas, Fort Worth,

Galveston, Houston, and San Antonio. Under terrible but typical financial burdens, the League struggled through its inaugural season, losing along the way every franchise but Dallas and Austin, which McCloskey had moved to San Antonio.

The League reorganized for 1889 and struggled again through an abbreviated season. These early problems did not discourage McCloskey and other backers, who seem to have accepted their losses as necessary in forming a new league.

An optimistic outlook in 1890 among League owners failed to sustain the League through that season, and McCloskey was unable to find backers for 1891. After taking a team of Texas refugees to California in 1891, McCloskey returned to manage the Houston franchise in a reorganized Texas League.

The 1892 season marked the end of the first era of professional baseball in Texas. The League again lost franchises during the season. It reorganized, tried a split season, and under McCloskey's guidance retreated to north Texas to finish the campaign.

McCloskey's apparent failure ended professional baseball in Texas for two years. From our perspective, it is easy to appreciate the obstacles that thwarted him. Virtually every league in organized baseball was plagued with unstable schedules and rosters. For that matter, the behavior of the owners suggests that some of them were unstable as well.

The Texas League tried to organize while the American Association and Brotherhood League were competing and disbanding, sending disruptive ripples throughout organized baseball. Not even the game itself was stable during this time. The final rules governing the dimensions of the field and the number of balls and strikes were being set. Fielding strategies were still primitive; for example, first basemen rarely left the bag except at the end of an inning.

John McCloskey returned to the Texas League to manage Dallas in 1897 and 1898. He secured his reputation in baseball by managing in almost every season from 1888 to 1932. He led Louisville and the St. Louis Cardinals in the majors as well as teams at all levels in the minors. He guided the Milwaukee

Brewers to a second-place finish in the American Association in 1909, his best finish in the higher echelons of organized ball.

McCloskey's great contribution was in carrying his organizational skills to remote parts of the country. When times were more favorable to building baseball teams, "Honest John" was able to prove his worth. After his labors in Texas and the south, McCloskey managed teams in Vancouver, Butte, Great Falls, Boise, Salt Lake City, and Ogden.

He tried several times to organize new leagues in Texas—a Rio Grande League in 1915 and a Panhandle League in 1931. Neither was particularly successful by conventional standards, but in another light McCloskey had a grand career. He spread an interest in the game he loved to some of the most remote parts of America. Compared with Kenesaw Landis, Ban Johnson, Jack Dunn, and Branch Rickey, John McCloskey was a minor actor. But even on his smaller stage, few have done as much to promote the national game beyond the limits defined by the financial interests of the major league owners.

FOLLOWING ITS COLLAPSE after the 1892 season, the Texas League was revived by another of the great minor league promoters, Ted Sullivan. An eight-team league was established for the 1895 season with clubs located in the familiar sites of Austin, Dallas, Fort Worth, Galveston, Houston, and San Antonio. Two other franchises were placed in Monroe and Shreveport, Louisiana.

At first Sullivan had little more success than McCloskey had had. Teams disbanded, schedules were revised, and new owners were recruited. Sullivan's efforts seemingly also ended in failure when the league was unable to field teams in 1900 and 1901, but Bill O'Neal's superb history of the league points out Sullivan's contributions to baseball in Texas before the turn of the century: "Over the years Texans had become accustomed to a high quality of baseball, and certain Texas cities had become accustomed to fielding a professional team. Several

Texas League players had appeared who boasted major league credentials, while a steady stream of them advanced to the big leagues. Rich Texas League traditions had been firmly established and would evolve expansively during the twentieth century."[1]

Sullivan worked again to revive the Texas League during the winter of 1901–2. The new league included teams in Corsicana, Dallas, Fort Worth, Paris, Sherman-Denison, and Waco. The Sherman-Denison franchise lasted just over a week before transferring to Texarkana, where it was on the receiving end of a 51–3 drubbing by Corsicana on June 15, 1902. Nig Clarke, Corsicana's catcher, went to the plate eight times and hit eight home runs. The most amazing part of the game by our standards was that the Texarkana pitcher, C. B. DeWitt, was left in for the entire game—his other role as part owner may explain the lack of relief. Equally incredible is that the entire game took only two hours and ten minutes to play.

At this time the American League was successfully challenging the National League monopoly, and the National Association had been formed to protect the interests of the minor leagues. The classification scheme that assigned minor leagues to their allegedly appropriate strata gave the Texas League a Class-D ranking, at the bottom of the heap.

The Texas fans did not seem to mind the low ranking, however, supporting their teams as enthusiastically as any community. Some San Antonio Bronco fans treated that championship team to a reception in a local bordello. Traditional rituals of a dinner, speeches, and a trophy were supplemented with hundred-dollar bills beneath each of the players' plates and, one assumes, the opportunities that a seraglio affords the wealthy.

The Galveston Sandcrabs were also acquainted with sins of the flesh. Their distinguished pitcher Eugene Moore used batting practice to belt home runs over the short right field fence. Players were required to recover those balls, and Bill O'Neal writes that Moore was delighted to play fetch since the Blue Goose Saloon was in the vicinity of his home runs.

Players could also be governed by gentler instincts. In 1910 the Houston Buffaloes found an abandoned baby on a train. The child became a ward of the team, with the players donating from meager salaries for the boy's care. Third baseman Roy Akin eventually adopted the lad.

Akin was a fine third baseman who played for several teams in the Texas League. In 1912, while playing for Waco against Houston, Akin made an unassisted triple play at third base. It is believed to be the only time in organized baseball that the ultimate fielding play has been achieved by a third baseman.

In these early years, the preeminent player in Texas was one of Akin's Cleburne teammates, Tris Speaker. A "Texas Leaguer" is a fly ball that drops between the infield and outfield. During Speaker's two-year apprenticeship with Cleburne and Houston, he developed his style of playing a very shallow outfield to catch bloop hits while relying on his brilliant speed to haul in the long drives. Speaker's career began as a very unsuccessful pitcher, but his batting skills and ability to steal bases quickly became apparent. At Houston in 1907 he took the Texas League batting championship with a .314 average, and at the end of the year he moved to the Boston Red Sox, where he began his twenty-two-year major league career.

Branch Rickey was another immortal who appeared early in the history of the Texas League. As a player, his impact on the circuit was negligible, but when he developed the Cardinals' farm system in the 1920s and 1930s, his teams in Texas would feature many future stars of St. Louis.

Less remembered is Big Mike O'Connor, who left a significant mark on Texas baseball. At six feet, five inches, he made an imposing target as a first baseman, and as a manager he was hard to ignore. O'Connor was a fixture from the first season of the Texas League in 1888 until his untimely death in 1906. He was the manager of the Corsicana team that destroyed Texarkana, and he himself went seven for eight with three home runs in that debacle. That team also established a League record with a twenty-seven-game winning streak. In 1896 he led the League with a .401 average for San Antonio, yet O'Connor never had an opportunity to play in the big leagues.

Piggy Page, Buck Harris, and Bill Bailey were among the great pitchers of the early Texas League, but its greatest career pitcher arrived at Beaumont in 1912. "Oyster" Joe Martina enjoyed a twenty-two-year career in professional baseball, most of it spent in the minor leagues, and most of that in Texas. On his way to recording 349 wins in the minors, Martina won at least twenty games in each of seven seasons. He also held a record for strikeouts in the minor leagues that stood for over sixty years. Oyster Joe had a remarkably durable arm. He often appeared in over forty games per season, and he frequently pitched over 300 innings. In a career that lasted from 1910 through 1931, Martina pitched in the majors in only one season. At the age of thirty-five, he was finally summoned to the big leagues, where in 1924 he had an undistinguished season with Washington.

Martina has achieved a mixed bag of fame in recent years. SABR included him in its first volume of minor league stars, and the second volume lists him among the fifteen all-time minor league all-stars. On the down side, Oyster Joe had something other than classic features, and he was picked by Bill James as the ugliest player in organized ball during the decade of the 1920s.[2]

FROM 1910 TO 1920, pitchers dominated the Texas League. Snipe Conley won twenty-seven games in 1917, including nineteen in a row, and he led his team in hitting with a .309 average. Hickory Dickson set a league record with a 1.06 earned run average in 1916. Eugene Moore was sober enough to strike out over 200 batters twice and to win twenty-one games in 1914. Bill Bailey, teamed with Joe Martina at Beaumont, won twenty-four games, with a league-leading 277 strikeouts, in 1919.

This was also an era of dynasties. Houston won the league title in 1909, a disputed co-championship with Dallas in 1910, the titles in 1912 and 1913, and a co-championship with Waco in 1914. Charles Rose led the pitching staff with over 100 wins during those championship seasons.

Andy Ware aided Houston with twenty wins in 1913 and twenty-six the following year. Bill O'Neal describes Ware as the minor leagues' Mordecai Brown. A childhood accident left Ware with a deformity of his pitching hand that he used to his advantage by putting a unique spin on the ball. Despite his own success and the great performances of Three-Finger Brown, Ware was never given the chance to pitch in the majors.

The weak-hitting Buffaloes were supplanted by the Waco Navigators, who added pennants in 1916 and 1917 to their 1915 title. O'Neal mentions three pitchers as stalwarts of the Navigators' staff: Eddie Donalds won sixty-five games from 1914–16; George Sage had two good seasons in 1914 and 1915 before posting a 6–14 record in 1916; and Cliff Hill steadily improved during these seasons from 10–5 to 15–8 to 23–14. Of these three pitchers, Donalds and Hill appeared in the majors, but each appeared in only one game for a few innings. Donalds was up in 1912 before his fine years at Waco, but not even his thirty wins in 1914 attracted big-league attention.

O'Neal describes catcher Emmett Reilly as having a "cannon for an arm," yet Reilly never appeared in the majors. Second baseman Walter Malmquist, "a flawless fielder," spent his entire career in the minors. Harvey Grubb "handled the hot corner superbly, but was weak at the plate." Grubb appeared in one game for Cleveland in 1912, did not bat, and never got another chance in the majors. Fred Wohleben "led the Texas League in home runs in 1913 and 1915," yet he never appeared in the majors. Archie Tanner had a career average of .280 in fourteen seasons, and he was "one of the great Texas League shortstops." He never played in the majors.[3]

Bob James, an outfielder, hit .295 in 1914, .313 in 1915, and .303 in 1916. James had the most extensive major league career of any of the Navigators. He had appeared in six games with the Cardinals in 1909, hitting .286 in twenty-one trips to the plate. His was another case of a Waco player who had a cup of coffee in the big leagues before starring on a championship team at Waco, heroics that the majors ignored.

What do we make of the apparent anomaly of minor league stars who never had a serious chance to make the majors? At first glance, perhaps not much. The Texas League at that time was the lowest rung on the ladder of organized baseball. A superb performance at that level did not necessarily indicate ability that qualified for the majors. Indeed, none of those Waco stars are included in the SABR volumes of minor league heroes.

Another limitation on the advancement of some of these players may have been the relative isolation of Texas from the major league havens. Travel was more imposing in those days for both players and scouts. It would have been much easier to miss a prospect than it has since become.

More significant, a perspective that views the Texas League from the vantage point of the majors is deceptive. It either mistakenly presumes that the Texas players were among the least skilled in baseball, or if that judgment is accurate, it fails to appreciate the beauty of the game in the setting of dust storms on the Texas plains and hurricanes along the Gulf coast.

The relative merits of the Dallas Hams and the Boston Red Sox were less important in Dallas than whether the locals would beat Fort Worth. The Houston-Waco rivalry was as intense for Texans as the Dodger-Giant rivalry was for New Yorkers. On its own terms, the Texas League did just fine. Gifted players battled for championships to the pleasure and frustration of their fans. How good they were compared to clubs in other leagues is an inevitable question, but perhaps it is also a trivial one.

IF FANS OF the Texas League cannot resist the urge to compare their teams with those of other circuits, they most likely would make a case for the Fort Worth Panthers of the 1920s. Rivaling the string of Jack Dunn's Orioles, the Panthers won their league championship in every year from 1919 through 1925.

By the time of the Panthers' dynasty, the Texas League had closed the gap between itself and other minor leagues. Beginning as a Class-D circuit in 1902, it was elevated to Class C in 1907, to Class B in 1911, and to Class A in 1921. A Double-A ranking had been established in 1908 for the American Association, the International League, and the Pacific Coast League; that remained the highest rating until a Triple-A classification was established in 1945.

The Panthers, then, were dominant in the Texas League when that circuit was just a stride behind the International League that was the playground of Dunn's Orioles during the same era. The timing of the two pennant streaks was not accidental. The draft exemption allowed talent to remain in the minor leagues, and the decision of the Double-A leagues to forgo the draft denied them the privilege of drafting from lower circuits. The Texas League thus benefited from the decision of its more exalted colleagues to go it alone.

As with the International League, the draft exemption simply opened the possibility for a dynasty; there was nothing inevitable about the dominance of either the Orioles or the Panthers. The key in both cases was the quality of the management. While Baltimore enjoyed the genius of Jack Dunn, Fort Worth was led by three men who achieved the same result.

Before the 1917 season, the Panthers were acquired by a stock company led by W. K. Stripling and Paul LaGrave, who became respectively the club president and its secretary and business manager. They retained Jake Atz as the Panthers' manager. Atz had been with Fort Worth since 1914, but he had yet to complete a season with the club.

In the first season under the new regime, the Panthers finished with a 91–70 record for second place, five games behind Dallas. The 1918 season was cut short by the "work or fight" policy that had been adopted after America's entry into World War I. A 47–39 record was good for another second-place finish, again five games behind the Hams.

The string of pennants began with a second-half title in the 1919 season. Fort Worth won more games than any other team for the entire season with ninety-four wins. Shreveport had captured the first-half championship and finished second over-all that year with eighty-one victories. Despite the Panthers' better record, Shreveport defeated Fort Worth in the postseason playoffs. It was the last time for seven years that any competitor in the Texas League would be close to the Pan-thers.

The utter dominance of the Panthers during their reign is easily seen by comparing their record with that of the Texas League runner-up for each year:

| Year | Teams | W–L Record | Games Back |
|------|-------|-----------|-----------|
| 1920 | Fort Worth | 108–40 | |
| | Wichita Falls | 85–63 | 23 |
| 1921 | Fort Worth | 107–51 | |
| | Houston | 92–67 | 15½ |
| 1922 | Fort Worth | 109–46 | |
| | Wichita Falls | 94–61 | 15 |
| 1923 | Fort Worth | 96–56 | |
| | San Antonio | 81–68 | 13½ |
| 1924 | Fort Worth | 109–41 | |
| | Houston | 80–73 | 30½ |
| 1925 | Fort Worth | 103–48 | |
| | Houston | 87–56 | 12 |

The Texas League continued with a split-season format dur-ing these years, but the Panthers routed the league with such consistency that no other half-season champion emerged to provide competition.

An important part of baseball in the south was the Dixie Se-ries, which began in 1920. It featured the champions of the Texas League and the Southern Association in a best-of-seven playoff, and it helped to enhance the appeal of baseball to southerners.

While the Orioles struggled in the Junior World Series, the Panthers continued their dominance in the Dixie Series. They defeated Little Rock four games to two with one tie in the inaugural match in 1920. That victory may have helped to promote the Texas League to equal Class-A status with the Southern Association.

In 1921 the Panthers beat Memphis, four games to two. They beat New Orleans, four games to two with one tie, in 1923. The next year they took Memphis again, four games to three with one tie, and in 1925 they beat Atlanta, four games to two. The Panthers' only defeat was a 1922 loss to Mobile. Their success in the Dixie Series suggests that Fort Worth was the class of an entire region of the country, and it naturally makes one wish that a series with the Baltimore Orioles had been arranged.

The most apparent difference between the Panthers and the Orioles is the respective fame of the players. While Lefty Grove and Jack Bentley were well known and eagerly coveted by major league teams, few of the Panthers even approached that level of acclaim.

Joe Pate and Paul Wachtel anchored the pitching staff over the six-year reign. Wachtel won more than twenty games in each of those years except 1923. It was his misfortune to be a spitball pitcher at the very time that the pitch was banned in the majors. His only chance in the big leagues was a two-game stint with the Dodgers in 1917. He performed terribly, but two years later he was a twenty-game winner with the Panthers. If he had been recalled to the majors in 1920, he would have won an exemption from the spitball ban. Wachtel's career spanned the period 1912 to 1930, during which he won 317 games in the minors. If the draft had been in place, Wachtel might have moved up in baseball's hierarchy. As it was, he remained another fine player who enriched the Texas League for many years, lacking the skills or the luck to move on.

Joe Pate enjoyed a career that was even longer than Wachtel's. Pate broke in with Corpus Christi in 1911, and he pitched in professional ball until 1932. He twice won thirty games for the Panthers, in 1921 and 1924. In the other years of the championship streak, he won a total of ninety-three games, and he regularly pitched over 300 innings. Pate's major league career consisted of two seasons with Connie Mack's A's in 1926 and 1927. By that time he was thirty-four years old, no longer at his peak. Even so, he posted a 9–0 record for Philadelphia in his first year before falling to 0–3 in his final season in the big leagues.

Pate and Wachtel may vindicate Commissioner Landis's support for the universal draft as a means of advancing talented players, but even at a market price, it seems sensible that some major league club should have taken a chance on these two.

Compounding the puzzling attitude of the majors is the acquisition of Lil Stoner by the Detroit Tigers after Stoner won twenty-seven games for the Panthers in 1923. The right-hander had gone 4–4 for the Tigers in 1922 but was brought back after his spectacular season in the Texas League. He stayed with Detroit through the 1929 season, when he was dealt to Pittsburgh, who kept him for one season before sending him to the Phillies, where he ended his career in 1931. Stoner had no decisions in the National League. During that time in the majors, Stoner compiled a record of 50–58 with an earned run average of 4.76. Despite such mediocre numbers, no one appeared to think that perhaps Detroit had selected the wrong Panther. Pate could win thirty games twice and be ignored, while a twenty-seven-win season earned Stoner a career in the majors.

Clarence "Big Boy" Kraft supplied the bulk of the Fort Worth offense. He enjoyed a spectacular season in 1924, when he hit fifty-five home runs, batted .349, and drove in 196 runs. In that year he was thirty-seven, and no major league team was interested. Kraft was another Texas Leaguer who had been given the proverbial cup of coffee by the Red Sox in 1914. He managed one hit in his three-at-bat major league career before he was sent down to Newark to resume his minor league career. Kraft's numbers suggest that he simply decided to start hitting home runs in 1921. Until that point in his career, he had hit a total of eighty-seven home runs in eleven seasons. In the four years that remained, he belted 150.

Kraft retired at the peak of his game. After the 1924 season, he left baseball to become an automobile dealer. He was one of the characters who endeared the Panthers to their fans. O'Neal quotes Kraft on the art of public relations: "You always want your name in the paper. If you're walking down the street and you haven't been getting enough publicity, hit someone in the nose." Perhaps that worked on a team that, according to its manager, could "drink any brewery dry at night and beat any baseball team the next afternoon."[4]

O'Neal also tells of Jimmy Walkup, a left-handed pitcher who frustrated Babe Ruth with three strikeouts in an exhibition game. For entertainment, Walkup "liked to fill a drinking straw with gunpowder, twist it at one end, light the other, and watch his homemade missile take off. When Walkup ignited one of his explosive straws in the direction of a slumbering Possum Moore, the big catcher leaped from his bed stark naked, jammed his foot into a spittoon, and angrily chased Walkup through the hotel."[5]

That brand of humor was prevalent throughout the League. When Wichita Falls faced Snipe Conley of Dallas in a game in 1922, someone doctored the ball with creosote. As Conley, a spitball pitcher, applied saliva to the ball, he inevitably applied creosote to his mouth. The resulting burn gave the Spudders the margin of victory in a 4–3 win.

PERHAPS SUCH ANTICS convinced Branch Rickey that Gashouse Gang material thrived in the Lone Star State. The Texas League became a critical part of his St. Louis Cardinal farm system, and Texas became part of the early training of many future major league stars.

The Houston club was acquired by the Cardinals in the early 1920s despite the opposition of independent owners in the Texas League. The Fort Worth dynasty offered some initial vindication for the independents, but by the end of the decade the force of the Cardinals' farm system was evident.

Dizzy Dean, Howie Pollett, and later, Harry Brecheen starred on the Buffalo pitching staff, while Ducky Medwick and Pepper Martin provided much of the offense. During the interwar years, Houston won Texas League championships in 1928, 1931, 1933, 1939, 1940, and 1941. As the Panthers had benefited from their independence from the majors, so the Buffs were enriched by Cardinals talent that overflowed St. Louis and Rochester.

The Cardinals did not monopolize star players in the Texas League. Carl Hubbell appeared for half a season for the last-place Beaumont Exporters in 1928. He compiled a 12–9 record and completed twenty of twenty-one starts. The New York Giants acquired Hubbell in midseason, and he became the greatest pitcher that the franchise had had since Christy Mathewson.

By 1932 Beaumont's fortunes had improved. Hank Greenberg was the Texas League's Most Valuable Player, an honor he secured with a .318 batting average, thirty-nine home runs, and 131 runs batted in. Like Hubbell, Greenberg did not languish in the minors. He moved to Detroit in 1933 and became one of the great power hitters of his time in the majors.

At the other end of his career, Grover Cleveland Alexander ended his professional career pitching for the Dallas Steers in 1930. The minors were not the opportunity for Alexander that they had been for Joe McGinnity, and he was out of baseball after that season.

During these years the Texas League remained a place with great players who never moved up to the majors. Among the most prominent was Homer Peel, who enjoyed a minor league career from 1923–46, with most of that time spent in the Texas League. Peel had retired after the 1942 season at the age of forty, but he returned in 1946 to play for Paris in the East Texas League. Even after that layoff, he hit .322 in 115 at-bats. His greatest year was in 1937, when he played for and managed Fort Worth and led the Texas League with a .370 average, with forty-eight doubles and 118 runs batted in. He compiled a career batting average of .322 in his more than 2,000 minor league games.

Peel played for a number of years in the Cardinal organization, so he undoubtedly was evaluated regularly as a major league prospect. Unlike some of the Texas all-stars, Peel had several chances to make the big leagues. The Cardinals called him up for two at-bats in the 1927 season, and he played in over fifty games for the Phillies in 1929. His .269 average earned him a trade back to the Cardinals, where he foundered. He then spent several years at Houston before joining the New York Giants in 1933. In the following year, Peel was sent back to the minors, where he remained for the rest of his career. Apparently he simply lacked the critical margin of skill that distinguished the best minor league players from the worst major leaguers. Certainly it is possible that the chances he was given were insufficient for him to prove himself, but compared to Pate and Wachtel, Peel was given ample opportunity.

If Homer Peel enjoyed the greatest career in the Texas League, the most spectacular inning was enjoyed by Eugene Rudolph Mercantelli, better known as Gene Rye. Playing for Waco in a game against Beaumont on August 6, 1930, Rye led off the bottom of the eighth with a home run. Waco batted around, and Rye came up with two runners on. He hit his second home run of the inning, but he was not finished. Waco batted around for a second time and presented Rye with the bases loaded when he went up for his third at-bat of the inning. Rye pulled another home run over the right field fence. As Robert McConnell describes it, "When the dust had cleared, Rye had set four Organized Baseball records for one inning: most total bases (12), most extra bases (9), most runs batted in (8), and most home runs (3)."[6] McConnell notes that the RBI mark was matched in 1947 by Ken Myers of Las Vegas, who hit two grand slams in one inning of a Sunset League game in 1947. Rye was part of an eighteen-run explosion by Waco in that famous eighth inning. Within a few years, he was out of the game, but Gene Rye had left his mark on the Texas League with three incredible at-bats.

◆ ◆ ◆

THE GREAT DEPRESSION was a time of enormous economic challenge to baseball teams at every level. The support of major league patrons was no guarantee of security for minor league teams. Marginal independents were in worse shape than clubs under the protection of the Cardinals or Yankees were, but money for leisure pursuits was virtually nonexistent.

Hard times were as prevalent in Texas as anywhere else. A once-thriving oil economy had collapsed. The price of oil had fallen to less than a nickel per barrel, and federal policies tried to restrict production even at that price. A fortunate few remained prosperous, but for most people the fifty cents needed for admission to a baseball game was hard to come by.

The combination of night baseball and postseason playoffs significantly helped to bolster the Texas League, which had begun to show some instability. In 1931 Galveston replaced Waco; the following year, Shreveport lost its ball park to a fire. The Wichita Falls franchise moved to Longview and then to San Antonio.

In 1933 teams were settled in Beaumont, Dallas, Fort Worth, Galveston, Houston, Oklahoma City, San Antonio, and Tulsa. Those eight cities constituted the Texas League until the mid-1950s, when the avarice of the major league owners unsettled the minors even more than the Great Depression had.

In the interim, the Texas League enjoyed the peak years of minor league baseball. That era was not without its own challenges, but at no time before or since have the minors been so prosperous.

During World War II, baseball was given more latitude to continue play than had been the case during the First World War. The major leagues played full schedules from 1942 through 1945, although many of their best players were performing military service. The minor leagues had a more difficult time continuing play. The teams were, of course, a prime source of men for the military, and restrictions on travel complicated the completion of schedules. Since minor league teams were located in smaller communities than major league franchises, local opposition to playing games while local boys were risking their lives was probably more difficult to ignore than it was in the big cities.

A record number forty-three minor leagues competed in 1940, and forty-one were still around in 1941. The effects of the war dropped that number to thirty-one in 1942, then to ten in the next two years. With the end of the war in sight in 1945, a dozen leagues resumed play.

The postwar period brought immediate prosperity to the minors. Forty-two minor leagues operated in 1946, and three years later an all-time record of fifty-nine leagues participated in the minor league game. Within a decade the minor leagues were shattered by television and the expansion and relocation of the major leagues.

The Texas League voted in 1942 to suspend operations, but a skeleton organization continued to protect the league's interests in the National Association. When peace was restored, the league resumed play, and record attendance marks were set.


PERHAPS THE MOST striking characteristic of baseball in Texas during the first half of the twentieth century was its self-containment. Over 100 communities from Dallas to small towns along the Mexican border were represented in Texas baseball. Rivalries developed that distracted Texans from major league pennant races and the World Series.

The stratification of baseball leagues compels comparisons of players and teams. Some of the game's greatest players appeared in Texas before moving on to major league careers that led to Cooperstown, so we can conclude that the quality of play was respectable. Why other players with comparable figures were ignored by the big leagues remains puzzling, but much is lost by evaluating the Texas League solely from the perspective of the majors.

Joe Pate and Paul Wachtel never made a dent in the majors while Dizzy Dean and Carl Hubbell made it big, but the Panther hurlers were as important to baseball fans in Texas as Dean and Hubbell were in St. Louis and New York. Homer Peel was known as the Ty Cobb of the Texas League, and he probably thrilled Texans as much as Cobb did Detroit fans.

Certainly a vital part of baseball or any competitive sport is the struggle to determine who is best. No doubt in head-to-head competition between Texas League teams and those of the American and National Leagues, the Texans would have been trounced; but, again, that is only one part of the beauty of the game. The struggle itself as much as the outcome is at the core of baseball's appeal. The integrity, imagination, effort, and color that players and fans bring to the struggle may not lend themselves to comparisons between leagues, but it is doubtful if fans anywhere appreciated baseball more than the Texans.

# Nine

# THE LOW MINORS

"THERE WAS A time in this country when every village and crossroad had a baseball team. Some were 'town' teams. Some were 'pickup.'

"There was one period after World War II when every town big enough to have a bank also had a professional baseball team, and the peak of excitement was reached when the bank was robbed or the baseball team won a pennant."[1]

Baseball, as Furman Bisher remembered it, was a game for small southern towns, an encapsulated world that existed for its own reasons apart from any interests of the major leagues. The majors represented the best players in the biggest cities, but the lower echelons of the minor leagues had their own devoted fans, memorable players, and spectacular games.

As hundreds of small communities all over North America came to lose their teams during the 1950s, one debate revolved around whether the low minors were really needed. Odds were calculated on the possibility of a player rising from Class D to the majors. If the odds were too long, then the league was considered superfluous.

To the town that watched its boys become young men pursuing greatness on the local diamond, the calculations of the major league executive neglected the most important factors. The townspeople shared the same bond as that of Yankee or Red Sox fans even when none of the local heroes approached major league caliber.

The low minors also seemed expendable because they often were so close to bankruptcy. Class-D leagues resembled the nineteenth-century game: teams would fold in midseason or transfer to another city, schedules would be cut short, and after one or two seasons, the league itself would disband, leaving memories and hopes for a resurgence during better times.

Robert Obojski has performed yeoman's work in assembling a record of every minor league in the twentieth century in his book, *Bush Leagues*. A sample of his findings shows how deeply knit baseball had become in small-town America.

At the depths of the Depression in 1936, the Alabama-Mississippi League placed teams in Anniston, Decatur, Gadsden, Huntsville, and Sheffield, Alabama, and Corinth, Mississippi. It was unable to survive its inaugural season. On the surface, the League was an utter failure, but in another light, it can be viewed as part of the larger community of baseball. Residents of Corinth might have rooted for the Cardinals or the Senators, or they might have followed Atlanta in the Southern Association. But for a few months, the people of Corinth had their own team, and that must have made the game itself more personal to them.

Another Class-D partial-season circuit was the Anthracite League of 1928. The towns of Hazelton, Mahanoy City, Mount Carmel, Shamokin, Shenandoah, and Tamaqua, Pennsylvania, were favored with franchises, with no noticeable detriment to the Pirates or Phillies. In the tradition of mineral leagues, the Copper-Country Soo League, another Class-D affiliate, came and went in 1905 with clubs in Calumet, Hancock, Lake Linden, and Sault Sainte Marie, Michigan.

These leagues were often more than mere trivia for baseball fanatics. The Cooper-Country Soo League lasted but one season, but the following year it joined with the Northern League, a three-year-old circuit, to form the Northern Copper Country League. Calumet and Lake Linden combined with Duluth, Fargo, and Winnipeg from the Northern League to form the new circuit. The Northern Copper Country League lasted for two seasons before it was reorganized back into the Northern League in 1908. The League failed to finish that season, but returned in 1909, in an altered state, as the Minnesota-Wisconsin League. The Northern League reappeared in 1913 with part of the then-extinct Minnesota-Wisconsin League. The new Northern League operated as a Class-C circuit from 1913 to 1916. It collapsed in Class D during World War I and reappeared from 1933 through 1942, moving back to Class C in 1941. After suspending operations for World War II, the Northern League was part of Class C from 1946 through 1962, and then it moved to Class A from 1963 through 1971.

This odyssey demonstrates that taking snapshots of the low minors in any particular year is misleading. Quite often communities that support baseball teams are hospitable to the sport over many years. The failure of one league to complete its first and only season does not mean that some of the towns will not be back in organized baseball in a few years.

In fact the resilience of baseball in the hinterlands is its most impressive quality even after a cursory glance. The major financial obstacles to the success of the low minors were world wars and the Great Depression, serious challenges to most industries.

The Evangeline League was a successful venture that is relatively easy to trace. It operated in Class D from 1934 through 1948 except during the war years. It then moved up to Class C from 1949 through 1957. Comprising primarily teams in Louisiana, the League included the towns of Houma, New Iberia, and Opelousas, Louisiana, among its members.

Thirty towns in Georgia were represented in the Georgia

State League, which sputtered through several incarnations until it settled in Class D from 1948 through 1956. The Kitty League included clubs in Kentucky, Illinois, and Tennessee. Another Class-D circuit, it ran from 1910–14, part of 1916, from 1922–24, part of 1935, 1936 through part of 1942, then from 1946 through 1955.

The Mississippi State League of 1921 was another apparent failure that simply became another league. The clubs in Clarksdale, Greenwood, Jackson, and Meridian, Mississippi joined the Cotton States League in 1922. That circuit disbanded after the 1923 season but reappeared at the Class-C level from 1936 through 1941, then from 1947 through 1955. The teams of the Mississippi State League were represented during much of the subsequent history of the Cotton States League.

What appears to be instability in the low minors might be better thought of as fluidity. The major leagues by contrast remained locked into their cities from 1903 through 1953, but a number of their franchises, including the Browns and the Dodgers, were bankrupt during some of those years. Rather than being run by the League, the minor league franchises simply hopped to another community or disbanded until times were more favorable.

The potential number of markets for minor league teams is extraordinary. The six towns in Colorado that have hosted minor league clubs seems about right, as do the six in Idaho, five in Montana, two in Nevada, and one in Wyoming. California's 56 minor league communities are impressive, as are New York's 59 and Texas's 101. But some incredible numbers of towns in other states have also sustained minor league baseball.

Alabama has had minor league baseball in thirty-three towns, not just in Birmingham, Mobile, and Montgomery, but in Brewton, Dothan, Eufaula, Opelika, and Selma as well. Illinois has had two major league teams in Chicago from day one, and the Cardinals draw attention downstate. But Illinois has also had fifty-one minor league communities in its history.

Georgia was shut out of the majors until the late 1960s, but thirty-eight minor league communities flourished in Furman Bisher's home state. Kansas has been home to forty-three teams, Kentucky to thirty, and Louisiana to twenty-one. Ohio has two major league teams, and others on its borders; but Ohio still has been the home to forty minor league clubs.

Oklahoma has hosted thirty-seven teams, but none in Mickey Mantle's home town of Commerce. Pennsylvania, a state with major league teams at each end, has fielded sixty-six minor league clubs. Virginia has had forty-two minor league teams, not just in Richmond, but in Big Stone Gap, Galax, and Roanoke.

The most remarkable state for minor league baseball must be North Carolina, which has fielded minor league clubs in *seventy* of its towns and villages. The North Carolina League lasted only until July of 1902 in the first attempt to organize baseball in the Tarheel State. The North Carolina State League, formed in 1913, operated from 1913–17, from 1937–42, and finally from 1945–52.

On a loftier plateau, North Carolina teams played in the Class-B Piedmont League, in the Class-A South Atlantic League, and the Class-AA Southern League. But again, the more impressive feature may be how deep and extensive the roots of baseball have traveled rather than how high the branches have reached.

Every state has sent players to the big leagues, but it is more remarkable that organized baseball has been played in the North Carolina towns of Angier, Cooleemee, Fuquay Springs, Kannapolis, Mayodan, and Snow Hill. Perhaps it is easier to understand how baseball has had such a grip on the country when the sport is seen from the small towns, where the game is played for local pride and the commercial machinations of the majors seem a world away.


BASEBALL HAS WOVEN a fabric not only through the small towns of America, but also across our national borders. The International League is, of course, the best example when it included Havana and Montreal in the 1950s. But the low minors have also had an international flavor from time to time.

The Arizona-Mexico League was a Class-C organization that operated from 1955–58. Of the thirteen cities that were included in that circuit, six were Mexican. Juárez, Mexicali, Nogales, and Tijuana are all border towns, Cananea is not far from the Arizona border, and Chihuahua is almost 150 miles south of Texas.

All of the Mexican cities except for Tijuana had previously been part of the Arizona-Texas League, an organization that operated sporadically at the Class-C and -D levels from the 1930s to the 1950s. In one of its incarnations, it was the Southwest International League of 1951–52, a combination of the Arizona-Texas League and the Sunset League of 1947–50.

A thorough integration of Mexican and American baseball was beyond the capacity of these leagues, but some inclusion of the Mexican game along the southwestern border was a recurring part of minor league baseball over several decades. The Mexican leagues themselves have been nominally a part of the National Association for a number of years, but those leagues restrict the number of foreigners who may play.

Affiliations between teams in the United States and Canada have been more extensive. Canadian teams were part of the very first minor leagues, and they played in the Pacific Coast League and the International League before major league expansion included Montreal and Toronto in the 1970s.

One Border League operated in Michigan from 1912–13 at the Class-D level, including five teams from Michigan and one from Windsor, Ontario. In 1914 the circuit operated for the final time as the Eastern Michigan League. Another Border League was a Class-C organization that ran from 1946–51, with teams in Quebec, Ontario, and New York.

The Canadian-American League operated at the Class-C level from 1936–42, then from 1946–51. Twenty towns participated in this league at one time or another, eleven in the state of New York, six in the province of Ontario, two in Quebec, and one in Massachusetts.

A Canadian League that made it to Class B for its final two seasons, 1914–15, was an all-Ontario contingent, but it included Erie, Pennsylvania, in the 1914 season. The Central International League was another small organization that played Class-C ball in 1912. It included Winnipeg during its sole campaign. Winnipeg was another town that proved the resilience of the low minors when it hitched up with the Northern League for over twenty-five seasons.

Victoria, British Columbia, was part of the Northwestern League for several years before World War I. After the war a Pacific Coast International League operated for a few years at the Class-B level, and teams included the towns of Vancouver and Victoria, British Columbia. The Michigan-Ontario League operated at Class B from 1919–1925.

The PONY League, comprising clubs in Pennsylvania, Ontario, and New York, operated in Class D from 1939 through 1956, even through World War II. The Western International League included teams in Washington, Oregon, Idaho, British Columbia, and Alberta. It ran at the Class-B and -A levels from 1937 to 1954, with time out for the war.

American and Canadian teams joined for parts of a season in the International League of Class D in 1908. The New Brunswick and Maine League made it through part of the 1913 season. Burlington, Vermont, joined the Provincial League for the 1955 season. The Quebec-Ontario-Vermont League played a partial season at Class B in 1924.

All-Canadian leagues included the Cape Breton Colliery League, an aggregate of five teams in Nova Scotia that played at Class D and Class C from 1937–39. The Eastern Canada League struggled through parts of 1922 and 1923. The Western Canada League began a roller-coaster ride in Class B at 1907, fell to C and D before World War I, came back at Class C in 1919, moved to Class B for 1920 and 1921, and disbanded.

The Quebec Provincial League was an all-Canadian contingent that tried to organize in 1940. Only three of six teams finished its only season. The Ontario League was a complete bust, as none of six teams could make it past July.

CAN WE LEARN anything important from what might appear to be a pedantic display of trivia? On the face of it, the low minors, whether in the United States, Canada, or Mexico, have consistently failed. They operated in virtual chaos without a reasonable chance of predicting future business conditions. One can claim that the elimination of these leagues during the 1950s and 1960s gave professional baseball a much-needed pruning that has stabilized the remaining leagues and made the evaluation of potential major leaguers more efficient.

That view is not unreasonable, but it certainly reflects the major league bias that stability and the training of future major leaguers are paramount values. From a less tidy vantage point, different lessons may be drawn that are at least as reasonable and perhaps less stodgy.

If we focus on the resilience of the low minors before World War II, we see networks of small towns in remote parts of America. Radio and newspapers provide information from the media centers, but television has not yet developed and transportation still requires effort. These towns are connected in part by an abiding interest in baseball, not just following teams in distant cities but also enjoying the occasional treat of watching a home team for a few seasons.

Whether a specific community had a baseball team in each and every year from 1903 to the present may have been less important than the presence of some team in the general area on a fairly regular basis. For example, seventy teams played in North Carolina in 1941; when the franchise in Cooleemee failed after that season, residents could travel twenty miles to the new team in the larger town of Statesville in 1942—a formidable but not impossible jaunt.

Teams in the low minors operated on the margin of local economies. A slight downturn would require people to tighten their spending, and recreational and leisure pursuits would most likely suffer. Remarkably, when hard times eased, baseball was swiftly restored to many communities.

These teams in forgotten towns may have advanced few players to the majors, but they developed the attachments of millions of people to the national game. Only someone with a very narrow perspective could fail to appreciate the contribution made to baseball by those players and their fans.

SINCE THERE HAVE been many more games in the minor leagues than in the majors, it is not surprising that some of the most spectacular records have been recorded in the minors. Add to the number of games the disparity of talent that met in the low minors, and the incredible becomes almost inevitable.

Fred Mangum recounted some of those events in the South Atlantic League in an article for *Baseball Magazine* in 1921. Mangum described a pitching duel between Scott Holmes of Augusta and Harry Kane of Savannah. Both men carried no-hitters into the tenth inning when Augusta finally broke through to win the game on a hit, a stolen base, and an error.

The only time that a double no-hitter over nine innings was achieved in the big leagues was in 1917, when Fred Toney of Cincinnati beat Jim Vaughn of the Cubs 1–0 in ten innings. But Toney had been even more spectacular in a game in 1909 in the Blue Grass League. Pitching for the Winchester, Kentucky, Hustlers against the Lexington Colts, Toney, in his first full professional season, took the mound on a rainy spring afternoon. He locked horns with a pitcher named Baker who scattered seven hits and six walks but no runs well into extra innings. Toney, meanwhile, held the Colts hitless while giving up only one walk. The game was finally decided when the Hustlers scored on a squeeze play in the bottom of the seventeenth inning. Toney's seventeen-inning no-hitter remains the longest in the history of organized baseball, most likely, one of those never-to-be-broken records.

Back in the South Atlantic League, Bugs Raymond pitched a variation of Toney's game on July 4, 1905. In Charleston, South Carolina, on that Independence Day, Raymond threw no-hitters in both the morning and afternoon games of a double header.

Three no-hitters were hurled on June 12, 1937, when Manuel Perez of Palestine in the East Texas League beat Kilgore, 5–0; Fred Marberry of Dallas no-hit the Galveston Pirates, 3–0, while Perez was working his magic; and that night, Bill Prince of Davenport in the Western League no-hit Cedar Rapids in a 2–1 victory.

John Cantley, who pitched for Opelika in the Georgia-Alabama League, put on the greatest hitting display by a pitcher when he hit three grand slam home runs and a single for fifteen runs batted in to lead his team to a 19–1 win over Talledega on June 5, 1914.

The hitters, of course, could also perform with a vengeance. In the first game of organized baseball played in Albuquerque, a record was established for total run production. The Albuquerque Dons clobbered the El Paso Longhorns 43–15 in an Arizona-Texas League game in 1932. The Dons' forty-three runs is short of the mark set by Corsicana, but combined with the scoring by the Longhorns, the fifty-eight runs is more than have been scored in any other game of professional ball.

New Mexico was also the site of the greatest season for home runs by one batter. In 1954, during the dying days of the low minors, Joe Bauman hit seventy-two home runs for the Roswell Rockets in the Class-C Longhorn League. Certainly the weather in that part of the country benefits hitters, and the pitching that Bauman faced would not have been the greatest. But the fact remains that other players have hit under those same conditions, and none of them has hit seventy home runs.

Bart Ripp's interview with Bauman for the 1980 *Baseball Research Journal* sheds some interesting light on the careers of players in remote leagues. Despite his remarkable slugging records, Bauman played only one game above the Class-A level in his career. He pumped gas in his service station during the day, then played for the Rockets in the evening. And the year after his record home run mark, he received the same pay that he had made the previous year.

Another neglected minor league hitter was Frank Huelsman, who five times led all of the minors in hitting, a record. Huelsman hit .392 for Shreveport of the Southern Association in 1901, and he matched that figure two years later while playing with Spokane. Two unspectacular years in the majors followed before Huelsman was sent to Montreal of the Eastern League. He spent 1907 with Kansas City, his last year out of the low minors. In 1911 Huelsman batted .411 for Great Falls in the Union Association, a Class-C organization at the time. In 1913 and 1914, he hit .423 and .424 respectively for Salt Lake City of the Union Association, which had been relegated to Class D. Despite those numbers, no teams in the majors or the high minors seem to have been interested in Huelsman. His career is another puzzle if we assume that the hierarchy of baseball always reflects the quality of play at the various levels. Either scouts could tell that Huelsman would have been a bust in a tougher league, or there may not have been as much difference among the various classes as one would be inclined to think.

John Spalding has found that the minor league batting champion almost always came from the low minors, and frequently that hitter batted over .400, as the table below shows.[2]

| Decade | Number of Batting Averages over .400 | Batting Champions from the High Minors |
|--------|--------------------------------------|----------------------------------------|
| 1901–10 | 2 | 2 |
| 1911–20 | 6 | 1 |
| 1921–30 | 10 | 1 |
| 1931–40 | 8 | 2 |
| 1941–50 | 6 | 0 |
| 1951–60 | 9 | 0 |

In sixty years the highest batting average in the minor leagues exceeded .400 forty-one times, and only six of those sixty champion batters were from the high minors.

No one could dispute that the .406 that Ted Williams hit in 1941 was more impressive than the .418 put up that same year by Lewis Flick of Elizabethton, Tennessee, of the Appalachian League. But the fans in Elizabethton were probably just as excited by Flick's heroics as Red Sox fans were by Williams's.

The same would apply to Joe Bauman. Is a home run record set in the New Mexico desert less exciting than one set in New York? Well, yes, it is for most of us; but if you happen to have lived in Roswell in 1954, Bauman's record might be the most dramatic event in baseball history to you. And, of course, if you are a fan, you would talk about that record many times to your children, your friends, and anyone else who would listen.

The appeal of baseball lies not only in the spectacular play by major leaguers immortalized by national media. It is also in the local player who, for a moment, rises to join the gods of the sport. He takes a community with him for that brief ascent, and they may remain eternally grateful.

In the elaborate calculations of organized baseball, Huelsman did not merit a chance in the majors after 1905, despite his batting titles. Lewis Flick was given a grand total of forty at-bats to prove his mettle in the big leagues; he hit .175 and was returned to the minors. But playing for Little Rock in a Southern League game against Memphis in 1946, Flick banged out nine consecutive hits in a nineteen-inning game. He probably made little impression in Philadelphia, but Flick left a strong legacy in Elizabethton, Little Rock, Milwaukee (where he won a batting title in the American Association in 1945), and Big Stone Gap in the Mountain States League, where he ended his career in 1951 with a .354 average.

Danny Boone was another great minor league player who spent most of his career in the low minors. The brother of the great Ike Boone, Danny was a pitcher for more than his first six seasons, and he made it to Detroit and Cleveland from 1921–23. Converted to the outfield, he tore up the Piedmont League, where he played for High Point from 1926 through part of 1931. He led the league in hitting for four of those years, and he twice led in home runs and runs batted in. Boone finished with a career batting average of .356. Not only was he neglected by the majors as a hitter, but he was overshadowed by brother Ike, who hit .370 over his brilliant career.

Buster Chatham, Moose Clabaugh, and Mervyn Connors are included in SABR's *Minor League Baseball Stars.* Each had a long career that was spent primarily in the low minors. Robert Crues established a record for organized ball with 254 RBIs in 1948. Crues played at the time for Amarillo of the West Texas–New Mexico League, and many of those runs were powered by his sixty-nine home runs that season.

A two-city franchise in the Northern League, Fargo-Moorhead, was the club where Frank Gravino hit fifty-two home runs in 1953, thirty-three more than the runner-up and more than four other *teams* in the league managed.

Pete Gray compiled a .307 batting average in the minors. He played for Three Rivers in the Canadian-American League, Memphis in the Southern League, Elmira in the Eastern League, Toledo in the American Association, and Dallas in the Texas League. In 1944 with Memphis, Gray led the league with sixty-eight stolen bases. This fine minor league career is especially incredible given that Gray played with one arm. His right arm had been lost in a childhood accident, yet Gray persevered to the point of playing for the St. Louis Browns during the 1945 season. His minor league records show that he was a fine ball player, not just a novelty brought to the big leagues by the player shortage of World War II.

Pete Hughes's twelve-year career in organized baseball was spent entirely in the low minors. He played from 1937–52, missing the 1942–45 seasons because of military service. In nine of those years he led his league in walks, and he had a career batting average of .350. The game had matured significantly by the time Hughes played, and his exclusion from the majors or the high minors is odd.

Joe Wilhoit set the record in organized ball for a hitting streak in 1919, when he batted safely in sixty-nine consecutive games for Wichita in the Western League. Wilhoit went to the Boston Red Sox for six games later that season and hit .333 but never appeared in the majors again.

Pitchers included among SABR's all-stars are George Boehler, who won thirty-eight games for Tulsa in the Western League in 1922, and Earl Caldwell, who began his career with

Temple-Mexia of the Texas Association in 1926. In 1948, at the age of forty-three, Caldwell was pitching in the American League. Five years later, he won the ERA title in the Evangeline League for Lafayette, where his son was his catcher.

Lefty George was another pitcher with incredible endurance. Born in 1886, he began his career in 1909 with Montgomery of the Southern League and York of the Tri-State League. Thirty-five years later, he ended his career back with York at the age of fifty-seven.

Clarence "Hooks" Iott posted some remarkable numbers in 1941. With Paragould in the Northeast Arkansas League, Iott struck out twenty-five batters in a nine-inning game. One month later, he fanned thirty in a sixteen-inning game.

Bill Thomas set career records for most games and innings pitched and for most games won and lost. He also gave up more hits and allowed more runs than any other pitcher in the game. From 1926 through 1952, Thomas pitched in 1,015 games and threw 5,987 innings, winning 383 and losing 346. He allowed 6,709 hits and 3,092 runs. Thomas is also associated with an allegation that he and other players on the Houma Indians of the Class-D Evangeline League conspired to throw games in the 1946 Shaughnessy playoffs. Thomas was one of the players charged with consorting with gamblers to rig the playoffs. Thomas denied the accusation, and he revealed that he had been approached during the season by a bookie who had sought to have some games thrown during the regular season. Thomas said he refused and had not even learned the bookie's name. An article by George Hilton in the 1982 *Baseball Research Journal* includes the conclusion of Judge Bramham, the president of the National Association, who had to rule on the charges:

In the case of the investigation here dealt with, there are positive allegations and circumstantial evidence to support them. On the other hand each of the players enter [sic] a vigorous denial. I have a very definite per-

sonal opinion in the premises, but do not find it necessary to predicate any finding of guilt as to this
allegation based upon that opinion. There is sufficient
other conduct detrimental to baseball established by
the record to justify the decision now rendered.[3]

The decision was to ban from baseball five Houma players, including Bill Thomas. Thomas protested, pointing out that he
had compiled a record of 5–0 in the playoffs. Three years later,
he was reinstated near the end of the 1949 season.

Hilton's article suggests that rumors of gamblers and fixed
games abounded in the Evangeline League that year. Gambling itself was apparently rampant in Louisiana and, with it,
suspicions of corruption. At the same time, no evidence specifically linking any of the Houma players with conspiracies to fix
games was offered. Thomas may have been the victim of a
clumsy attempt by Bramham to emulate Landis's handling of
the Black Sox scandal. At the very least, Thomas was denied
the most elemental requirements of a fair hearing, but that was
hardly unusual for players in those days.

In the fiftieth-anniversary history of the National Association, L. H. Addington described Judge Bramham's handling of
the Pitts case in 1935. Edwin Pitts had been incarcerated at
Sing Sing, where he starred on the prison baseball team. When
he was released, he was signed by Albany of the International
League. Bramham intervened to block the contract, and Addington's list of explanations are another example of the pa-
tronizing attitude that governed the game.

Bramham, according to Addington, had been informed that
Pitts was not talented enough for the International League.
There was one obvious way to find out, but Bramham had
other objections: "Bramham felt the player was being shown
off, as in the case of a circus freak, and that he should not be
subjected to that sort of treatment, just to draw a few crowds
at the gate. He despised that sort of exploitation. Furthermore,
he did not believe it a healthy situation to take a man just out

from behind the 'gray walls' and possibly pair him up as a room-mate with some other member of the club."[4]

A revised explanation is probably more accurate: Bramham saw the former convict as an unsavory influence on the game; whatever attention Pitts drew would be similar to that of a sideshow; and since Pitts probably was not good enough to compete, he should not be given the chance. No doubt Bramham believed he was acting in the best interests of the game, and his motives were sincere. But obviously there was no confidence that Pitts's teammates were mature enough to resist any corrupting influence that he might have. Baseball orthodoxy assumes that players always need the close supervision of the statesmen-owners and executives who alone possess the qualities required for governing.

Addington mentioned one more factor that influenced Bramham in this case: "He was tipped off by what he termed a reliable source that a National League club was the prime mover in behalf of Pitts, and the Minors were simply being used as a guinea pig. If Pitts 'got by' and drew big crowds in the Minors, then the idea was that he be called in for a swing around the circuit by his original promoters. Bramham literally [sic] 'burned up' at that."[5]

Bramham's blocking of Pitts was appealed to Commissioner Landis, who reversed the decision and then talked Bramham out of resigning. The unfortunate Pitts indeed was not up to the quality of play in organized ball, and a few years after his release from prison, he was killed in a fight.

One common element of the Pitts case and the allegations about the Evangeline League was the reliance on hearsay. Rumors from "reliable sources" seem to have been enough to start the wheels of baseball justice turning. Another point that both cases shared was the great concern with appearances. A sport that had endured the Black Sox scandal required protection against even the appearance of corruption, but sometimes prudence seems to have been replaced with hysteria. Finally, in both cases, concern about the rights of the players was negligible. They were treated simply as the objects of decisions by their betters.

♦ ♦ ♦

THE DEMISE OF the low minors turned on a battle between two visions of baseball. The losing stance, treasured the game in the small town as much as the games of the big cities. The view that prevailed considered the minors significant only to the extent that they contributed to major league baseball.

John Steadman, a writer for the *Baltimore News-Post*, reflected on his own experience as a minor leaguer in an article for *Baseball Digest* in 1955. The romance of the game was captured in his memories about the minors:

> It's where kids cry when they told they aren't good enough. Where fading veterans finally face the grim reality that time is running out. Where the man who drives the team bus usually acts as trainer. Where the uniforms stay dirty a couple weeks between cleanings.
>
> Where infields are baked like macadam or else are as soft as sand at the seashore. Where the lights aren't any brighter than candles and balls hit into the night often go temporarily out of sight. Where the grandstands hug the playing field and fans exercise their undeniable right to cheer or jeer.[6]

Steadman's fondness for that time was shared by many fans. Don Trenary of the *Milwaukee Journal* wrote that, "the best baseball may be played in the majors, but the wildest takes place down where the players never shave for television."[7] One example that Trenary cited involved George Brunet, whose incredible career in organized baseball lasted for more than thirty years. While pitching for Little Rock of the Southern Association, Brunet reversed Orel Hershiser's achievement. In 1957 from June 21 to August 3, his teammates failed to score a run while Brunet pitched. He lost eight straight through the 52⅓ innings that he worked without support.

The experience of the low minors was summarized by Jerry Coleman, who played for the Yankees, managed, and is now a broadcaster. Reflecting on his summer in Wellsville, New York, during the 1942 season, Coleman said, "It was a great, great summer . . . the best I've ever had in baseball. After that, it became only a matter of winning and money became too important."[8]

Early in the 1950s, the effects of television could be seen as the minors steadily collapsed, but not everyone was troubled by the trend. Gerry Hern of the *Boston Post* wrote in 1954 that the reduction in the number of minor leagues was "a blessing."[9] His objections to the low minors turned on the claim that most of those teams could not beat a good high school club. He lamented inept players turning pro when they could have gone to college on an athletic scholarship. Hern rejected completely the emotional gloss on the memories of Steadman and Coleman: "Why are there so many minor leagues? Local pride and boosterism. Why are the leagues folding? They were artificially created, pumped and expanded, when they didn't need to exist in the first place. And because they didn't arise from a need, they will disappear gradually without a sound. Does the steady collapsing of minor leagues mean a loss of interest in baseball? No."[10]

Others had contended that the low minors were indispensable to baseball at all levels. L. H. Addington described the importance of the low minors in an article in *Baseball Magazine* in 1941. Of the Class-D leagues, he wrote:

They offer opportunities to thousands of kids who want to be ballplayers. The AA's and A-1's could not possibly take care of these boys until they have had some of their rough edges sandpapered off.

The bigger fellows might go along for several years if there were no D's, but the pinch would soon begin to tell. The score or more of D leagues in baseball today are life blood to the game. If they should disappear, the absence would be felt all up the line and would eventually reach the majors.[11]

Stepping back from the debate for a moment can restore perspective. One important point to remember is that the low minors expanded and contracted with adjustments in local economies. Operating at the margin of organized baseball, the lower classifications did not have the stability that characterized the majors and the higher minors. Another point to recall is that the alternatives to the low minors also varied in their capacity to develop major leaguers. Industrial leagues, colleges, semipro leagues, and the military were even less reliable than Class D.

In essence, the debate over the value of the low minors is a debate over their purpose. If the game that ultimately matters is the major league game, then minor leagues are important to the extent that they add to the stable growth of the big leagues. If the chance to attend or to play organized baseball is more important than an emotional affiliation with a major league franchise, then the minors are intrinsically important, regardless of the effects on the majors, and the more of them there are, the better it is for baseball and for the small-town hosts.

# Ten

# THE NEGRO LEAGUES

Whenever leagues prospered outside of organized baseball, the major league owners and their minor league allies brought them to heel. The offending league was branded an outlaw, and implied threats of player raids left those circuits feeling lonely and exposed. A reconciliation could be expected, with the maverick league soon back in the fold of the organized game. With one spectacular exception.

From 1920 to the late 1940s, black baseball players who had been shunned from organized ball competed in leagues that in some cases filled major league parks such as Yankee Stadium. These leagues suffered the same economic upheavals that the white leagues endured, but the game itself prospered in the black communities of the nation's great cities.

The history of those leagues and their heroic players has recently become better known because of several excellent accounts of this neglected chapter of American sports. For our purposes, the Negro leagues need to be examined because they offer a unique perspective on minor league baseball.

Like the minors, the Negro leagues showed that excellent baseball that was passionately followed by devoted fans was being played far beyond the confines of the major leagues. Even in the nineteenth century, black players were making their marks.

Frank Grant played with Buffalo in the International League from 1886–88. In 1887 he hit eleven home runs while batting .353 and stealing forty bases. Grant was out of organized baseball in 1891 after only six years and a career batting average of .337.

An article by James Delaney, Jr., in the 1982 *Baseball Research Journal* records some of the sentiments about blacks in the International League at that time. Delaney describes the atmosphere of racism and enlightenment that somehow coexisted. The release of Bud Fowler and a pitcher named Renfroe was noted in the local paper under the heading, "Gone coons—Fowler and Renfroe." The same article then characterized Renfroe as "a gentlemanly fellow, who deserves to do well."[1] The leading newspaper in Binghamton, the *Daily Leader*, printed marginally literate descriptions of black players that ranged from crude to vile. The paper then attacked an umpire who had been quoted as saying that on a close play he would rule against any team with black players. When the International League decided in the middle of the 1887 season to ban the hiring of black players, the *Daily Leader* wrote that the League had made a monkey of itself and asked if it planned to bar blacks from attending the games as well.

These events in the International League occurred four years after the color line had been drawn in the major leagues. An exhibition game between Chicago of the National League and Toledo of the Northwestern League was delayed when Cap Anson announced his refusal to take the field if Toledo used a black catcher, Moses Walker. Toledo had planned to rest Walker, who had been taking a pounding behind the plate, but the Ohio team refused to be intimidated by Anson, and Walker played right field. Toledo apparently refused to pay the guaranteed fee to Chicago if the game were cancelled, forcing Anson to back down.

In the *Baseball Research Journal* of 1977, Merl Kleinknecht records fifty-five black players who were in minor league ball in the nineteenth century. Some of them played on all-black teams such as the Cuban Giants, but a few played on otherwise white teams, especially in the International League. (The Cuban Giants played in the Middle States League in 1889 and the Eastern Interstate League in 1890. The instability of these leagues prevented the Giants from establishing their credentials thoroughly, but indications are that this was certainly a competitive franchise.)

The last black player in organized ball in this period may have been Bert Jones, who pitched for Atchison in the Kansas State League in 1898. After a few outings, Jones appears to have been dropped from the team because of objections from a fellow pitcher. Jones then went to the Chicago Unions, another all-black franchise. No black then played in organized ball until Jackie Robinson joined the Montreal Royals, a Brooklyn Dodger farm team, in 1946.

This racist exclusion was probably the worst decision in the history of baseball, and it is naive to blame it on the bigotry of one man. The late nineteenth century featured the development of Jim Crow laws and other measures intended to demean black people. Anson's racism was certainly repugnant, but by itself it could not have led to such a sweeping policy. American institutions of all kinds were willing to adopt policies that promoted the alleged superiority of whites over blacks. The ban on blacks in baseball was simply one of more notable examples of white bigotry.

As the Walker brothers, Bud Fowler, Frank Grant, and other black stars were gradually excluded from organized baseball, all-black teams such as the Cuban Giants adjusted to white racism as best they could. The Cuban Giants were a group of black waiters from a Long Island hotel. The "Cuban" dodge was intended to make them appear more exotic, a goal they also fostered by speaking in gibberish while on the field. The Cuban Giants happened to be a fine baseball team. With few opportunities to compete against white clubs, they set a pattern for black teams by traveling across the country to play wherever the contest was profitable.

Barnstorming teams like the Giants operated on the fringes of professional baseball. In organized ball, when a franchise is forced to move from its home, the ultimate tragedy has occurred. But barnstorming teams had no home, only the road. Through the first two decades of the twentieth century, such was the fate of black baseball, yet the sport produced legendary players and moments.

Andrew Foster, like Comiskey, Griffith, and Spalding, was a gifted player and organizer; unlike them, he was black. In 1902 Foster pitched against and beat Rube Waddell and the Philadelphia Athletics. He was thereafter known as Rube himself, and he became the man who finally shaped black baseball into settled franchises, always dreaming that one day the game would be integrated.

Smokey Joe Williams was another great black pitcher of that era. He twice defeated Walter Johnson, a claim few white pitchers could make, and he shut out the Phillies when they were National League champions in 1915.

The outstanding black player of this time was John Henry Lloyd, a shortstop who frequently batted over .400. Such statistics are almost meaningless given the irregular competition and playing conditions. Contemporary accounts are the best evidence of ability available, and one concerning Lloyd is compelling. In his ground-breaking book, *Only the Ball Was White*, Robert Peterson includes a conversation between Honus Wagner and a white St. Louis sportswriter in 1938. Wagner asked the writer for his opinion of the best baseball player in history. "If you mean in organized baseball," the writer said, "my answer would be Babe Ruth; but if you mean in all baseball, organized and unorganized, the answer would have to be a colored man, John Henry Lloyd."[2]

Peterson also found that when Ty Cobb's Detroit Tigers traveled to Cuba for a short series in 1910, some of the American black players surpassed Detroit's Hall of Famers. Cobb hit .371 in five games and Sam Crawford batted .360 in twelve games; but Lloyd hit .500 and two other black players, Grant Johnson and Bruce Petway, hit .412 and .390 respectively.

As in white baseball, part of the joy of the game was arguing about the best players. For every fan who thought John Lloyd was the best black player they had seen, another might choose Oscar Charleston. Donn Rogosin claims that Charleston would have been picked as the best black player of the segregated leagues by his fellow players.

Many of these black stars are described in terms of a white equivalent. Lloyd was considered the black Wagner for his brilliant hitting and play at shortstop. Charleston was compared with Babe Ruth. Like the Babe, Charleston was a gifted fielder in his youth; also like the Babe, when Charleston got older he grew more stout, which limited him in the field although his bat remained powerful.

From any rational perspective, the limited direct competition between white and black players left inconclusive their respective abilities. But such rationality certainly should have given blacks the opportunity to put the lie to the racism that forced them to the edges of the game. Unfortunately, the rational perspective did not prevail in those days. Given a choice between adding legendary talent to the game or staying mired in a comfortable prejudice, baseball's leaders chose bigotry.

John McGraw was one who tried to break the color barrier, or rather, slide around it. In 1901, when McGraw was managing the Orioles, he came across a hotel bellboy named Charlie Grant in Hot Springs, Arkansas. Grant had played on a black team in Chicago, and when McGraw saw him in a pickup game, he realized at once that Grant had major league skills. McGraw, the little Napoleon who terrorized umpires and warred with Ban Johnson, suddenly was filled with tact. He was eager to promote Grant to the Orioles but was reluctant to battle the ignorance of his peers. McGraw reconciled his eagerness with his timidity through a scam. He rechristened Charlie Grant "Charlie Tokohoma" and announced that the lad was a full-blooded Cherokee. Grant cooperated in the ruse, but a skeptical baseball establishment never bought it. Grant remained on black ball clubs, and McGraw never tried to sign another black player.

AS GREAT AS Foster, Williams, Lloyd, and other black stars were, bringing them to the major leagues would have been very big news. Playing in any of the ten big-league cities would have put the players in a national spotlight. Such attention meant that a club with a modicum of moral courage would have been doing the country the great service that was deferred until 1947 when Jackie Robinson first played for Brooklyn. No one in the majors had such fortitude until Branch Rickey acted at the end of World War II.

As obnoxious as the major league indifference was, the bigotry of the minor leagues was even more inexcusable. With so many more teams and leagues, some of them defiantly independent, it remains difficult to understand why no minor league president would hire some of the best talent in professional baseball. Two explanations come to mind.

The first is that baseball's racial barrier was created by a small but powerful group who did not care that fans would delight in a team that would be significantly improved by the inclusion of black stars. The second possibility is that the leaders of organized baseball were simply reflecting prevailing attitudes in America, and that fans would not have been particularly delighted to have a John Lloyd on their team because his color counted more than his ability.

The baseball anecdotes that were published early in this century commonly included crude racial and ethnic references. An issue of *Baseball Magazine* in July 1919 included a collection of tales from the Pacific Coast League by Warren Brown. Brown described two games between major leaguers and convicts

who were incarcerated at Folsom and San Quentin. The pitcher
for Folsom was described by Brown as "a big, long-armed colored chap, who thought he was just about the 'bestest pitchah
that ever was.'" The pitcher was subsequently referred to as a
"smoke," and Brown noted that he was pitching very quickly
to the big leaguers who were pasting him. After one sharp hit,
Brown concluded, "The pitcher could hardly wait for the ball
to get back to him. He grabbed it, jumped on the rubber and
was about to let it go, when a little colored man in the
'bleacher' section piped up: 'Take yo' time, niggah; take yo'
time. Yo's in heah fo' TWENTY YEAHS!'"[3]

In Brown's story of the San Quentin game, Swede Risberg
belted a couple of home runs. Brown wrote of the second
homer, "As the ball sailed on its way, one little colored convict
in a group near first base turned to a companion and sighed.
'Boss, ah suah would like to be sittin on dat ball.'"[4]

In our time, Al Campanis and Jimmy the Greek were fired
for making less inflammatory remarks than Brown's. But at
that time similar demeaning stories about other racial and ethnic groups were common. Humor that turned on dialects was
aimed at blacks, Irish, Scandinavians, Germans, Italians, and
any other groups that could be distinguished in the melting
pot cliché.

For baseball and other businesses that were dominated by
Jim Crow, taking the times into account does not explain the
racism that kept blacks from fair opportunities. If the humor of
that day did not discriminate, the business did. The particular
business of baseball had already produced stars with a variety
of ethnic backgrounds, but all of them were white.

Blacks were consigned to an inferior caste, treated the same
in some superficial respects but rebuffed whenever they asserted their equality. Baseball was as good an example of that
institutionalized discrimination as existed in America. From the
major league teams in the country's great cities to the marginal
clubs in the small towns of the low minors, no one wanted
black players.

On the clubs in every league that desperately hung on

through the competition of the Federal League and the drain of World War I, there was no place for the black ball player. The Federal League itself went bankrupt without considering the obvious way of improving the quality of its teams.

The Cubs, Giants, and Pirates waged a bitter pennant race in 1908 that was decided by the narrowest of margins, but none of them thought they needed another great pitcher or hitter. Minor leagues folded and some major league teams survived on a shoestring, but that terrible pressure still did not realize the economists' assumption that people behave rationally in a marketplace. Bigotry, ignorance, and indifference overcame the formidable forces of justice, decency, and the clear path to money.

BY 1920 RUBE Foster was prepared to find a more permanent place for blacks in American baseball. Foster had become the power behind black baseball in Chicago, and he organized the Negro National League in 1920, consisting of his Chicago American Giants, Chicago Giants, Cuban Stars, Dayton Marcos, Detroit Stars, Kansas City Monarchs, St. Louis Giants, and Taylor ABCs.

Foster's plan was to establish and operate a baseball league that would command the admiration of whites. By offering an exciting and profitable game, Foster believed that integration would have to follow. He was especially wary of white intrusions into his league and of the many sharp promoters who would have been eager to exploit the venture for their own purposes. To preserve the integrity of his league, ownership was generally restricted to blacks. Only the Kansas City team was owned by a white man.

The creation of the Negro National League did not confine black teams to limited schedules and cities. Barnstorming continued to be as important as ever, with many clubs playing over 200 games a year. But the league did elevate black baseball above semipro leagues and other traveling shows like the House of David.

The Negro National League was no more stable than many of the low minors. Franchises changed regularly, league standings were sometimes incomplete, and other statistics, so vital to the fans' discussion of the game, were erratically compiled. Rube Foster's contribution to baseball was not so much the record of his league but its place in a long journey to bring justice to baseball.

By having regularly scheduled games in some of the largest cities, Foster provided a showcase for players who no longer would compete in total obscurity. John Henry Lloyd got his chance to play before larger crowds and some reporters. Smokey Joe Williams, who was forty-four years old in 1920, continued to pitch until 1932. Some of the other stars of an earlier day received some acclaim during the country's "Golden Age of Sports."

Other black players arrived during the 1920s and 1930s, the most famous being Satchel Paige. Acclaimed by Dizzy Dean and other Hall of Famers as the greatest pitcher they had ever seen, Paige finished behind Smokey Joe Williams in a 1952 poll of thirty-one experts on the Negro leagues when they selected their all-time list.

Paige's notoriety grew from his distinct personality as much as from his baseball talent. Paige was famous for being late to the ball park after racing through red lights, for having a casual understanding of contractual obligations, and for being one of the best pitchers of his generation.

As the legend of Satchel Paige has grown, it has become difficult to determine exactly how good he was. There are stories of how wild he was when he first came up and other stories of how he always had had pinpoint control. Beyond dispute was his longevity, twenty-seven years of professional ball, including three shutout innings in the major leagues when he was fifty-nine years old.

Paige was such a commercial attraction that his appearance could guarantee a capacity crowd for the Kansas City Monarchs and other teams for whom he played. To take advantage of his appeal in the latter part of his career, he pitched two or three innings in almost all of his teams' games rather than taking his place in a rotation.

Known for his carefree attitude, Paige nevertheless was no clown. He refused to pitch in towns where Jim Crow laws were imposed. His famous stunt of calling in his outfielders before striking out the side may have been triggered by racial remarks from the major league all-star team he was playing.

The distortion of baseball's racism is evident in Paige's numbers. His major league record was 28–31 for a career that began in 1948 at the official age of forty-two. In the Negro leagues, Paige was 73–30. These numbers do not indicate either his greatness or his importance to the game.

Paige's treatment suggests that without a fair chance to make the big leagues his enormous skills were diverted to professional exhibitions, exciting for those fortunate to see him but shallow compared to the setting he was meant for. Perhaps he was not the equal of Smokey Joe Williams or Bullet Joe Rogan. Tragically, that means only that two more great stars were lost to organized baseball.

If Satchel Paige was the most famous pitcher of the Negro leagues, the preeminent catcher was Josh Gibson. It is claimed that he once hit a home run out of Yankee Stadium—a feat never achieved by Ruth, DiMaggio, Mantle, or anyone else.

Gibson grew up in Pittsburgh playing semipro ball for the Crawford Colored Giants. In Hollywood fashion, he was watching a night game between the Kansas City Monarchs and the Homestead Grays, Pittsburgh's entry in the Negro National League, when his chance came. The teams were playing at night with a poor lighting system that caused the Grays' catcher to get his signs mixed up with the pitcher. Unfortunately, the pitcher was Smokey Joe Williams, who split the catcher's finger with a fastball. The backup catcher was already in the game playing the outfield, but Judy Johnson, the Grays' manager, noticed Gibson in the stands and brought him in to catch. A star was born.

A gifted hitter, Gibson apparently had to work on his fielding. Robert Peterson found a range of opinions about Gibson's ability as a catcher. Some remember him as marginal, while Walter Johnson was quoted as believing Gibson to be better than Bill Dickey.

Tape-measure home runs enhanced his reputation as the great power hitter of the Negro leagues. Since a season in those leagues consisted of fewer than sixty games, Gibson won home run titles with six or eight homers. None who saw him doubted that he would have been a phenomenal player in the major leagues.

Gibson may have hastened the day of baseball's integration as Rube Foster had intended. Peterson writes that Clark Griffith, the owner of the Washington Senators, flirted with signing Gibson and his teammate Buck Leonard in the late 1930s. Although Griffith could never commit himself, Peterson writes, "Griffith must have been sorely tempted to sign the two black men. His Senators were usually mired deep in the American League's second division, and when they were on the road he could look out of his office and watch Gibson and Leonard busting the fences in his park."[5]

Thinking about the Dodgers without Robinson, the Giants without Mays, or the Braves without Aaron is another way of appreciating what baseball lost through its bigotry. In the past forty years, the character of many great teams has been defined by their black stars. How much mediocrity was endured for generations because of the stupidity of baseball's rulers.

Buck Leonard, Cool Papa Bell, Judy Johnson, and Ray Dandridge are a few of the better-known stars of the Negro leagues. So many other great athletes played in near obscurity. A perceptive and bold owner of any team in organized baseball could have competed with the Yankee dynasty by doing what baseball executives are supposed to do: field the best team they can.


FOLLOWING BASEBALL THROUGH the careers of its first black stars offers a radically different view of the game than the sanitized version that the game's established powers promote. The low minors were luxury itself compared with baseball on the barnstorming circuit. Semipro ball, industrial leagues, and school baseball mixed with black players and major league stars as a love of the game and a chance for a few extra dollars lured fans, players, and promoters to these games.

Since Foster's true purpose was to display black baseball to America, the irregularities in scheduling and standings were of secondary importance. For instance, in 1923, the Monarchs won the pennant of the Negro National League with a record of 57–33. The Detroit Stars finished in second at 40–27, playing twenty-three fewer games than the pennant winners did. These disparities would be inconceivable in organized baseball, but in the Negro leagues, they were simply a sign of marginal franchises struggling to survive in a hostile market.

In 1923 the Eastern Colored League was established with the same characteristic of floating franchises and irregular schedules. This league lasted until spring of 1928. Beginning in 1924, a World Series was played between the two Negro leagues, and the National League won three of the four series.

The Negro National League survived until 1931, five years without Foster's leadership and one year beyond his death. The League was reorganized in 1933 by Gus Greenlee of Pittsburgh. Greenlee's business interests were not directly represented by the chamber of commerce—he was one of the kingpins of Pittsburgh's numbers racket. Nor would his associates have been invited to take tea with the queen. The revival of black baseball during the depths of the Depression was bankrolled by black gangsters.

Their reputations deeply troubled the virtuous Landis and Rickey. It is curious that they feared the corruption of a game that they refused to recognize. The moral hypocrisy of white baseball was nothing new to Greenlee, and he further offended the sensibilities of organized baseball by flaunting and enjoying his wealth.

The Negro American League was established in 1937, and it continued to operate until 1960. The Negro National League collapsed with baseball's integration. The histories of these leagues are perhaps the best modern example we have of what baseball was like in the nineteenth century. Preserving the integrity of schedules and rosters was just as difficult for black owners in the 1930s as it had been for white owners half a century before.

Organized baseball solved the problem through monopoly and coercion. Black baseball struggled for survival throughout its history, to be undone when the major leagues finally did the right thing. Racism was something the black players and owners could overcome. Since organized baseball integrated, black players have found the riches and honors of the game fairly accessible. Black executives have found the front offices of the game harder to reach.

SINCE SO MUCH of black baseball was an exhibition, it should not be surprising that the most popular event in the Negro leagues was their East-West All-Star Game. Donn Rogosin explains that the Negro World Series followed seasons that could not be taken seriously as championship competition, and that a series required more money and time than poor people could afford.

The East-West game was perfect for highlighting the players whom the fans worshipped. From 1933 through 1950, the game was played in major league stadiums and drew crowds of 20,000 to more than 50,000. As the great event in black baseball, the all-star game drew more attention from whites than any black sporting event outside of boxing.

ANOTHER ASPECT OF the game that was ignored by most of organized baseball was its Latin dimension. Just as in the Pacific Coast League with its extraordinarily long seasons, warm weather south of the border allowed players to compete all year long. In the myopia of the northeast establishment, baseball was played from April to October in one quadrant of the country. Donn Rogosin points out:

In the first half of the twentieth century, jockeys, fighters, and above all, baseball players engaged in sports exchanges of such significant proportion that it is perhaps appropriate to speak of a North American sports environment stretching from the Panama Canal to the Canadian prairies.

In a typical year, white players would play white players in the summer and blacks would play blacks, but in the winter the situation was different. Then the best black and white players competed in special attraction games throughout the land, and in Latin America they were often teammates.[6]

Baseball's elite reacted nervously to this reality. Commissioner Landis decreed that major leaguers who participated in these games had to understand clearly that they were not competing in a normal major league franchise. The obvious competitiveness of the black players was such that Landis wanted to stress that these games were simply exhibitions.

The Latin game exposed the full lunacy of baseball's segregation. Light-skinned Cubans, such as Rafael Almeida and Armando Marsans, were accepted into the major leagues before World War I, while their dark-skinned neighbors were shunned. Rogosin describes Luis Tiant's poignant memories of his childhood in Cuba while his father pitched in the Negro leagues of America and tried to discourage his son from becoming a ball player because of the degrading treatment the elder Tiant had received.

Cuba became a place where white major league stars played freely against the best of the Negro leagues. Beyond what was the norm in the United States, white and black players socialized in Cuba during the winter season. This contact helped to eliminate the ignorance that caused segregation. The white players saw that many of the blacks were their equals on the field and that after a game the interests of healthy young men tended to be similar, regardless of race.

As baseball developed throughout the Caribbean, new opportunities arose for black players to improve themselves through winter baseball. The Latin game matured to the point that Mexican interests prepared to challenge the major leagues in the United States with their summer schedule. After World War II, Jorge Pasquel hoped to add black and white players from the United States to teams in the Mexican League.

Through intimidation, the majors kept Pasquel from signing such American stars as Stan Musial. Like the Pacific Coast League, the Mexican League tried to change the structure of organized baseball after World War II, but the primary interest of the major league owners continued to be the protection of their own privilege.

The Mexican League failed to change the organization of the game, but it made an important contribution to baseball's integration. The black players increasingly lived the way white players always had. It had been one thing to endure discrimination in the United States and know it was wrong. In the Latin game, black players were celebrated as sports heroes, making it unlikely that they would accept the demeaning status offered in the United States. Rogosin summarizes the influence of this experience on the black players:

In Mexico they lived in fashionable neighborhoods and made excellent money. . . . Some of the players partook of the cultural opportunities available in Mexico City, either by wandering the pyramids or by visiting the remarkable Museum of Anthropology, located in an area where many of them lived. Most learned Spanish; some even became fluent. Bill Wright of the Baltimore Elite Giants found such freedom that he never came back. Willie Wells summed up his attitude toward Mexico when he said, "We are heroes here . . . [while] in the United States everything I did was regulated by color. Well, here in Mexico I am a man."[7]

As Rogosin's chapter on Latin baseball concludes, the experience from Cuba to Mexico answered the doubts that had been raised about blacks playing baseball. The easiest questions to resolve were those about the abilities of the black athletes. Social issues were more stubborn, but they too were put to rest. Roy Campanella handled white pitchers in Mexico, settling questions about authority on the field. White and black players became friends, ignored one another, or fought—just as baseball players have always treated one another.

Rube Foster had hoped that the Negro leagues would prove through their excellence that blacks should be brought into organized baseball. Latin American baseball became a laboratory where the excellence was displayed for any fair-minded person to see.

THE INTEGRATION OF organized baseball after World War II was one of the important events in American cultural history. Jules Tygiel astutely describes it as the beginning of the civil rights movement. Most accounts of the decision to sign Jackie Robinson stress the moral courage of Robinson and Branch Rickey, and that is as it should be. But there are other dimensions to the story that should not be lost.

Donn Rogosin notes the general tendency to understand this historic event in personal terms: "The popular perception was that Branch Rickey's benevolence and Jackie Robinson's courage had joined to shatter the color barrier. Baseball integration was *not* perceived as an inevitable consequence of the history of Negro baseball and changing race relations in the United States, a view that would have emphasized the social rather than individual dimension of baseball's integration."[8]

Rogosin believes that neither Rickey nor Robinson appreciated the important role that the Negro leagues had played in this drama, even though Robinson had been lured away from the Kansas City Monarchs. The credit due the Negro leagues has been established by Rogosin, Robert Peterson, and others, but the treatment of those leagues by organized baseball is important here as another example of how the major leagues operated when they found something they wanted.

At its core, the great contribution of organized baseball has centered on preserving the integrity of rosters and schedules which allowed the game to develop commercially. The merging of that preservation with monopolistic practices has been a mistake, stemming from arrogance and greed that were evident again in the game's finest hour. When Jackie Robinson was signed by the Brooklyn Dodgers, no compensation was offered to Kansas City. In effect, the Monarchs' roster was raided.

Branch Rickey's explanation was simple: the Negro National League was no league at all. Tygiel quotes Rickey as saying, "They're simply a booking agents' paradise. They are not leagues and have no right to expect organized baseball to respect them."[9] The nefarious backgrounds of many of the Negro league owners offended Rickey the moralist, and the inability of the Monarchs to do anything about their loss undoubtedly encouraged Rickey the businessman.

The contracts that players signed in the Negro leagues did not have a reserve clause, and it had proven difficult to keep such free spirits as Satchel Paige on a team even for the duration of his contract. On the other hand, owners had not always lived up to their obligations, so the business side of the Negro leagues was indeed chaotic.

Still, there was understandable annoyance with Rickey's method. As it happened, the Monarchs were a rare example of white ownership in the Negro National League. Tom Baird, one of the owners, announced that Kansas City would fight the loss of Robinson. The threat of court action over baseball's antitrust exemption always chilled the major league owners, and in 1945 that concern was especially acute. The Pasquel brothers were planning their own raid of the majors, and the Pacific Coast League was considering a break to form a third major league. Another assault on the ordered universe of organized baseball was the last thing the owners wanted.

Larry MacPhail and Clark Griffith were two of the owners

that Tygiel cites who warned against the manner, if not the fact, of Robinson's signing. At one point, every major league owner except Rickey had expressed in writing his opposition to integration. The major league magnates were seeing their privileged world threatened over an issue that they did not even support.

At the same time, players and owners in the Negro leagues were having their fondest dreams realized in a way that left them uneasy. Among players who were elated that they might soon get a chance to play in the majors, one question recurred: why Robinson? The consensus was that this former All-America football player and track star from UCLA was something less than the best player in the league.

The sun had clearly set on the careers of Oscar Charleston, Cool Papa Bell, and Judy Johnson; but Josh Gibson was thought to have some good years left, and Satchel Paige was simply beyond time. Robinson was a shortstop without a major league arm. He was a good hitter and fine base runner, but with only one year of professional baseball to his credit, he was not the obvious choice to a lot of people.

Rickey may have seen in Robinson's character the other qualifications that this heroic effort would require. To their credit, Robinson's teammates helped him learn to play the right side of the infield where his arm would not be a problem. He may not have been their choice for the pioneer, but they understood the importance of his mission, and he had their support.

More perplexing was the question of what Robinson's breakthrough would mean to the Negro leagues themselves. Would these clubs develop black talent only to lose it to the majors without even the negligible draft compensation that the minor leagues received?

The owner who faced the greatest dilemma was Effa Manley. Racial discrimination was compounded in this case by the fact that this owner was a woman. She was the wife of Abe Manley, a numbers racketeer from Jersey City and, with him, co-owner of the Newark Eagles.

204 • THE MINORS

As described by Rogosin, Effa Manley was born of white parents in a family with six half-brothers and -sisters, all of whom had black fathers. Effa's stepfather was black, and she was very active in the earliest fights for integration. A treasurer of the NAACP in New Jersey, this remarkable woman did not accept the limitations that a biased culture prescribed.

While Branch Rickey had a different explanation for signing Robinson for every occasion, Manley did not buy any of them. Rickey could claim either that he was only doing it for the money or that God had compelled him. He had several positions between those two, with variations on all the themes. Perhaps from her time with Abe and his associates, Manley knew theft when she saw it. The Negro leagues were full of potential major league ball players, and the major leagues were going to take them for nothing.

Branch Rickey turned out to be rather ruthless in his emancipation of black ball players. He reportedly was troubled by Effa Manley's criticism of his raids, and according to Murray Polner's biography, he had his aides determine if players such as Don Newcombe were actually under contract to the Newark Eagles. Polner concludes that "the Negro Leagues had no written contracts, only unenforceable and vague verbal agreements on a game-by-game or annual basis."[10]

The contracts were unenforceable precisely because black baseball had been pushed to the margins of American business. The legal niceties that Rickey was looking for were impossible given the conditions under which the Negro leagues were forced to operate.

Polner then writes that Rickey asked the players themselves if they were bound to contracts with their Negro league clubs. Offered the chance to more to the big leagues, the players, not surprisingly, said no. All of these maneuvers were undoubtedly legal, but the law for baseball (especially the antitrust exemption) simply codified the privileged status of the major league owners. Whether justice was done is a far more doubtful issue.

The Negro league owners tried to respond through new contracts that included reserve clauses. The owners then tried to convince Commissioner Happy Chandler to enforce these agreements against major league raids. Chandler agreed on the condition that the Negro leagues clean up their ownership to meet the sensibilities of organized baseball. In other words, Chandler told them to sell their clubs to people that the major leagues approved (major league owners, perhaps?), and the contracts would be enforced.

After losing Don Newcombe to Rickey without any compensation, Effa Manley pressed her claim that the majors were simply raiding the rosters of Negro league teams. She found some support from Bill Veeck, a maverick owner, who purchased Larry Doby's contract from her in a move that integrated the American League.

Hoping that a precedent had been established, Manley was outraged when Rickey signed Monte Irvin, a future Hall of Famer who was the bright young star of the Newark Eagles. Manley tried to block the transfer through her lawyers, prompting a brutal response from Rickey. He informed Irvin that Manley had claimed him and the Dodgers were unable to bring him to the majors. Rickey took full advantage of Manley's dilemma. If she wanted the major leagues integrated, it would be on Rickey's terms, and those terms would soon destroy her business.

Manley tried instead to sell Irvin's contract to a major league franchise, and she was finally successful. After being rebuffed by George Weiss and the New York Yankees, she worked out a deal with the Giants, who paid a fraction of what Irvin was worth. The arrangement was so inequitable that Irvin himself had to take a cut in salary from $6,500 to $5,000.

The new economic reality killed the Negro National League within two years. The Negro American League survived until 1960, existing only as a curiosity.

THE INTEGRATION OF organized baseball is one of the legitimate accomplishments of the sport. Few businesses in America were serious about racial justice before World War II, and the major leagues were among the quickest to move after the war.

But the way that the majors went about this change showed that there was an important difference between integration and racial justice.

Branch Rickey probably was sincerely offended by the hoodlums who owned the Negro league teams, but there were few opportunities for these people in corporate America at that time. No doubt they were not all gangsters with hearts of gold, but their racketeering, like drug peddling now, was one of the few accessible ways to wealth in a culture that determined value by what one owned and how much money one made.

The signing of Jackie Robinson was perhaps baseball's finest moment. But the means by which organized baseball accomplished this fact were less than admirable. These players were able to become major leaguers because the Negro leagues had given them the chance to develop their games. Compensating the black teams for the players they were losing would not have been charity but justice, and it would also have been good business because teams such as the Monarchs and Eagles were in a better position to find more black players.

The majors' handling of the Negro leagues, outside of organized baseball, should have been instructive for the minor leagues. When the major league owners found a new resource, the only thing that kept them from exploiting it was their own bigotry. Despite Robinson's immediate success, as well as that of other black players, the majors were not fully integrated until the Red Sox signed Pumpsie Green in 1959.

With the exception of Bill Veeck, the other owners never considered more than their immediate financial gain. No one seriously proposed integrating the business side of the Negro leagues into organized baseball. Taking the best black players for little or no compensation was the extent of the major leagues' appreciation for the Negro leagues.

Very shortly, other opportunities to increase profits would develop. Television, franchise movement, and expansion could also be handled in several ways. The money that would be generated could be used to strengthen baseball at all levels across the country to the ultimate benefit of the major leagues;

or the majors could use their power to grab every dime they could, regardless of the consequences. They chose the latter course, and most minor leagues found themselves as helpless as the Negro leagues had been. Within a few years, those minor leagues would join the Negro leagues as romantic footnotes to increasingly greedy history.

# ◆ Eleven ◆

# THE PCL AND
# THE MAJORS

Aт THE END of World War II, the Pacific Coast League anticipated the coming boom years of baseball and tried to
become a third major league. The idea made a lot of sense.
The west was already one of the fastest-growing areas of the
country, and every sign suggested that postwar growth would
accelerate. But, as with other sensible ideas in baseball, this
one was doomed because it threatened the major league
owners.

In 1941 the majors had shown their indifference to the PCL's
integrity by preparing to ship their worst team, the St. Louis
Browns, to the PCL's largest market, Los Angeles. The
Browns' move to Los Angeles was suspended when America
entered the war.

Before the majors could try again, Clarence "Pants"
Rowland, the president of the Pacific Coast League, decided to

emulate Ban Johnson by creating a strong minor league to break the major leagues' monopoly. Unlike Johnson, Rowland did not have to invade another league's territory. He had to defend his own turf in California, Oregon, and Washington and secure recognition that these cities and their franchises could shortly be the equal of those in the American and National Leagues.

Pacific Coast League boosters were encouraged because some of the greatest players of the 1930s and 1940s had developed in the west. The DiMaggio and Waner brothers played in San Francisco before moving to the majors. Lefty Gomez and Fred Hutchinson were among the star pitchers on the Coast. But the Pacific Coast League is also distinguished by the number of great players who never made it big in the majors. Seven of the top fifteen minor league stars singled out for distinction by SABR played the bulk of their careers in the Pacific Coast League.

Perhaps most prominent among that select group was Russell "Buzz" Arlett. Born in 1899 in Oakland, California, he had a brilliant career for his hometown Oaks. Arlett broke into the League in 1918. He posted a 4–9 record as a pitcher and compiled a batting average of .211 with one home run. That inauspicious beginning was the only unimpressive year in a twenty-year career.

Arlett pitched in a league-leading fifty-seven games in 1919, winning twenty-two of them while batting .292. In the next three years, he won twenty-nine, nineteen, and twenty-five games. Twice during that stretch he led the League in innings pitched, including a remarkable 427 innings in 1920.

During the 1923 season, his arm went bad, but this gifted athlete simply switched positions and became a leading hitter. That year Arlett hit .330—the first season that he hit over .300. His lowest average after that year would be .313. Arlett also developed as a power hitter. In 1923 he hit nineteen home runs, where as his previous best had been five.

He remained with Oakland through the 1930 season. In those last seven years his home run totals were: thirty-three, twenty-five, twenty-five, twenty, twenty-five, thirty-nine, and thirty-one. He drove in over 140 runs in five of those seasons, including 189 in 1929, which failed to lead the League. The extended PCL season distorts those numbers somewhat, but these players had to have been great athletes to produce over such a long stretch.

An article by Gerald Tomlinson in the 1988 *Baseball Research Journal* considers the inevitable question of why Arlett remained in the minor leagues. Tomlinson notes that Arlett was considered a poor fielder, but his offensive production should have made him worth a gamble, especially since he was a switch hitter.

Another explanation seems to be the independence of the Oakland franchise. Like the Orioles, the Oaks were free to negotiate with the majors at market rates, and Arlett's employers were not offered the kind of money they thought he was worth. According to Tomlinson:

> The Oakland owners, independent operators in that free-wheeling, pre-farm-system era, felt they had a bonanza on their hands in this handsome pitcher-turned-slugger. They wouldn't sell him to the majors for a penny under $100,000. Now, Babe Ruth was worth that kind of money in 1920. Lefty Grove's spectacular five-year stint in the International League was deemed to be worth it in 1924. But Buzz Arlett, the mightiest Oak, simply didn't figure to attract a hundred thousand dollars.[1]

One opportunity to go to the Brooklyn Dodgers was lost when a dispute with an umpire earned Arlett a mask across the face and a bad cut above the eye. After the 1930 season, the Phillies acquired Arlett, and he got his one chance in the major leagues at the age of thirty-one. Buzz posted some impressive numbers. He hit .313 and finished in a tie for fourth place in home runs with eighteen. His slugging average was .538, good for fifth in the league behind Klein, Hornsby, Hafey, and Ott—all future members of the Hall of Fame. Yet the 1931 season was Arlett's only season in the majors.

Fielding remained a problem for him, and apparently his batting tailed off as the season progressed. Tomlinson concludes, "Like so many other great minor league sluggers—Ike Boone, Smead Jolley, Moose Clabaugh, to name a few—Buzz never overcame his problems with the glove. And in those pre-DH, pre-defensive specialist days, a bad glove could be too much to bear."[2] Still it remains incredible, as Tomlinson reports, that when the Phillies put Arlett on waivers there were no takers.

Arlett spent the 1932 and 1933 seasons in Baltimore, where he made a great impact. In that first season, he led the International League with fifty-four home runs, 144 runs batted in, and 141 runs scored. On both June 1 and July 4 of that year, Buzz hit four home runs in one game. As great as that season was, Arlett missed thirty-one games with a bad shoulder, preventing him from notching some all-time records in the International League.

His last three full seasons were spent with the Minneapolis Millers, and he again managed to lead his league in home runs with forty-one in 1934. When he retired in 1937, he was the greatest home-run hitter in the history of the minors. Tomlinson points out that "from 1918 to 1937, he hit 432, not counting his 18 homers for the Phillies. Next in line are Nick Cullop (420), Merv Connors (400, most in the low minors), and Joe Hauser (399)."[3]

Arlett's career contrasts interestingly with that of Dave Kingman, who had an extensive career in the majors in spite of a bad glove and a low batting average. Kingman stuck on the basis of his tremendous power. Arlett might not have hit so many home runs in the majors, but he seemed to be a better hitter for average than Kingman. The differences between them may say something about the greater reliance on home runs in the modern game.

Ike Boone was a contemporary of Arlett who played for four seasons in the Pacific Coast League during the 1920s. Boone was an outfielder who played from 1920 through 1936. His career took him from the Georgia State League to the majors with stops in the Southern and Texas Leagues. He played in the International League longer than anywhere else, but his performance in his PCL years merits mention here.

In 1926 Boone joined the Missions, the former Sacramento franchise that had moved to the Mission District of San Francisco. He had just completed two seasons with the Boston Red Sox, where he hit .333 and .330. His defensive limits kept him from staying in the majors, but he continued his terrific hitting in the high minors.

In 172 games, he batted .380 for the Missions in 1926, earning himself a trip up to the Chicago White Sox in 1927. That season was a disappointment. Boone had only fifty-three at-bats, and he hit .226, the lowest average he would ever post.

Back with the Missions, he hit .354 in 1928, and then he had one of the greatest years ever in organized ball. In 1929 Boone appeared in 198 games, collecting 323 hits with fifty-five home runs, 218 RBIs, and a .407 average. All of those hitting figures led the League. His mark of 553 total bases is the highest ever in organized baseball.

Boone began the next season on the same tear. After eighty-three games, he had twenty-two home runs, ninety-six RBIs, and an average of .448. He was picked up by the Brooklyn Dodgers and never returned to the PCL. He alternated over the next three seasons between cups of coffee in Brooklyn and longer stays in the International League. At the age of thirty-seven, he won the International League batting title in Toronto with a .372 average.

Boone's lifetime career batting average was .370, the highest ever recorded in the minor leagues. Ike had a brother named Danny who was quite a player himself. Danny played from 1919 through 1933, hitting .356 over his minor league career. Unlike his brother who labored almost exclusively in the low minors, Ike Boone posted most of his marks in the International League, the American Association, and the Pacific Coast League. In 1923, the one year he played in the Texas League, Ike led the circuit in runs, hits, doubles, triples, RBIs, and batting average. He is the only twentieth-century player to hit over .400 in the Texas League, posting a .402 average that year.

Smead Jolley was another great Pacific Coast League batter of the 1920s. Like Buzz Arlett, Jolley started as a pitcher. He never compiled the numbers that Arlett had had before his arm injury, and by his second year Jolley was playing the outfield to keep his bat in the lineup.

His first three seasons were played in several leagues in Texas. Jolley moved to San Francisco in 1925, where he played with the Seals until 1930. He led the PCL in hitting with averages of .397 and .404 in 1927 and 1928. He fell off to .387 when Boone had his incredible 1929 season.

Jolley was also sold to the White Sox, where he began a four-year stay in the majors. His big league average was .305, but he was another defensive liability. In 1934 he was back in the PCL with the Hollywood Stars. In two seasons with the Stars, he hit .360 and .372 before he was dealt to Albany of the International League. He took the league batting title there with an average of .373.

His next batting championship was back in the Pacific Coast League in 1938, won with a .350 average while playing for both Hollywood and Oakland. He ended his career in 1940 and 1941 with successive batting crowns with Spokane of the Western International League.

Jolley's lifetime batting average in the minors was .366, good for third place on the all-time list behind Boone and Ox Eckhardt. This great player was described as "a slow runner and a defensive liability," but his hitting was close to unsurpassed.[4]

Arnold "Jigger" Statz was another PCL star of this era. Statz began his career with the New York Giants in 1919. He had only sixty at-bats that season but hit .300. The next year he played briefly for the Giants and was traded to the Red Sox, who moved him to the Los Angeles Angels after three hitless at-bats.

Statz's entire minor league career of eighteen seasons was spent with the Angels, although he had two more shots in the majors. In 1922 he went to the Chicago Cubs and played well for several seasons, batting .297, .319, and .277 in his three full seasons with the club. In 1923, when he hit .319, he also stole twenty-nine bases, had 209 hits, and drove in seventy runs.

His numbers tailed off in 1925, and he was sent back to the Angels. He hit .354 for Los Angeles in 1926 with a league-leading 291 hits in 199 games. That earned him a chance with the Brooklyn Dodgers, but Statz could not cash it in. He was back with the Angels for good in 1929. In his remaining fourteen years, Statz became a leading base stealer in the PCL. He led the League with forty-three steals in 1936 at the age of thirty-nine. His bat remained lively as well, and he finished his minor league career in 1942 with a lifetime average of .315.

His durability contributed to several PCL records. Statz holds the League record for games played with 2,790, runs with 1,996, hits with 3,356, doubles with 595, and triples with 137. Statz was never much of a power hitter, but his speed and batting skill made him a great offensive threat. Unlike Boone and Jolley, Statz was a fine outfielder, but when given the opportunity he could not hit well enough at the major league level.

Oscar "Ox" Eckhardt played six of his fourteen seasons in organized baseball in the Pacific Coast League and thrived on that circuit. He took the PCL batting title four times, including a .414 average for the Missions in 1933. Eckhardt also did not get a chance to play in the majors until he was in his thirties. He pinch-hit for the Boston Braves in eight games in 1932, at the age of thirty-one.

After winning the batting crown for Mission with a .399 average in 1935, Eckhardt moved to Brooklyn, where he hit .182 in forty-four at-bats. He was dealt to Indianapolis of the American Association, and he played for another four years in the minors. His lifetime minor league batting average of .367

again raises the question of whether some major league team could not have taken more of a chance on Eckhardt.

As it was, the Pacific Coast League included some of the best hitters in minor league history during the 1930s. Arlett, Statz, Boone, Eckhardt, and Jolley were perennial stars who provided a base of very high quality, making even more impressive the bursts of Lazzeri and DiMaggio.

Among the notable pitchers in PCL history was Herman Polycarp Pillette. He established a record by pitching for twenty-three years in one league. Pillette's career is another puzzling case as far as his treatment by the majors is concerned. While pitching for Portland in 1921, Pillette won thirteen games but lost a league-leading thirty games while giving up 378 hits and compiling an earned run average of 4.20. For some reason (durability?), Pillette made it to the Detroit Tigers in 1922, where he went 19–12 with a 2.85 ERA. He tailed off further during the next two seasons and was back in the PCL to stay in 1925.

He won twenty games for Mission on two occasions, but his numbers were less than overpowering. In a career from 1917 through 1945, Pillette precisely broke even in the minors. He won 264 games and he lost 264 games. His major league mark was slightly better, at 34–32.

Frank Shellenback had a more impressive career pitching in the Pacific Coast League from 1920 through 1938. He set the League mark with a career total of 295 wins. On five occasions he won more than twenty games. His lowest ERA was 2.85; usually, it was over 3.00, and in 1933 he won twenty-one games for the Hollywood Stars with an earned run average of 4.53. The duration of the League's season may have been more draining on the pitchers than on the hitters.

THE GREAT TEAM in the history of the Pacific Coast League was the 1934 Los Angeles Angels. Under manager Jack Lelivelt, the Angels compiled an incredible record of 137–50. That .733 winning percentage was the best in League history.

The Angels' outfield included Jigger Statz, who hit .324 with sixty-one stolen bases. He was joined by Marvin Gudat, who hit .319, and Frank Demaree who led the League in hitting with a .382 average. Demaree also took the titles for home runs, with forty-five, for RBIs, with 173, and for runs scored, with 190.

Jim Oglesby played first base and hit .312. Jimmy Reese played second and batted .311. Gene Lillard was the third baseman, and he hit .289 with twenty-seven home runs. Carl Dittmar played short, batting .294. Gilly Campbell caught 145 games and hit .305 with seventeen home runs.

Fay Thomas led the pitchers with a record of 28–4. Louis Garland and Emile Meola also won twenty games. J. Millard Campbell won nineteen games, and the other pitchers included Emmett Nelson (14–5), Dick Ward (13–4), and Roy Henshaw (16–4). Every pitcher on the staff had an ERA of less than 3.00.

For postseason play, the League compiled an all-star team that the Angels dispatched in six games. The League itself was a powerhouse at the time. It included not only Ox Eckhardt, Smead Jolley, and Babe Dahlgren, but Joe DiMaggio, who had hit safely in a record sixty-one games in 1933.

Bill James ascribes the reputation of the 1937 Newark Bears to its proximity to New York media and the team's affiliation with the Yankees. He reasons that the Angels must have been better than the Bears because Los Angeles was an independent franchise playing in a stronger league. James doubts that the Angels were the match of Jack Dunn's Orioles, but he picks them as the strongest team of the 1930s.

POPULATION GROWTH IN the west was great enough before World War II to encourage new stadium construction. Wrigley Field in Los Angeles, Sick Stadium in Seattle, and Seals Stadium in San Francisco were all built well before World War II, and all became temporary homes for major league clubs in the 1960s and 1970s. Even greater growth was expected after the war with the return of men who had enjoyed the beautiful climate before shipping out to the Pacific.

At the 1945 winter meetings, Pacific Coast League president Rowland petitioned his fellow minor leagues to approve the PCL request to become a major league. After winning their support, he went to the majors with a bold proposal to make the first radical change in the major league organization since the turn of the century.

This step was but one of several indications that baseball after the war would be a different game and a different business. Players gained some leverage by organizing a union that, while dormant for twenty years, would become a powerful force under the leadership of Marvin Miller. For a short time, Mexico beckoned (as Japan does now) by offering tantalizing salaries to the game's greatest stars. In the most important change, Jackie Robinson broke baseball's color barrier in 1946 by signing with the Dodger organization and playing his first season in Canada with the Montreal Royals of the International League. The major league owners ignored the union, brushed aside the Mexican challenge, and reluctantly came to grips with racial integration.

Compounding the problem of the Pacific Coast League for the majors was Rowland's demand that all eight teams of the PCL be elevated to the majors. Teams such as the Los Angeles Angels and the San Francisco Seals were obvious possibilities for inclusion in the major leagues, but other clubs were less attractive. The San Diego Padres were surrounded by Mexico, the desert, the Pacific Ocean, and Los Angeles. The Hollywood Stars had transferred from Salt Lake City only in 1925, and they were more of a curiosity than a strong franchise. The Oakland Oaks were successful after the war under the management of Casey Stengel, but whether the Bay Area could support two major league franchises remains unclear even today. The Sacramento Solons, Portland Beavers, and Seattle Rainiers completed the eight-team league, and none of those communities appeared to be ripe for a major league franchise.

At the 1945 meetings, the major league owners rebuffed the PCL petition. The same request was reintroduced the following year, and though the request itself was denied, the PCL did make some gains. The majors agreed that if one of its teams were to relocate in a PCL city, the club would have to pay indemnities to the local team and to the rest of the PCL.

That concession was significant for the PCL because it created a barrier to a move by one of the marginal major league franchises. When the St. Louis Browns finally relocated in 1953, it was to Baltimore, not Los Angeles. Similarly, when the Braves left Boston in 1952, they moved to Milwaukee; and when the Athletics departed Philadelphia in 1954, they went to Kansas City.

From their strong position in 1947, the PCL again demanded exemption from the major league draft, a move that alienated other minor leagues, which would be left to bear the burden of an increased demand for players from the major leagues. When the majors refused to grant the exemption, the PCL responded with proposals to extend the length of time a player was exempt from the draft from four to six years and to increase compensation to the club from $10,000 to $25,000.

The other minor leagues were by now growing impatient with the PCL's demands. They alleged that the League's record attendance was due as much to its extended season as to the strength of its markets. They passed the PCL request on to the majors but without the three-fourths majority that the bylaws required.

Al Wolf of the *Los Angeles Times* offered the opinion in the fall of 1947 that major league baseball on the West Coast was still a dream. He wrote that the major leagues would not likely give the PCL the draft exemption necessary to boost the quality of the West Coast teams to competitive levels with the American and National Leagues. Wolf also argued that adequate ball parks for big-league games were far in the future.

An alternative to upgrading the entire league was the transfer of a major league team to the West Coast. Wolf noted that, if only one team came, it would have to leave for road trips that would last over a month on at least three occasions over the course of the season. He allowed that bringing a second team to the coast would help alleviate the scheduling problem, but he saw no such transfers in the foreseeable future.

Wolf mentioned some other hurdles to bringing in an existing team, such as the opposition of Pacific Coast League owners, and he dismissed playing baseball in the Los Angeles Memorial Coliseum (the Dodgers' first home in Los Angeles) as "an utterly impractical daydream."

The most significant part of his article was its conclusion: "We Californians might just as well settle back and enjoy what we've got. Besides, it's good fun, the minor league Coast ball. So far as we're concerned, it'll do handsomely until something better comes along, if and when, that is."[5] Wolf suggests some of the content that had led earlier westerners to refer to the major leagues simply as the eastern leagues. While admitting that he wanted major league ball on the West Coast, he was still able to appreciate how the game had developed in that part of the country without being among the anointed of baseball's hierarchy.

The 1947 major league winter meetings confirmed Wolf's skepticism about a change of status for the Pacific Coast League. Commissioner Happy Chandler, Landis's successor, had considered the PCL goals for a year. His reply was a proposal that the major leagues expand to ten teams in each league, with the four additional teams located in Los Angeles and San Francisco.

Chandler's position was consistent with the history of the major leagues treatment of the minor leagues. After cultivating the western market for a hundred years, the PCL was to be brushed aside and its most lucrative cities grabbed by the reigning powers of the east and midwest. Chandler's plan failed at that time because of two dissenting votes in the American League. The National League had voted its unanimous approval.

THE TOP OFFICIALS of organized baseball could not conceive of the PCL as an equal, but the leadership of that league remained convinced that they were in the minors only because of the manipulation of the majors. The PCL case was advanced by Bob Cobb, principal owner of the Hollywood Stars.

Cobb had worked his way up from head waiter to owner of the Brown Derby restaurants, and he was one of the most popular men in southern California. In an interview with H. G. Salsinger of the *Detroit News*, Cobb rejected the majors' offer to move franchises west. He charged that the proposal was simply a ruse to deflect attention from the Pacific Coast League's demand for equality. He stated that the differences between the major and minor leagues were "size of parks, attendance, prices of admission and players' salaries. That's about all."[6] Achieving parity with the American and National Leagues depended on one thing, exemption from the major league draft. Cobb insisted that a six-year moratorium on the draft would allow the PCL to bring their rosters and their parks up to the major league level.

Cobb was not asking for any favors. He told Salsinger that the PCL had done a lot for baseball and had weathered disasters from the San Francisco earthquake to epidemics and floods without any support from the major leagues. "Did they ever vote, say $100,000, to help us rehabilitate? All they ever did was lift our best players by drafting them."[7]

Cobb gave the hypothetical example of a PCL team with three star players. At the end of one season, one of those players could be drafted to the majors for the $10,000 fee. At the start of the next season, a second player could be lost in the same way, and at the end of that season, the third star could be gone. "Had we put the three players on the auction block they would have brought more than $100,000," he noted. "The draft took them for $30,000. We did not want the $30,000 and we would not have sold them for more than $100,000. We wanted to keep them. Had we been a big league club we could have kept them; being a minor league club we had to watch them arbitrarily taken from us, with ownership rights abruptly severed."[8]

Cobb claimed that fifty-seven players in the big leagues had been drafted or purchased from the PCL. He offered to buy them all back for the original purchase price plus 10 percent, and he then repeated his call for a six-year suspension of the draft. Cobb concluded his remarks by disparaging the American Association and the International League as lacking the class of the Pacific Coast League.

Cobb's perception of the PCL's place in organized baseball was unique. As sensible as his arguments were, they could not compel the majors to yield their privileged position, and the arrogant attitude that Cobb demonstrated toward other minor leagues won few friends in those circuits. Organizationally, the Pacific Coast League was as isolated as it had been geographically.

The rejection by the majors in 1947 and the weakening support from the other minor leagues led the PCL to curtail its ambitions for several years. When it raised the issues again in 1950, it reverted to its threat to withdraw from organized baseball. The ultimatum won a few platitudes from the game's moguls, but the threat had to be repeated in 1951 before the majors reacted.

As the deadline to the ultimatum approached in 1951, Al Wolf offered another pessimistic assessment of the PCL's position. The pressure of organized baseball was said to be ruffling some of the PCL's executives: "As the Coasters nervously await the response to their bold bid, 'tis said they jump every time somebody mentions the ill-fated Federal League of 1914–15, sweat at every fresh indication that this player and that manager will balk at signing an 'outlaw' contract, shiver at grapevine reports that the majors will benignly accede to their demand but ostracize them when it comes to working agreements and player deals." Wolf correctly understood that the threat of withdrawing from organized baseball held risks for the PCL as well as for the majors. He also pointed out that attendance and revenues had dropped for the second straight year. Wolf concluded with the observation that the PCL officials were "belligerently optimistic. . . . But right now, it appears to us the Coast League is facing a multi-angled crisis. We hope, sincerely so, that a happy ending latches itself onto this pillar of gloom. But we haven't got one in stock."[9]

The crisis was defused when a new commissioner, Ford Frick, raised the PCL's status with a unique Four-A classification. This largely symbolic gesture was accompanied by a policy for elevating other leagues to that level and for bringing Four-A teams into the major leagues. The threefold test for entering the majors required a league to have a market in all of its cities of at least 15 million people, each franchise to have a stadium with a capacity in excess of 25,000, and total attendance in excess of 3.5 million in each of the previous three years.

The Pacific Coast League achieved the first two conditions but failed the third for reasons beyond its control. The 3.5 million test had been met in the PCL for the years 1947–49, but by 1950 the effects of television were being felt as the majors could not resist the millions that television and radio offered. The effects of broadcasting were devastating for every minor league but especially so for the PCL.

In the case of television, the Pacific Coast League shared some of the responsibility for its problems. The PCL was not terribly wise in its use of the medium, and the case of the Hollywood Stars provides a good example. The Stars had moved to southern California from Salt Lake City after the 1925 season. This club never did find its niche in Los Angeles. It played in Wrigley Field, the home of the PCL Angels, a team that in 1934 fielded one of the finest minor league clubs ever. After the 1936 season, the Stars moved to San Diego and became the Padres. Another struggling franchise, the Mission team of the San Francisco area, moved to Los Angeles in 1938 and took the name the Hollywood Stars.

This club caught on by including celebrities such as Bing Crosby and Gary Cooper among its stockholders. The Stars also had their own ballpark built in 1939. Gilmore Field was a wooden bandbox that seated fewer than 13,000, but it put fans close to the field and gave the team an identity distinct from that of the Angels.

Although the Stars did not win a pennant until 1949, they thrived in Gilmore, drawing competitively with the strongest teams in the League. In 1946 PCL attendance peaked, with 3,716,718 fans for the eight teams. The Stars and Angels combined for over a million attendance, with the Stars edging their neighbors by 12,000.

Such figures encouraged the League in its claim that it belonged with the American and National Leagues, but the numbers almost immediately began a decline that would not be reversed for years. In 1947 the Stars televised their first game. The following year, they were televising every home game and cutting their attendance by one-fifth for their troubles.

The majors began to broadcast a game of the day nationally over radio, but the televising of minor league games proved to be very damaging even though relatively few people owned televisions in the late 1940s.

Through the 1950s, the Stars maintained a working relationship with the Pittsburgh Pirates. The association developed after Branch Rickey was forced from the presidency of the Brooklyn Dodgers, and assumed the same post at Pittsburgh. Bob Cobb, the owner of the Stars, was a great admirer of Rickey and shifted the Stars' major league affiliation from the Dodgers to the Pirates when Rickey left Brooklyn.

During the 1950s, Rickey built the foundation of the Pirates' 1960 championship team. In so doing, he used the Stars as he had Rochester and Montreal for the Cardinals and Dodgers. In ten years the Stars went from being one of the glamor teams of a circuit with major league ambitions to one more team in Branch Rickey's farm system.

When major league baseball came to southern California in 1958, the Stars' fate was sealed. They moved to Salt Lake City, the town they had left in 1926. The Stars became the Bees, the principal farm team of the California Angels.

THE PACIFIC COAST League in the post–World War II era operated in a twilight zone. It rode the crest of minor league prosperity but failed to crack the major league monopoly. Shunned by the big leagues and unwilling to accept minor league status, the League began to split internally.

James Crusinberry reflected in *Baseball Magazine* in June 1951 that fans in Los Angeles and San Francisco were becoming indifferent to their teams because they had fallen under the spell of a "major league voodoo."[10] With every rumor of franchises moving or league meetings, fans in the principal markets wanted to know when major league baseball would arrive.

In the smaller communities of San Diego, Seattle, Portland, and Sacramento, there were no delusions about becoming part of the majors. Despite the differences in population, Crusinberry found that games in the smaller cities drew larger crowds than those in Los Angeles and San Francisco, where fans had been saturated by a month of major league exhibition games.

Crusinberry found that the press in California, like the fans, ignored the local teams to report on major league games thousands of miles away. At the peak of its success, the PCL was divided between cities that relished the game as it was and those that were distracted by the future.

A personal view of how the League's struggles could affect the ball players was offered by Kevin "Chuck" Connors, the first baseman of the Los Angeles Angels and the future "Rifleman" of television fame. Connors was one of the PCL players who exercised an option to exempt himself from the major league draft. He explained in 1952 that he had been motivated by family considerations and local business opportunities.

Connors acknowledged that it might seem foolish on the face of it to limit his chances of playing in the major leagues, but he saw that in his own case it was more likely that he would be drafted to bolster another Triple-A club in a major league farm system. He anticipated that, if drafted, he would have to move merely to remain in the minors while his wife and children would have to endure a serious disruption of their lives.

In the minors, especially at that time, a player needed to have a job in the off-season and also to plan a career for the time after his retirement from baseball. Connors claimed that "when I came out and publicly stated I would sign the 'no-draft' clause, I was immediately offered three good jobs in Southern California. Business firms aren't interested in hiring ballplayers who may be here one month and gone the next. They are interested in those who indicate they are settling permanently in the locality."[11]

These jobs included public relations, and they assisted Connors in his fledgling acting career. Other players owned local businesses that in the long run would prove more significant financially than their baseball salaries. Today a ball player would do well to sacrifice a few seasons traveling because of the salaries that are available in the major leagues. But at that time the dream of a major league career could be more costly.

By the early 1950s, the PCL had reduced its schedule from the interminable seasons of the past. Air travel made the road trips more pleasant, and Connors added to the impression that the game itself was thriving in the west even without major league status. "On the West Coast, the press, radio and television coverage is as good as in any big-league city. I consider this important because it determines the degree of public interest in the game. Fans out here are as rabid as those in any other section of the country." Connors, a native of Brooklyn, rhapsodized about his new home. "Major-league ball on the Pacific Coast is something worth fighting for. Just picture this: I live in my own home in the San Fernando Valley the year around. I can play golf and go fishing every day if I want to. I'm two hours from ski country, 20 minutes from good swimming, two and a half hours from a bull fight. I'm near many lucrative income sources. Do I want to be drafted—away from all this—to play baseball in, say, St. Louis? Not me."[12]

Connor's optimism proved to be unwarranted. The demise of the League was evident by the mid-1950s. Bill Conlin reviewed the financial health of each of the clubs, beginning with the gloomy assessment that "in a span of three years the Coast

League has run the course from solid entrenchment to disaster's brink. You haven't read it elsewhere but this pillar knows—and can prove—that only six clubs were committed to start the season in 1954 as of last October when the P.C.L. held an emergency meeting in Los Angeles."[13] Conlin concluded that the only stable franchises were the Los Angeles Angels and the Seattle Rainiers. The other clubs were beset with financial problems, weak owners, dilapidated ball parks with no capital to rebuild, and no marketing strategies to combat the intrusion of television and other competition.

This ominous condition seemed to reverse itself in the next two years. Al Wolf reported in *Baseball Digest* in January 1956 that the League had improved dramatically. The San Francisco Seals were purchased by the Boston Red Sox, providing needed capital and management to that franchise. The Oakland Oaks moved to Vancouver, where they enjoyed an enthusiastic reception. Portland finally replaced their park with a new facility. The Padres were purchased by a tuna-packing company that had the sense to hire Ralph Kiner to operate the club. Hollywood continued to benefit from its affiliation with the Pirates, and the Angels remained the class of the League.

The League presidency was assumed by Leslie O'Connor, who had worked for Commissioner Landis for twenty years. O'Connor not only was well-versed in the administration of the game, but he shared Landis's appreciation for the integrity of the minors.

The improved prospects for the League were also noticed in a journalism class at Long Beach State. Fred Claire, who would serve as the Dodgers' general manager and become the *Sporting News* Executive of the Year in 1988, was, in 1955, an aspiring sportswriter who wrote a paper that was published by *Baseball Magazine*. Claire mentioned approvingly the injunction by Commissioner Ford Frick curtailing speculation about major league moves to the West Coast. He added that several clubs had regained their independence after being farm affiliates, and that this independence was vital in upgrading the League further. Claire noted that California had produced more major league players than any other state, and that the PCL had employed such distinguished managers as Casey Stengel, Fred Haney, Charlie Dressen, and Paul Richards. The future of the League looked bright, and Claire anticipated a renewed push for major league status by the PCL.

THE MID-1950s were the last time that anyone could dream of the Pacific Coast League as a major league. After the 1957 season, the Brooklyn Dodgers and New York Giants moved to Los Angeles and San Francisco, depriving the League of its two principal markets.

The PCL was dropped back to Triple-A status. The Angels, now a farm team of the Dodgers, moved to Spokane. The Seals, now owned by the Giants, moved to Phoenix. The Hollywood Stars returned to their old home in Salt Lake City.

The worst having happened, the League adjusted to the trauma rather successfully. Robert Obojski points out that PCL attendance in 1957 was 1,708,000 and that, for the first two years of the new era, it held at about 1,500,000.

Further moves by the major leagues distorted the League beyond recognition. In 1961 the Sacramento Solons became the Hawaii Islanders. Two years later, when the American Association collapsed, the PCL picked up teams from Denver, Dallas–Fort Worth, and Oklahoma City while losing Vancouver.

This trend passed beyond absurdity in 1964 when the PCL took in Indianapolis and Little Rock. The League that a decade before had aspired to the pinnacle of organized baseball was now a twelve-team caricature that stretched from Hawaii to Indiana.

The expansion and restructuring of the major leagues in 1969 restored some sanity to the minors. The addition of Montreal and San Diego to the National League and Kansas City and Seattle to the American League had a billiard effect on the minors. The American Association was revived at the Triple-A level, ending the distortion of the Pacific Coast League. The PCL was again an eight-team circuit with northern and southern divisions. A sign of the new times was the attendance record of Hawaii in 1970, where the 462,217 fans set the standard for all of the minor leagues that year.[14]

The major league potential of the West Coast at the end of World War II is evident from the presence of major league franchises today in virtually all of the old Coast League cities. Three teams continue to share southern California, two struggle in the Bay Area, and Seattle more or less supports the Mariners.

The issue was not whether the West Coast could support major league baseball, but how the majors would expand to the coast. Had the Pacific Coast League become a third major league in the late 1940s, it undoubtedly would have been the weakest of the majors for a decade or more. In time, with its character, traditions, and rivalries intact, it would have made a special contribution to major league baseball.

Instead, the majors engulfed the West Coast by transferring three of its historic franchises and creating three new ones. Baseball in the west is a hodgepodge of clubs from the eminent Dodgers to the marginal Mariners with little to suggest the deep traditions of the game in that part of the country. A comparison between the failure of the Pacific Coast League and the success of the Western League in its earlier challenge to the major league monopoly suggests an important lesson about baseball management. Ban Johnson led a league with strong and innovative ownership. He attacked a bloated and inept National League in its own markets. He saw what he wanted and took it. The PCL lacked sufficient leadership without a president as capable as Johnson, and most important, challenged the majors at the time of their greatest strength. With the introduction of television revenues, before the days of free agency, the 1950s were a time when the major leagues combined the opportunities of the new era with the coercion of the past.

The Pacific Coast League failed because it had asked for equality rather than seizing it. While it may have been in the best interests of the major league owners to facilitate the elevation of the PCL, the likelihood that baseball owners would overlook short-term gains for more permanent rewards has never been a very strong possibility.

• Part Three •

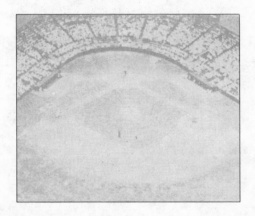

# FALL AND RISE

*THE MAJOR LEAGUES did not gently assimilate the minor leagues; indeed, adjustment of the American and National Leagues to postwar America could hardly have been more devastating to the minors. The ultimate result was a collection of destitute minor leagues that were the fortunate but ragged survivors of bewildering economic forces.*

*The debate over the purposes of minor league baseball had been resolved. Providing the game to small-town America was now undeniably a secondary consideration to providing players to the major leagues. Every source of economic self-sufficiency had been stripped from the minors, and every inclination to independence had been routed.*

*In fairy tales, the admirable victim is magically rescued just before its demise. Such was the case with minor league baseball. After pumping some life into the minors, the major leagues decided to dump their impoverished wards on local owners. With that decision, the minors were revived. Today more teams and more leagues play to more people than at any point since the minors' Golden Age. Movies and books celebrate the minor league game for its simplicity and beauty.*

*The major leagues are also enjoying a new burst of popularity. Major league owners, some of whom are among the great prima donnas of sport, are responding to this popularity with the most tiresome arias. Fans who work for a living are subjected to millionaires pleading for sympathy, begging for stadiums, and threatening all who oppose them.*

*The minors have been responding to their popularity by having a good time. Fans are entertained and respected, and the integrity of baseball is nurtured. The majors may try to spoil the party as they redefine their relationship with the minors after the 1990 season but one can hope that a sensible perspective will prevail.*

# ⋅ Twelve ⋅

# THE MINORS
# COLLAPSE

No PERIOD IN the history of the game has been more disastrous for minor league baseball than the 1950s. In 1949, nearly 42 million people paid to watch teams compete in fifty-nine minor leagues. Ten years later, attendance barely surpassed 12 million, and only twenty-one leagues operated.

Television, new leisure activities, major league franchise movement, air conditioning, and other factors have been accurately blamed for drawing fans away from the ball parks of small-town America. As plausible as these explanations are, they seem too trivial to account for the destruction of such an important part of organized baseball.

Certainly, it had been true enough that the minors operated at the margin of the sport's economy—hard times had always taken a toll on the minor leagues. But in the 1950s the minors were destroyed not by a recession but by a prosperity that they should have been able to share. With the Pacific Coast League petitioning for major league status and with future major league cities in both the American Association and the International League, why were the minors so decimated by a period of good fortune for the game?

The short answer is that the collapse of the minors was but one result of major league greed. The prosperity that baseball has enjoyed may seem to confirm the wisdom of policies that were in fact catastrophic. But grasping after short-term gain has cost us most of our minor league teams, historic rivalries at both the major and minor league levels, strong bonds between communities and their teams, and elegant ball parks that enhanced the game. In exchange we have been treated to domed stadiums, plastic grass, designated hitters, spasmodic expansion and franchise relocation, and other tricks that seem to ensure the privileges of the major league owners but inevitably erode the foundation of the game for everyone. The problem with baseball in recent years is not that a game has become a business, for it was always a business. The problem is that the business is run with so little regard for its heritage.

Major league owners are not villains who have schemed to cheapen the game, but they are responsible for many of the travails of baseball including the reckless destruction of the minor leagues. More generous policies that sought to accommodate the reasonable interests of all parties to the game would have still produced unprecedented wealth with less turmoil for everyone.

THE DECISIONS OF the major league owners that destroyed the minors were not made thoughtlessly. In the 1950s serious examinations of the business of baseball by those outside the game raised questions about the game's most hallowed commercial assumptions. The legality of the reserve clause was twice challenged in court, and on two other occasions congressional committees held comprehensive hearings concerning baseball's economic structure and behavior. The first of these hearings included the state of the minor leagues in 1951, as the beginning of their decline was becoming apparent.

The congressional report noted that minor league clubs tended to be either farm teams or independent franchises, but that a third category was also important, the independent club with a working agreement or affiliation with a major league team.

The report rejected Branch Rickey's contention that farm systems had saved the minor leagues. The data that the committee reviewed were less than comprehensive, but they did appear to show a surprising pattern: "Until 1950, the net cost to the major leagues of owning minor league subsidiaries never exceeded $400,000; 1933 and 1943 appear to have been the costliest years. In normal times, however, the major leagues have operated their minor-league subsidiaries at a profit; from 1939–42, 1944–47, and 1949, the net flow of funds was not from parent club to subsidiary, but from the minor affiliates to the majors.[1]

Since the figures are limited to a few years, any conclusions based on them should be cautiously drawn, but the apparent fact that the minor leagues were actually subsidizing the majors during the years just after World War II is intriguing. In that period the minors reached the peak of their prosperity. The data supply further evidence that raising some of the minor league franchises to major league status could have been justified on economic grounds.

TELEVISION WAS THE most obvious villain in the minors' demise. For that matter, television was hurting even major league attendance. The Cleveland Indians had set attendance records in the late 1940s under Bill Veeck's inspired ownership. By 1956 the Indians' attendance had dropped by two-thirds, even though Cleveland had one of the best teams in baseball in the 1950s.

Branch Rickey distinguished between radio and television by contending that radio enticed the fan to the park while television gave the game away for nothing. Rickey's point was poetic but not especially accurate. Broadcast revenues from television were so alluring that teams sacrificed attendance for their cut of the sponsors' purses.

At the end of World War II, major league baseball was prepared to be cautious in expanding its television coverage. The majors decided in 1946 to restrict broadcasting to the home territory of each team. This policy, known officially as Rule 1 (d), defined the "home territory" as "the circumference of a circle having a radius of fifty (50) miles, with its center at the baseball park of such baseball club."[2]

Rule 1 (d) did not prevent a club, such as the Hollywood Stars, from killing its own attendance through the overly generous use of television, but it did protect the minors from an electronic invasion by the major leagues. Ironically, it was not major league greed that subverted the rule, but the U.S. Department of Justice.

Following complaints by several radio stations, the Antitrust Division of the Justice Department reviewed the legality of Rule 1 (d). The extensive broadcasting of major league games was expected to be a lucrative service that those stations could offer to markets all over America. The self-restraint of the major leagues threatened to cost those stations substantial profits. Major league representatives discussed their concerns with the Justice Department, and an amended Rule 1 (d) was adopted in 1949. This new policy limited the broadcasting of major league games to those hours when a minor league team was playing in its home territory. The compromise pleased no one. The minors began their precipitous drop in attendance. Two stations brought suit against the major leagues. And the Justice Department continued to smell blood on the antitrust question.

At the end of the 1951 season, Rule 1 (d) was abandoned, and each club was allowed to decide for itself where, when, and how its games would be broadcast into minor league territories. The accelerated decline in minor league attendance led to the introduction of federal legislation to restore the earlier restrictions, but the effort was futile.

Senate hearings in 1953 gave officials at all levels of baseball a chance to register their concerns about television. Commissioner Ford Frick testified in favor of restoring the old controls on broadcasting, and he expressed the familiar position of organized baseball concerning its antitrust status: "Baseball cannot be treated as an isolated group of leagues or clubs. Each is interdependent on the other; we are both competitors and partners. We have the major leagues and the minor leagues; the minor leagues cannot exist without major leagues; the major leagues cannot exist without the minor leagues." Frick then laid the blame for the minor leagues' television crisis squarely with the Justice Department. "We eliminated [the broadcasting restrictions] because we were high-pressured by the Department of Justice at a time when we were already faced with 5 or 6 litigations, and when we did not want litigation by the Department of Justice and the United States Government to come in and be added to this terrific pile which we already faced, and not because at any time we had the slightest doubt as to the legality of our position."[3]

George Trautman, president of the minor leagues' National Association of Professional Baseball Leagues, testified that in one city on the West Coast, five major league games were broadcast on radio each day, from 10:30 in the morning to 11:00 at night. Trautman understated, "That is a lot of baseball in one community."[4]

Not only was the quantity of the broadcasts beyond reason, but their hype also created problems. The early radio games were often re-creations by local announcers from a wire service's running account of the game. (Before his stints as an actor and a politician, Ronald Reagan was employed as such an announcer.) Accuracy was not the paramount objective of these broadcasts. As Norris West, public relations director of the San Francisco Seals complained to the Senate, "Broadcasters make the recreated game sound sensational, souping up the plays, and so forth. Actually, most folks out here have never seen a major-league game; so they have no way to know if they are really that good. But they go out to our games, and see nothing quite that sensational quite so frequently as the broadcaster recreating gives them."[5]

Frank Shaughnessy, president of the International League, made the same point for the eastern markets: "A lot of this stuff comes in under the wire, is dramatized to beat the band. The shortstop makes the most wonderful catch in the world. It makes our game look a little bad, and most the time we play better ball than they do."[6]

Shaughnessy offered evidence to support his claim that the drop in minor league attendance was directly attributable to the abandonment of broadcasting restrictions. And the Senate committee received letters from minor league officials all over the country urging a restoration of some barrier against the tide of major league broadcasts, but Congress declined to help.

The broadcasting example demonstrates the complexity of the major leagues' treatment of the minor leagues. To say that the majors were driven by greed implies that, with cunning and indifference, they took deliberate measures to wrest wealth away from the minors. Such a conclusion simplifies and distorts their actions.

From the beginning of organized baseball, the majors had succeeded by imposing order on chaos. Their version of order for fifty years was monopolistic control, but changed conditions in America were threatening that monopoly. Broadcasting represented an unknown technology about which the major league owners were unsure.

Some, such as Branch Rickey, wanted little part of it, while others, including Walter O'Malley, foresaw immense profits. Rule 1 (d) reflected a collective decision to proceed cautiously with broadcasting. The minors were not protected out of the goodness of anyone's heart, but because no one could be sure of the long-term effects of the new technology.

When the broadcasters and the government threatened baseball's antitrust status, the game's sacred cow, the majors were forced to accept a market economy—a condition they had labored to avoid throughout their history. The ruin of the minors followed not so much from the majors' venal decisions as from their inept calculations of self-interest within the new market of baseball broadcasting. Sometimes good intentions are not sufficient.

FRANCHISE RELOCATION IN the 1950s was another blow to the minors. The Braves, Orioles, and Athletics picked off the historic minor league communities of Milwaukee, Baltimore, and Kansas City. The Dodgers and Giants broke the geographic bounds of major league baseball when they moved to the West Coast after the 1957 season.

These five new major league markets opened up new opportunities to the majors. New demographic patterns after World War II showed the potential of minor league communities. In 1950 metropolitan Los Angeles was larger than any major league cities except New York and Chicago. San Francisco–Oakland was a bigger market than Pittsburgh, St. Louis, Washington, Cleveland, and Cincinnati were. Baltimore, Minneapolis–St. Paul, and Buffalo were larger than Cincinnati. Milwaukee, Houston, and Kansas City were only slightly smaller than Cincinnati.

The most obvious value of these cities was in absorbing the surplus of teams from such cities as Boston, Philadelphia, and St. Louis, which could no longer support two major league franchises. The change of scene worked instant magic for the Braves, and the other travelers of the 1950s profited from their moves as well.

The availability of these large markets also triggered thoughts of major league expansion. At the fore of the expansion movement was Branch Rickey. Along with William Shea, Rickey was working to return a National League team to New York. Rickey had a broader goal than New York. He became the president of the Continental League, a paper organization that challenged the American and National Leagues for the future of the game.

Murray Polner listed the cities that this new league comprised, and the high rollers who would own the franchises:

"Twenty great cities cannot be ignored," he [Rickey] told everyone who would listen. Rounding up wealthy investors—Joan Payson Whitney, Jack Kent Cooke, Lamar Hunt, Craig Cullinan, Max Winter, Bob Howsam and others—with the promise of tempting tax writeoffs, shelters, and depreciation, he formed the new league with franchises in Atlanta, Buffalo, Dallas–Fort Worth, Denver, Houston, Minneapolis–St. Paul, New York and Toronto. Eventually, he planned to expand to Honolulu, Montreal, New Orleans, San Diego and Seattle.[7]

Although the Continental League never played a game, it was important because of its influence on the majors. Of Rickey's targets, two-thirds that once hosted a minor league team now are homes to a major league franchise:

| City | Minor League Affiliation, 1961 | Current Major League Affiliation |
|------|-------------------------------|----------------------------------|
| Atlanta | Southern Association | National |
| Buffalo | International League | None |
| Dallas | Texas League | American |
| Denver | American Association | None |
| Honolulu | Pacific Coast League | None |
| Houston | Texas League | National |
| Minneapolis | American Association | American |
| Montreal | International League | National |
| New Orleans | Southern Association | None |
| New York | None | Both |

San Diego        Pacific Coast League        National
Seattle          Pacific Coast League        American
Toronto          International League        American

Of the thirteen cities envisioned for the Continental League, twelve had a minor league team in 1961 when the Continental League had planned to open. Eight of those twelve cities now have major league franchises. Rickey had picked his sites well.

For the minor leagues, the loss of those cities along with Milwaukee, Baltimore, Kansas City, Oakland, Los Angeles, and San Francisco meant that the high minors were shorn of significant sources of revenue.

The minors were thus caught in a squeeze. Television and other distractions eroded attendance at the minor league parks while the majors planned to move into the most lucrative minor league cities. One way out of the minors' problems was to expand the majors by upgrading the best minor league franchises.

This plan, a modification of what the Pacific Coast League had advanced, could have added perhaps four of the top minor league teams every few years until the expanded majors had absorbed all of the available talent.

Triggered by the threat of the Continental League, the majors expanded in 1961 and 1962. The new franchises were located in Los Angeles, New York, Houston, and Washington, D.C. The erstwhile Senators moved to Minneapolis–St. Paul and became the Minnesota Twins. The new Senators struggled for a few years and then moved to Dallas–Ft. Worth in 1972, becoming the Texas Rangers.

Other franchise shifts included the Braves' move to Atlanta after the 1965 season, the Seattle Pilots' transformation into the Milwaukee Brewers after one bankrupt season on the Pacific Coast in 1969, and the Athletics' move from Kansas City to Oakland in 1968.

Subsequent major league expansion occurred in 1969 when

the Montreal Expos and the San Diego Padres were added to the National League and the Seattle Pilots (Milwaukee Brewers) and Kansas City Royals joined the American League. The current roster of major league teams was completed in 1977 when the Seattle Mariners and Toronto Blue Jays expanded the American League to fourteen teams, while the National League remained at twelve.

A structural accommodation to the increase in franchises was made in 1969 when the major leagues split into western and eastern divisions of six teams each. Scheduling had been affected by the initial expansion in 1961, as the old 154-game schedule was replaced by the current 162-game season. The move to seven teams in each of the American League's divisions has made a hash of their scheduling since one of the teams in each of the divisions must play the final weeks of the season against the teams in the other division.

This scheduling problem is one symptom of the problems with the growth of the major league game since the 1950s. Simply put, the game has grown in a stumbling manner that avoided sensible planning in favor of spasms of greed. As Red Smith was fond of observing, "Baseball must be a great game, it survives the people who run it."

Consider the abuse of several of the great minor league cities. The Athletics played in Kansas City from 1954 through 1967. They were a terrible club, never finishing higher than sixth and even placing behind the expansion Angels in that club's first year.

Within a few years of arriving in Oakland, the A's compiled one of the great teams of the modern era. From 1972 through 1974, they won three straight World Championships, the only team other than the Yankees ever to do that. Did the liberation from Kansas City have anything to do with that achievement? Of course not.

Kansas City had been a great baseball town when the Blues played there in the American Association. The Blues had established traditions and a heritage that were tossed aside when the Athletics arrived. When the Royals filled the major league void, Kansas City again showed it would support a good team when the Royals became a power in the American League West.

The Athletics' move to Oakland suggested that there had been something wrong with Kansas City. Actually, there had been something wrong with the ball club. Just as it is easier to fire a manager than a roster of players, it sometimes is easier to blame a community rather than a front office when attendance declines.

Milwaukee is an even sorrier case than Kansas City. The Braves' visit from 1953 through 1965 never included a losing season. After the championship years of the late 1950s, the Braves dropped to the middle of the National League as the Aaron-Matthews-Spahn team aged, but they never finished below .500.

The Braves left for Atlanta because they received a sweeter deal on a stadium and television receipts. But the owners who approved the move neglected to consider that the greatest stadium in the world will not draw crowds to see a poor team. The Braves now ponder a move from Atlanta, while the Brewers prove that Milwaukee is a terrific baseball city.

The Giants' case is another example that defies logic. When the team won pennants in 1951 and 1954, they made money, and they could have expected to make more if they had stayed in New York. With Willie Mays at his peak and Juan Marichal, Orlando Cepeda, and Willie McCovey on the way, the Giants were another team that moved just as it was improving.

When the Mets were created to return National League baseball to New York, they played for two years in the Giants' old stadium, the Polo Grounds. The Mets then moved to Shea Stadium in Flushing, Queens. The obvious question is, why didn't the Giants do what the Mets did? The Giants have never been completely settled in San Francisco, playing in perhaps the worst open-air stadium in baseball. For thirty years, New Yorkers have questioned the Dodgers' move from Brooklyn when the transfer that made no sense was that of the Giants.

Certainly some of the moves have paid off for baseball and

the new markets. The Dodgers' success in Los Angeles has been remarkable. Montreal and Toronto have been stable homes for the Expos and Blue Jays. Anaheim has been a lucrative base for the California Angels, who needed to escape the shadows of the Dodgers to establish themselves in southern California.

Such successes are exceptional, however, as many other major league teams are periodically rumored to be searching for greener pastures. The Giants, A's, Mariners, and Padres have considered moves at various times, proving that the West Coast is not necessarily a gold mine. The Astros, White Sox, and Pirates are other clubs that have considered moving because their current homes were thought to have lost interest in baseball. New regimes have shown that cities such as Pittsburgh had lost interest only in bad baseball.

The restlessness of the major league franchises is largely attributable to owners, whose interest in baseball is focused on financial schemes related to the travesty of government-built stadiums. Few of these owners are serious about providing communities with family entertainment—competitive teams playing in clean, safe stadiums.

Since free agency liberated players from the reserve clause, some owners have spent money with abandon in the hopes of securing a championship. Frustrated when money proves to be no substitute for excellent management, owners bitterly blame the Players Association, arbitrators, or fans for the effects of their own decisions. This erratic behavior has created an unstable climate for the minor leagues by making their largest cities potential targets of a franchise move.

Through hindsight we can imagine a different scenario. In the years after the war, the major league owners might have recognized that the business of baseball was on the verge of unprecedented change. A population boom, economic prosperity, new opportunities for blacks, the growth of suburbs, the role of automobiles, more leisure time—all of these developments suggested that the game that had struggled for fifteen years through depression and war was about to enjoy good times.

By the early 1950s, the two-team city was clearly on the way out. Franchises were going to move, and minor league cities would inevitably be affected. But the major league policy on franchise relocation had all the reason and logic of a pinball. Even the Dodgers' great success in Los Angeles came despite Walter O'Malley's ignorance of the rights of county taxpayers to review his agreements with local officials. Other moves from Seattle, Milwaukee, Washington, D.C., and Kansas City were followed by expansion into those "failed" markets.

The expansion policy of the majors demonstrates their contempt for the minors most clearly. Rather than build on the heritage of the great minor league teams in the Pacific Coast League, the International League, and the American Association, the generations of loyalty to the home team were skimmed like cream for the enrichment of major league owners.

Generally, millionaires looking to enjoy the status of major league ownership were awarded the new franchises whether they had proven themselves as serious sports executives or not. Established minor league owners, who had made money in cities such as Seattle, were bypassed in favor of dilettantes.

The expansion teams were stocked with the most marginal players, and pathetic performances were inevitable during the new clubs' first few seasons. The New York Mets captured their first World Series seven years after their creation largely because of the skill of their general manager, George Weiss.

Of the ten teams that have been added to the major leagues since 1961, almost all have become competitive clubs. Only the Mariners and the Rangers have failed to win division titles, while the Mets and Royals have taken World Series crowns. By this standard, expansion has been a success. The new franchises do seem to rise from their status as doormats to challenge for the division within relatively few years. But a different expansion policy would have been better still for baseball. That policy would have upgraded minor league franchises to the major league level.

Certainly the majors need to be limited. Not every team should be able to give itself major league status. But the decisions of the major league owners on expansion made no sense for anyone. Not only were baseball fans and minor league franchises abused, but the major leagues have a lopsided foundation of franchise allotment that has produced inevitable problems.

The presence of two teams in the Bay Area of northern California has meant a struggle for both the Giants and the Athletics, even during Oakland's championship years. The absence of a team in the nation's capital has deprived the game of one of its great traditions. The scheduling problems in the American League have confounded pennant races, and the fickle movement of such clubs as the Athletics and Braves complicates any community's attachment to its team.

While baseball's economy is currently booming, several years ago the game made some wretched decisions to alleviate financial distress. Two of these choices were the designated hitter rule and the domed stadium. The DH was adopted by the American League to infuse more offense into the game and, it was thought, attract more fans.

The ruse has been successful in the sense that every league in organized baseball but the National League has adopted the device. Purists abhor such specialization because it eliminates painful strategic choices such as pinch hitting for an effective pitcher late in a game. The DH allows fading or injured stars to extend their careers, but such momentary comfort defies the nature of sports, in that one generation must move on to make room for the next. The designated hitter is a cheap attempt to avoid the inevitable. The essence of baseball's appeal has been its similarities with life itself. Its seasons, its vagaries, traditions, loyalties, and eternal hopes have been reviewed by its many poets. The DH is another quick fix in an age that demands instant gratification at the expense of tradition.

The domed stadium is another contrivance that promotes short-term gain. The first such structure was the Houston Astrodome, which opened in 1965. A team publicist described the virtues of the new facility: "Gone will be the gripes of the players on the bad lighting, gone will be the mosquito-spraying chores, gone will be the sweltering heat that sent over 100

fans to the first-aid room during a Sunday afternoon doubleheader, and gone will be the stiff wind blowing in from
right field that frustrated so many lefthanded hitters."[8] Sounds
great. But nature was not so easily conquered. Despite the hor-
rible heat and bugs, Houston had fielded a team in the Texas
League from 1917 through 1958. The minor league record
throughout the south demonstrates that teams could operate
successfully despite the less than favorable conditions in that
part of the country.

The choice to be made involves the lengths to which humans
should go in subjugating nature to improve comfort, and that
can be a tough call. Such efforts may have passed from common sense to hubris if the activity to be enjoyed is changed
significantly for the worse by our modifications. In Houston it
was. The plastic roof created such glare that it had to be
painted a dark color to absorb the sunlight. Taking offense at
that adjustment was the grass field. It died. To the rescue came
the Monsanto Chemical Company, which installed the first ar-
tificial-turf field. Even the Black Sox scandal produced some
useful reforms; Astroturf stands alone as the single worst development in baseball.

No one, perhaps including the architects, ever claimed that
Borchert Field or Sulphur Dell were ideal baseball parks. The
bizarre fields of the minor leagues were charming because men
bowed to nature in order to play the game. The travesty of
artificial grass is that its advocates claim that it improves the
game.

The only improvement is in the owners' treasuries. The National League, which to its credit has resisted the DH, has suc-
cumbed to the allure of cheaper maintenance and fewer
rainouts. Of the twelve National League parks, half use plastic
grass even though the Astrodome is the only stadium that is
incapable of using the real thing.

The American League has shown more resistance to plastic,
but in addition to the artificial surfaces in Kansas City and
Seattle, it has added two domed stadiums in Seattle and Min-

neapolis despite the long, successful history of minor league baseball played outdoors on real grass in both of those cities.

The Canadians may be leading the way to the next phase of stadium design. The Expos and Blue Jays both have stadiums with retractable domes, a device that Walter O'Malley considered for the Brooklyn Dodgers back in the 1950s. Such expense and effort makes one wonder what was so terrible about a few rainouts.

These remarks are not intended as simply another blast at the DH and Astroturf. The point is that these decisions are not aberrations from baseball's otherwise sensible course but part of a trend that ignores common sense and heritage in favor of the quick buck. Baseball cannot stand still in time, and this is not a nostalgic call for the game as it used to be. Turning back the clock also restores the stagnating effects of the reserve clause and even carries us back to the days of Jim Crow. Baseball has always been a business, and that point should not be lost in romantic recollections. But that business, as many minor league franchises showed, could operate profitably in rainy climates, with bugs harassing the fans, on sandy fields, and in sweltering heat or swirling winds. The integrity of the game could be preserved, and the team could still make money— that point has been proven again and again by minor league baseball.

If you wanted to watch baseball in Seattle, you might have had to endure a shower or two during the game. In Texas and Georgia during July and August, you could count on sweltering weather even after night games were introduced. In Minneapolis and Montreal, a snowstorm in April was not out of the question. Those simply were the conditions in those towns. Few people probably enjoyed the heat or the bugs, but if you wanted to see baseball, you put up with them. And you still do.

For all of the alleged improvements, the modern major league stadium has not dispelled all of the discomforts. Astroturf has actually made fields hotter in the summer. The enclosed multipurpose stadiums in St. Louis, Cincinnati, and

Philadelphia restrict air flow. Bugs, humidity, and rain continue to follow the dictates of nature rather than the preferences of players, fans, and club owners.

WHAT, THEN, HAS been gained by economic growth based on short-term interest? Very little that could not have been achieved more securely through more enlightened policies. Reasonable standards that would have allowed teams in the Pacific Coast League, the American Association, and the International League to enter the major league ranks would have made more sense than the mindless expansion that is motivated primarily by a panicked attempt to preclude a congressional review of the antitrust exemption.

Wouldn't the admission of so many minor league teams to the majors have diluted the available talent to an unacceptable level? Not if a radical proposition had been followed: let the Braves, Browns, and Athletics go out of business. That is the same "radical" notion that every other business in the marketplace faces. Why was sustaining the St. Louis Browns so essential that the real Baltimore Orioles had to be bounced by the worst franchise in the history of the major leagues? Why couldn't the real Orioles join the American League to replace the Browns? Why couldn't the Brewers of the American Association have joined the National League to replace the hapless Braves? Or the Kansas City Blues replace the Athletics? Because allowing major league failures to collapse was unthinkable, it was inevitable that the minor league successes would be destroyed.

Since the National League trimmed its membership from twelve teams to eight, the major league roster of teams has never declined. What a curious record compared with the continual adjustments made in the minor leagues during the same period. At first glance, the major league franchises might be presumed to have been more solvent, but teams such as the

Brooklyn Dodgers were occasionally owned by the banks when they reached financial collapse.

The major league owners simply refuse to let their teams die. The Athletics were as dismal in Kansas City as they had become in Philadelphia, but the American League allowed another move to Oakland rather than disband the franchise. From the sporting perspective, the owners preserved the great A's team of the early seventies; but in business terms, they simply made life harder for the Giants. Since both the Giants and A's have considered moves to other cities, it is conceivable that the Bay Area will someday be without any major league team. Such are the outcomes when decisions are made haphazardly.

Rational long-range planning is no panacea for the ills of any industry, but baseball would profit from some of this medicine. As the reality of the postwar era became clearer, the major league owners should have considered where they wanted the game to be in five, ten, and fifteen years. The risks and opportunities should have been carefully considered and weighed. This method would have provided some standard against which to review the specific decisions that cumulatively have made so little sense.

No such planning was done, and the bandages that the major leagues offered the minors were inadequate. Restrained use of broadcasting and revisions of the draft were perennial proposals that failed to reverse the decline in attendance.

After the 1956 season, John Holway proposed an ingenious solution in an article in *Baseball Magazine*. "Let the majors offer to play selected mid-week or Saturday dates in near-by minor league cities as part of four-team double-headers."[9] Holway was inspired by the impact of major league barnstorming in minor league cities. He reviewed a series of such games where overflow crowds swamped minor league ball parks. During the regular season, Holway noted, both major league teams and nearby minor league clubs often played to a fraction of their parks' capacities. In one example, an Indians' game against the Yankees in May drew fewer than 7,000 to Municipal Stadium, whose capacity was about ten times that amount. At the same time, 150 miles away in Columbus, the Jets played Miami before fewer than 3,000 in a park that could seat 14,000.

Holway anticipated three benefits: "1) the majors could double or triple their own revenue on many slack playing dates; 2) the desperate minors would get a life-giving injection worth three or four average playing dates, and 3) millions of fans, otherwise denied a chance to see big league stars in person, could enjoy the thrill of a major league pennant race."[10]

To help the minors, Holway proposed revenue sharing for those teams with inadequate parks and also for those clubs too far from major league franchises to merit a visit. The players were thought to benefit not only by the increased revenues but also by breaking up long tedious train rides between major league cities.

After reviewing the first six weeks of the 1956 season, Holway found forty-five major league dates that drew fewer than 10,000 fans in cities with nearby minor league parks with more than 10,000 seats. By combining the weak dates of both the majors and minors, Holway had cleverly found a way to improve revenues for all the teams.

Needless to say, his idea was never tried. It rested on nimble scheduling, imagination, and an appreciation for teams beyond one's own. Holway decried the emerging pattern: "The Braves, Orioles and Athletics have taken dramatic advantage of the hunger for major league ball outside the traditional big league towns. *But they profited at the expense of the minors which lost three valuable franchises.* [Holway's emphasis]"[11]

Impulsive is an apt description of the major leagues behavior during the 1950s. They had not yet learned how to use television wisely, so their own attendance declined with that of the minors. With some cooperation and vision, all of organized baseball could have reversed at decline. By choosing instead to cannibalize the minors, the majors only postponed their own reckoning.

In 1959 another solution to the minor league decline was considered. This measure would have allowed teams to sign local players and to sell them when they were ready to move up.[12] The rationale was that local fans would better support the home team if it included players that were known from Little League or high school ball.

This plan, introduced by a committee headed by Cleveland Indian executive Frank Lane, would also have included something for everyone. The minors would have enjoyed a boost in attendance. The player would have received a third of his selling price with each transaction. And the majors would have been able to draw players from a revitalized minor league system. Again, the plan failed to get the necessary support from the major leagues.

Having rejected ingenuity and good sense, the major leagues had to fall back on cash infusions to sustain the minors. In 1956 a stabilization fund of half a million dollars was created with donations from each of the sixteen major league clubs. Three years later, a new fund was created to help pay for player development and minor league marketing.

By 1962 the collapse of the minor leagues had stabilized at 10 million fans attending games in twenty leagues. The majors then tidied the mess that had evolved for almost fifteen years. The new "Player Development Plan" epitomized the triumph of the farm system over the independents. The teams that had survived the rout of the 1950s were reorganized into Class AAA, which remained unaffected for the moment; Class AA, which merged the old Double A with Class A; the new Class A, which absorbed the remaining B, C, and D leagues; and a Rookie classification, which was created for first-year players.

As Robert Obojski puts it, "The main point of the entire reorganization plan was that baseball executives agreed that it did not make much sense to maintain the old system of seven classifications with only eighteen to twenty leagues operating."[13] Obojski's conclusion is fair enough from the perspective of the major league owners in the 1960s, but the question remains: how sensible is that perspective?

Every few years, the owners appear to keep asking "What do we do now?" At the same time, they continue, perhaps unwittingly, with policies that aggravate their problems. The same pattern continues in the present day with player relations. Salaries for players are affected either by frantic spending to win it all now or by collusion to freeze spending. Then, when the Basic Agreement expires, the owners declare that the prevailing arrangement is intolerable.

So too with the minor leagues. By the early 1960s the major league owners could see that their own interests were compromised by weakened minor leagues. The majors intervened to support the minors so far as the majors themselves would benefit. Not surprisingly, the majors focus on only one of the minor leagues' historic purposes.

The role of the minors in providing professional baseball of the best quality to the smaller cities and towns of America does not fit into the plans of the major league owners. That purpose is only a happy by-product of farm systems, one that can be radically altered whenever it suits the purposes of the majors.

The independence and integrity of the minor leagues was destroyed during the 1950s without a serious attempt by the majors to save that area of organized ball. Only when the inevitable repercussions became apparent did the major leagues begin to help. And then the assistance took the form of a dole rather than a serious change in the relationships among the leagues.

One of the peculiar and charming features of minor league baseball is that it refuses to stay for long in any one condition. From being a ward of the major leagues, the minors have begun to revive. New owners are drawn to teams as they realize the bounty to be made in the reselling of clubs.

Under the current agreement with the majors, the principal operating expenses of the minor league clubs are assumed by the major league patron. The great capital investment, the ball park, is increasingly made by communities through their public treasuries.

Freed from significant expenses, the new owners can concentrate on having fun for a few years before realizing a handsome profit. Whether the team makes money each year or not, the owner can be confident that the value of the franchise is appreciating. Minor league baseball has become a place where the rich can enjoy the pleasures of ownership without the burdens.

# • Thirteen •

# THE REBOUND

THROUGH THE 1960s and 1970s, the minor leagues remained as fashionable as an Edsel. Baseball itself seemed out of touch with a larger culture that had become frantic and violent. Professional football, the pundits said, was now the national pastime. A sport without a clock, clipboards, and concussions seemed passé.

Minor league attendance inched from about 10 million per year to about 11 million, but that was roughly one-fourth of what it had been in the late 1940s. In 1973 a mere eighteen leagues operated, with only 130 teams. But from that dreary position, the minors have begun a renaissance.

In 1990 about 200 minor league teams will take the field. They can expect to play before more than 20 million people, a great improvement over the sixties and seventies. The high minors have retained historic teams in some cities, and they have also adjusted to new business conditions. The Triple-A Alliance is one of those adjustments that has recently been introduced to the high minors.

The Alliance is a new affiliation between the International League and the American Association. According to Randy Mobley, its secretary-treasurer, the Alliance is something less than a merger of the two historic leagues.[1] The administration of the Leagues was joined after the 1987 season when the American Association was looking for a new president and saw some advantages to hiring the International League's chief, Harold Cooper.

The Alliance has meant savings in administrative costs, but Mobley points out that the Leagues make their key business decisions independently. That distinction notwithstanding, interleague play began in 1988, another example of minor league innovation.

In 1989 the umpires of the American Association and the International Leagues were combined. The advantages include lower traveling costs, since many trips can be made by car rather than airplane. Another benefit may be that greater harmony may reign on the field because clubs will see the same umpire on fewer occasions.

The International League currently operates teams in Columbus, Pawtucket, Richmond, Rochester, Scranton, Syracuse, Tidewater, and Toledo. The Alliance office does not keep records of how many of the clubs are making money, but the opinion of the league officials is that every club is stable.

The Tidewater Tides, despite a small market, are one of the more successful minor league teams. The Tides are the New York Mets' top minor league team, and they have several major league prospects. The Tides drew only 181,667 in 1988, but they still made money because they have a favorable stadium lease.

The other member of the Alliance, the American Association, has recovered from its bashing in the 1960s, but it may face new challenges to its prosperity. The AA has teams in Buffalo, Denver, Des Moines, Indianapolis, Louisville, Nashville, Oklahoma City, and Omaha. All are thought to be stable franchises, and Denver and Buffalo may even be headed for the majors.

The Louisville Redbirds became the first minor league team to draw one million fans, during the 1983 season. Attendance declined last year to 574,000 under new ownership, but the financial health of the franchise is believed to be even more secure now. Sometimes minor league attendance swells because of postgame rock concerts and other attractions. League officials think the smaller numbers for Louisville are more realistic than the magical million mark.

Two of the Association's cities are potential major league markets. Buffalo and Denver both entertain hopes of being included in the National League expansion that is anticipated in the 1990s. Under the management of the Rich family, the Buffalo Bisons drew over one million fans to their new stadium in 1988 and 1989. That attendance figure exceeds those of the Atlanta Braves, the Chicago White Sox, and the Seattle Mariners for the same years, even though the Bisons played ten fewer home games and their facility, Pilot Field, holds fewer than 20,000.

Alliance officials would be reluctant to lose either Buffalo or Denver, but the major league aspirations of those owners take the curse off the prospect. At last the majors would be recognizing the achievements of minor league operators rather than assuming that anyone could make money in those towns, even the marginal franchises of the American and National Leagues.

The Pacific Coast League is also enjoying renewed prosperity, but it also must make some adjustments to secure its future. Currently the PCL consists of ten teams. The Northern Division includes clubs at Calgary, Edmonton, Portland, Tacoma, and Vancouver. The Southern Division comprises Albuquerque, Colorado Springs, Las Vegas, Phoenix, and Tucson.

Bill Cutler, the PCL president, confirms that the ten-team structure is cumbersome.[2] Five-team division races make for awkward and expensive scheduling, with the possibility of a Canadian team traveling to Arizona for a single series. The expansion to ten teams was caused by the American League's expansion to fourteen teams and the necessity of establishing Triple-A farms for Toronto and Seattle.

The savings that the Triple-A Alliance teams have enjoyed have eluded the PCL because of its alignment. Cutler notes that travel is the principal opportunity for cutting expenses, but those savings are difficult to achieve under the league's current alignment.

All of the PCL teams are reportedly stable, with some of them generating annual profits. Phoenix is the only market in the running for a major league expansion team, so the devastation that so distorted the League in the 1960s is unlikely when the majors next expand.

DOUBLE A CURRENTLY includes three minor leagues, the Eastern, Southern, and Texas Leagues. Both the Eastern and Texas Leagues have eight teams, while the Southern League lumbers with ten. All of those clubs have a major league affiliation.

Carl Sawatski, president of the Texas League, says that every club in his league is sound and that "five or six" are making a little money.[3] He makes no apologies for those profits but rejects the belief of some in the majors that minor league franchises are rolling in money.

Sawatski anticipates that the higher prices for minor league clubs will soon stabilize. Some of these new owners, he maintains, are "buying romance" and paying more than the clubs are actually worth.

Jimmy Bragan, president of the Southern League, echoes Sawatski's point that teams are breaking even or making a little money.[4] His league benefits from four or five exhibitions between major league clubs and their Double-A farms.

Class A has five leagues. The California League has ten teams, including the Stockton Ports, thought to be the inspiration for "Casey at the Bat." The Reno Silver Sox and the Salinas Spurs are independent clubs, while the other teams have working agreements with a major league patron.

The Carolina League is an eight-team association with the Peninsula Pilots of Hampton, Virginia, the only independent. The Florida State League is an administrative nightmare. Fourteen teams are arranged in three divisions. Many of these teams, like the Vero Beach Dodgers and the Port St. Lucie Mets, occupy elaborate major league spring-training facilities. The markets in the League are unbalanced, as indicated by the St. Petersburg Cardinals' attendance record of 170,534 for 1988, as compared with that of the Winter Haven Red Sox, who drew 27,746 in the same year.

The Midwest League is another fourteen-team conglomeration that is divided into two seven-team divisions. Balance is a problem in this circuit also. The Peoria Chiefs drew 207,294 in 1988, while the Wausau Timbers managed only 55,255. All of the clubs in the Midwest League have working agreements with major league clubs.

The South Atlantic League was another casualty of the 1950s. It has now operated continuously since 1960. Twelve teams, all with major league affiliations, are divided into two divisions. In 1988 attendance ranged from 168,675 for the Greensboro Hornets to 35,067 for the Sumter Braves.

Two Class-A leagues play short seasons. The New York–Penn League is celebrating its fiftieth year in operation. Its season begins on June 16 and ends September 4. Twelve teams play a seventy-eight-game campaign that cuts expenses during the least profitable months when schools are in session.

The Northwest League has been active since 1946. Its eight teams, located in Idaho, Oregon, and Washington, play seventy-six games during the summer. Though more manageable than other low minors, the disparity in the markets is notable. Spokane was once a Triple-A city, and its Indians, operated by the Brett family, drew 113,143 in 1988, trailing the Eugene Emeralds, who attracted 137,372. At the other end of the spectrum only 15,015 saw the Bellingham Mariners in 1988.

The Pioneer League and the Appalachian League are in the

Rookie League classification, and they also play shortened seasons. Attendance figures offer some indication of the vicissitudes of minor league baseball. In the Pioneer League, the Medicine Hat Blue Jays of Alberta, Canada, drew 10,553. The Salt Lake Trappers, an independent franchise, drew 176,217 in that old Pacific Coast League city.

The Arizona League and the Gulf Coast League operate some co-op franchises that are used by several major league clubs, and they also share some facilities among teams to help cut expenses. Dominican summer and winter leagues have been established recently as well to help develop the new gold mine of baseball talent in the Caribbean.

WHILE NOT QUITE enjoying the glory days of the late 1940s, minor league baseball is definitely recovering. Its resurgence can be explained by several factors, and not surprisingly the minors and the majors stress different implications in the revival.

Throughout the minor leagues, club and league officials stress marketing as the principal reason for the new appeal of their game. Several executives claimed that in the past some clubs simply opened their gates and expected crowds to arrive. The clubs were unprepared when television and other competition challenged their historic hold on the entertainment dollars of small towns.

Now a team is promoted more seriously. A minor league club is treated as a business twelve months a year. This aggressiveness is not really a new phenomenon. Innovation has always been a staple of minor league baseball. Night games and the Shaughnessy playoffs are two of the best examples.

Cavorting chickens and sideshows were introduced at the minor league level and were disdained by some in the majors until the subsequent profits were tallied. The majors now include special promotions at many of their own games.

Perhaps the late 1940s introduced some lethargy into the minors. Farm systems covered the major operating costs, and the postwar boom may have made prosperity seem inevitable. When their fortunes plummeted in the 1950s, the minors were unprepared to react.

An ironic boost to the minors' marketing efforts may be the growth of the major league game. Going to a major league game has become something of an ordeal. Parking now costs four dollars at the Angels' stadium. Ticket prices have risen to cover the greater operating costs, but the new stadiums offer poor seating to the general public.

Season ticket holders occupy most of the box seats in many major league parks, so the occasional visitor is relegated to a nosebleed section or the bleachers, where the intimacy of the old ball parks is only a memory. Add to this the inconvenience of traffic and the dreary tales of drugs, lawsuits, and labor unrest among players and management, and the major league appeal dims somewhat.

The largest minor league parks are about one-fourth the size of the major league stadiums. In some of the smaller towns, the facility may resemble the field of a high school or community college team. A close connection with the game is almost guaranteed, and Carl Sawatski of the Texas League is just one minor league executive who stresses the importance of keeping the park clean and safe for families. Parking is rarely a problem, nor are ticket prices. Jimmy Bragan says that a family of four can attend a Southern League game for less than ten dollars. Admittedly, the major league players are better, but the quality of the high minors is quite good, and the low minors can offer exciting games.

Jimmy Bragan explains the minors' revival in classical terms. He notes that so many people have played baseball at some level that there is a bond between the game and a broad market. The consistency of rules and playing conditions contributes to that appeal. Bragan adds that the novelty of television, a devastating factor in the 1950s, has subsided, and people are now more interested in attending an event in person.

If a fan is interested in bearing witness to a team, the major league game is worth the expense and the trouble. But if the point of seeing a game is to relax and have fun, then the minors may have the better of it.

Harold Cooper notes that many minor league teams have upgraded their stadiums in recent years. This construction has been financed by public treasuries, and that raises the question of whether such spending reflects the same kind of mindless commitment to teams that has characterized major league stadium building. But Max Schumacher of the Indianapolis Indians contends that minor league teams lack the resources to build their own parks. The minors, in his view, are closer to nonprofit enterprises, like museums and libraries. A town may decide to provide a stadium to expand the cultural opportunities of the community.

Bill Cutler of the PCL points out that the minors face a serious obstacle in promoting their game. The players do not stay in one place long enough to generate an identity for their team. He mentions that Jose Canseco and Mark McGwire both played for the Tucson Tigers but that few were aware of the "Bash Brothers" at the time. Canseco played a few games in 1989 in the Southern League while recovering from a wrist injury, and the stands were packed. For a change, stardom that developed in the majors returned to help the farms.

If a major league club is struggling, the chances of a prospect remaining in the minors to develop his game are remote. Just as the Giants pulled Willie Mays from the Minneapolis Millers, the top minor league players may be rushed to the majors in the hope that they will be ready to contribute. When major league teams fall out of a pennant race, their farm teams will inevitably be examined closely by impatient fans and reporters. If talent is discovered ripening in Triple A, a clamor may ensue to bring the putative savior up.

The one way that a minor league club can develop a strong identity is if the major league team is loaded and successful. The Tidewater Tides are probably the best current example. The Mets are so stocked with pitchers and infielders that major league talent is on display in Norfolk.

The same was true when the Dodgers were set in the late 1970s. Their Albuquerque team had Mike Marshall, Greg Brock, Candy Maldonado, Mickey Hatcher, Orel Hershiser, Alejandro Peña, and other future major leaguers, who compiled staggering numbers while waiting for the call up to the LA club. That pattern recalls the Newark Bears, who prospered while the Yankee dynasty gelled across the Hudson.

THE MAJORS, OF course, see the minor league revival differently. With the major leagues picking up the costs of the player contracts, the principal operational cost of the minor league franchise has been financed. The majors see their underwriting as a principal foundation of the minor league game.

Minor league officials such as Cooper and Cutler counter that the minors develop the major leagues' stars. From this perspective, the paying of minor league contracts is only fitting, since those players who advance to the majors are not sold at a market price.

In addition to picking up the players' salaries, the majors also pay the Triple-A clubs a fee of $25,000, for what is termed "special consideration." This amount was originally paid to compensate for the impact of television on the minors; in the 1950s, the high minors received $5,000 per club. Bill Cutler points out that the $25,000 currently paid reflects neither the effects of inflation nor the enormous increase in the majors' television receipts.

What the major leagues see are minor league franchises purchased by people looking for quick financial gain. The value of some of the minor league clubs is skyrocketing, yet the majors continue to pick up the player costs as they did when the minors were struggling.

Joe McIlvaine, vice-president in charge of baseball operations for the New York Mets, maintains that some minor league clubs make more money than some major league teams.[5] He charges that the minors "cry wolf" about their finances based on their lean years, which have now passed. Frank Cashen of the Mets adds that the minors have been attracting owners who are interested in financial gain rather than developing the club.

The same point could be made about many of the major league owners. Harold Cooper contends that new major league owners are not true baseball people. Their ignorance of the game has led some of them to believe that the minor leagues are rolling in money. Jimmy Bragan adds that few major league executives mention the extraordinary increases in the prices their clubs get when they are sold.

The minor league executives see different conditions in their game than the majors do. They see stable franchises that may be making modest profits or breaking even. This improvement over past conditions is seen as an achievement in spite of the majors rather than because of them.

THE GREATEST DIFFERENCE now between the majors and minors is the majors' staggering wealth. In the past the difference in salary between a marginal major leaguer and a career minor leaguer was slight. Players may even have chosen to stay in the minors. Those days are gone, as a few years in the majors at even a minimal salary could set a player financially for life.

The minors have always paid attention to money because their teams are generally shoestring operations, but major league teams have created their own money pit. Back in the 1960s, cities all over America were induced to build new stadiums for their sports franchises. Billions of tax dollars were spent to pick up the major capital investment for sports teams.

These massive subsidies opened the gates to owners who bought teams as a hobby. They had made money in less glamorous ventures and now they wanted to have fun. Freed from the expense of stadiums, the major league owners had unprecedented money in their pots when the players were finally freed from the reserve clause.

Free agency and arbitration have combined to put major league ball players in the same tax bracket as rock stars. It may always have been disappointing for a player to go down to the minors, but now the move can prove to be financially devastating.

These new owners have changed the business of baseball far more than the players' union has. The payment of high salaries to acquire the one or two players who could make a difference in a pennant race is a decision that one owner might make but that will consequently affect future contract talks for every team.

To acquire the revenues to pay those higher salaries, the leagues have obtained lucrative broadcast contracts and have collected the new money from merchandising rights. The owners may breathe a sigh of relief when they gain those windfalls, but all the gain represents is a bigger pot for the players to share. The owners and players do not yet have a balanced relationship, and no amount of money alone will establish peace in player relations.

The traditional function of the farm system has not changed greatly since Rickey's day. "Quality out of quantity" still guides the major league teams that prefer to acquire the players they need from within their own system. And players that are not needed by the parent club can be traded for other prospects or for established veterans.

On reflection of some new realities is the importance some teams place on teaching their young aspirants more than the fundamentals of the game. Charlie Blaney, director of minor league operations for the Los Angeles Dodgers, says that the Dodgers try to prepare their players for all phases of the game.[6] Financial advice, year-long conditioning, press relations, comportment, and emotional and spiritual support are all part of a package of developing young players for the big leagues.

Frank Cashen of the Mets adds that the great influx of Latin players requires attention to their needs.[7] Language classes and instruction in the culture of the United States help these players avoid being isolated.

After the current Player Development Contract expires at the end of the 1990 season, a new agreement defining major league–minor league relations will have to be reached. The majors are enormously impressed with their own financial woes and also with the minors' revival. At the same time, the minors see the majors floating on a sea of television revenue, and they want a more generous share. As far as the majors paying player salaries, the minors see that as a fair price for the development of the major league stars of tomorrow. The discussions should be interesting.

The critical issue of who should pay the players is related to baseball's new television agreement. A new era of technology is arriving, and it is not clear if anyone is examining the lessons of the past to determine how best to use television in the future.

A new agreement between major league baseball and two television networks will change significantly the way that baseball is offered nationally. Under a contract that was negotiated by former commissioner Peter Ueberroth, CBS will have exclusive rights to regular-season games, the League Championship Series, and the World Series. CBS will pay $1.1 billion over four years for these privileges, up from the $1.25 billion that NBC and ABC had paid over six years in the previous contract. The most noticeable effect for the average viewer will be the reduction in regular-season broadcasts. Rather than the current offering of at least one game every Saturday during the regular season, CBS plans to broadcast only about a dozen games all season.

From the network's standpoint, the key to the contract is the exclusive right to all postseason broadcasts, since they draw the top advertising revenues. Regular-season games are not so lucrative, and arguments about the pleasure the NBC games have brought to millions over the years have been unpersuasive to those who negotiate these ten-figure deals.

The slack in regular-season broadcasts will be picked up by ESPN. The cable station will pay $400 million for the rights to broadcast 175 games each season for four years. This contract is much more of a wild card for the minor leagues than the CBS pact. The reduction in network telecasts very well may benefit the minors, but the impact of cable is far more difficult to assess.

Currently about half the homes in America are wired for cable broadcasts. Some areas are too remote to finance the technology, but dense markets in New York City are also without cable because the wars over dividing the bounty are as yet unresolved. The baseball package will, one presumes, spur the growth of cable, though its expense will limit baseball's availability when compared to so-called free television broadcasts.

When ESPN is received, viewers may be offered a "Game of the Day." One hundred seventy-five games per year constitute more than one team's season, and the incentive will be to show the games with the widest appeal. A local minor league club might be competitive against a Mariners–White Sox game, but the incentive for ESPN will be to show the glamor franchises as often as possible. Sitting in an air-conditioned living room watching the Dodgers, Yankees, or Red Sox may be far more appealing than going to the park to cheer the local team during the dog days of August.

Bill Cutler fears that the majors will saturate the national market with these cable broadcasts. In the worst case, the 1950s will repeat themselves, with ESPN having the same impact that radio and television had decades ago. In that scenario, the current minor league revival will prove to be just as hollow as the minors' prosperity of the late 1940s.

Max Schumacher of Indianapolis is more hopeful that the minors will be able to compete against the cable broadcasts. He points out that many clubs have faced superstation broadcasts of major league teams for several years. Schumacher is another minor league official who ascribes the minors' recovery to their own marketing. He claims that clubs have become hardened to the factors that were so destructive in the past.

The new cable broadcasts are difficult to assess. The super-station analogy is limited because the Chicago Cubs and the Atlanta Braves have been the two principal users of such broadcasting, and even Ted Turner has stopped calling the Braves "America's Team." An aggressive, creative marketing strategy with first-rate announcers and innovative camera work covering teams with national followings could be far more challenging for the minors than a Braves-Astros game ever was.

Carl Sawatski says that Texas League games are already burdened with competition from the superstations. He adds that there is no way to tell what the effects of the ESPN games will be, but that cable is currently hurting the league.

A further complication in the broadcasting wars is the future of local television contracts. True to form, George Steinbrenner has roiled the waters with a new package with the Madison Square Garden Cable Network, which will have exclusive rights to Yankee games for twelve years starting in 1991, at a cost of $500 million.

The Yankees, Mets, and Dodgers are head and shoulders above other teams in having consistently popular teams in huge broadcast markets. If they exploit that advantage, teams such as the Milwaukee Brewers and the Cincinnati Reds may be unable to keep pace. The ultimate concern is that the wealthiest few teams will sign the best free agents and reduce competition, to the detriment of all.

This fear has been voiced since the beginning of free agency, and to date it has proven groundless. Owners who have been adept at making money have not always been so skilled in spending it wisely on ball players. The major leagues have been more competitive and more prosperous than ever before. But the television money takes baseball revenues to a new level, and continued competition is not guaranteed.

Conceivably, a team in a small media market might feel pinched enough to look to a national cable outlet. As the Red Sox are a kind of regional team for New England, other clubs might focus on the Gulf, the Northwest, the Rockies or the desert states. Extreme pressure to keep up with the wealthiest teams in the largest cities may add to the offerings of major league baseball on cable stations.

That pressure would require the minors to devise even more inventive ways to promote their game. Such a competition between the majors and minors might prove to be similar to that between theater and television. For reasons already mentioned, the minor league game might be far more appealing for fans at the ball park than the expensive, more remote major league game. The issue may be whether to see baseball in person or to stay home. The first choice will favor the minors; the second may clobber them again.

THE ABILITY OF the minors to compete with the majors in the years ahead may turn on the quality of play that the minors offer, and that question will be affected significantly by decisions that the National League makes about expansion. As more top minor league players move to the major leagues, fewer stars are available to entice fans in the smaller communities.

Competition for players has swung slightly in favor of the minors in recent years. The decision to drop major league rosters from twenty-five to twenty-four players has, in effect, placed an entire major league team in the minor leagues, scattered throughout Triple and Double A. The addition of clubs to the majors will move that phantom major league club back up and draw as well on every prospect currently in the minors.

Harold Cooper of the Triple-A Association chides the majors for failing to prepare for this phase of expansion. He argues that the number of Class-A teams should be increased now to get players ready when expansion begins in the 1990s. There has been some growth in the low minors in the past few years, but no indication that the increase is tied to plans for expansion.

Harry Dalton of the Milwaukee Brewers counters that the

terrific expense of supporting farm clubs as well as paying major league salaries precludes a major league team from carrying as many farm teams as it would have when Branch Rickey was alive.[8] Dalton believes that when the next round of major league expansion occurs, the new franchises will be given sufficient lead time to develop its players.

National League expansion awaits the adoption of a new Basic Agreement between the owners and players. Labor relations in the major leagues are so bad that it is impossible to plan beyond the expiration of the current contract at the end of 1989. Once a new labor agreement has been adopted, a new Player Development Contract will be negotiated, and then the agenda can turn to expansion.

At least two teams are likely to be added to bring the National League even with the American League. The problem is that the American League is already at an awkward size with its two seven-team divisions. William Hulbert saw over 100 years ago that eight teams were ideal for a league. The majors might then consider adding four teams to the National League and two to the American League to create four eight-team divisions.

Whether at that point the majors will be able to resist introducing wild-card playoffs is doubtful. The Shaughnessy playoffs were resisted at first by many minor league executives; but for marginal leagues playing in the Depression, they were a great boost. They have remained important to the financial success of the minors over the past fifty years.

What has been essential for the minor leagues has become a warped necessity for major sports other than baseball. The National Basketball Association and the National Hockey League go to great trouble and expense to eliminate a handful of woeful teams who cannot qualify for postseason play. The NCAA basketball tournament used to invite sixteen teams; now sixty-four teams are asked. The NFL adds four wild-card teams to its six division champions for its playoffs.

Money, of course, is the irresistible lure that turns championship playoffs into sideshows. Baseball is now the only major sport whose division winners are awarded more than home field advantage in an interminable postseason tournament. Baseball's regular-season champions are awarded the only prize that should matter: the opportunity to see which one of them is the best. No sub-.500 clubs need apply.

Assuming that the majors will be looking to add six teams, the next question is, where will they get the players? One hundred forty-four players will be added to major league rosters, and a cry will go up that the game is being diluted with minor leaguers. This is a twist on the refrain that baseball was at its best during the 1950s when only sixteen teams competed for the entire available labor pool that finally had expanded to include blacks.

The minors currently include the phantom major league club caused by the twenty-four man roster, and a few teams such as the Mets have major leaguers stockpiled on minor league clubs. Under the most optimistic assessment of the labor force, the addition of 144 players will diminish, for a time, the quality of the major league game. Inevitably the high minors themselves will be drained, and the differences among Triple and Double A and Class A will be harder to discern.

The compensation is that more cities will have major league baseball. Whether that benefit outweighs the drop in quality is an intriguing question. The combination of weaker leagues with wild-card playoffs seems clearly unwise. The Shaughnessy playoffs are a useful device for struggling leagues. If a similar playoff system were adopted by the wealthy majors, it would be a very regrettable sham that would diminish the value of the regular season beyond repair.


THE PRESENT CONDITION of the minors is about as good as it will ever be. For the moment, leagues are growing, and franchises are stable. Some clubs are making a little money, and more and more people are discovering the game. Attendance is up, as is the interest in ownership. If conditions do not change drastically, the future of the minors looks good.

Calamitous change is, however, something the minors can almost count on. Major league owners who insist that the minors pick up more of their costs, television agreements that pit attractive major league games against local teams, expansion that removes important minor league markets and dilutes talent on every team—all of these are factors on the horizon for the minors.

# Fourteen

# LESSONS

INTEGRITY IS THE most impressive quality of minor league baseball. For over a century, the major leagues have schemed to control the minors through every sort of organizational device. Draft compensation, farm systems, working agreements, territorial compensation, special consideration, and the Player Development Contract have been life supports from a mugger to its victim.

The welfare of minor league baseball is further complicated by the fact that, while the major league owners always intend to promote their own interests, they do not always do even that very well. Ignoring talented players such as Oscar Charleston and Josh Gibson is only the most notorious example. Their inability to bargain responsibly for free agents is only the most recent example.

If shabby treatment by the majors were not bad enough, the

minors have periodically trashed their integrity themselves. The mad rush into the League Alliance, the compliant beginnings of the National Association of Professional Baseball Leagues, its pressure on the American Association and the Pacific Coast League to become "legitimate," the refusal to help the Orioles withstand the Federal League, the minors' inexcusable acceptance of the racial barrier, the embrace of the draft, the lack of support for the PCL after World War II, and the meek acceptance of their fate as the low minors were destroyed during the 1950s—all constitute a dreary litany of inferiority.

The majors have robbed the minors of their integrity, and the minors themselves have given it away. But that integrity stubbornly returns and elevates the minor league game to a special place in baseball. The decisions of baseball's rulers to protect their own privilege are not always as important as the determination of a few owners, players, and fans to be stewards of the game.

A key to the minors' integrity had been their role in providing baseball to the small towns of America. This purpose once coexisted with their function of developing players for the major leagues. Under major league ownership, offering the best possible game to fans in smaller communities has become a distant secondary goal to providing phenoms to the majors.

As the value of these minor league clubs sank steadily to the bottom of baseball's market, the major league owners did the smart thing. They unloaded these properties on locals who, as it has been said, were trying to buy romance. From this effort to find a new home for their unwanted dog, the majors infused the minors with a new boost of integrity. From this attempt by local owners to capture a little glory, the minors recovered their soul.

The return of independent ownership to minor league clubs presents a dilemma to the majors. The minors' new prosperity is trying to the major league owners, who must be galled that they dumped these teams just before they started raking in money. On the other hand, it is entirely possible that the minors' revival was *caused* by their new freedom from the majors. The decision to return to working agreements to control their farm teams was not so much a stroke of bad luck or ill timing as it was the instrument of renewal.

Minor league teams are now worth a lot of money because there are a number of wealthy people looking to get into the game. It is their competition that drives up the price of the club, and the higher prices give the new owners an incentive to run the club in a way that cultivates the fans' loyalty.

To recover total control of the minors, the major leagues would have to shell out millions of dollars per club, and with that monopoly restored, the value of the minor league teams would likely plummet, since no market would exist to sustain the high franchise prices of recent years. Teams that would cost millions to purchase would return to a value measured in the thousands.

The majors' ownership dilemma gives the minor leagues a measure of operating independence. Farm systems that are based on working agreements are more binding for the minors than total independence and draft exemption used to be, but under a working agreement the minors have more freedom than they had when they were owned outright by their major league sponsor.

Specifically, if the major leagues apply the screws too hard in the upcoming contract negotiations, or if they are too cavalier in their manipulation of minor league rosters, the current minor league owners can simply sell their clubs, collect their sizable profits, and leave the majors to deal with the same economic mess they had in the 1950s and 1960s.

At the present time, there are no outright rebels in the minors. No one foresees the kind of revolt that the PCL threatened forty years ago. The current minor league owners seem content with the fundamentals of their relationship with the majors, but they are prepared to press their interests on important issues.

An open rebellion is not in the cards for the minors regardless of the provocation, and the reason simply is money. As recently as the Pacific Coast League's postwar challenge, it was plausible that the high minors could compete with the majors for players. Even in 1970, the minimum salary for a major league player was less than $10,000 and the superstars were paid less than $200,000. The explosion of salaries that free agency and arbitration unleashed have taken the major league labor market out of the minors' reach. When the PCL included six future major league markets, it was in a position to grow into a competitive major league. When the American Association included Milwaukee, Kansas City, Minneapolis, and St. Paul, it too had major league potential. With Baltimore, Montreal, and Toronto in the International League, what has become the Triple-A Alliance would have had a solid foundation in major league communities.

Now those cities are lost to the minors. Attendance and broadcast revenues are too limited even in the high minors to compete with the American and National Leagues. Minor league owners are making substantial profits from the eventual sales of their investments, but they do not generate the operating revenues needed to pay major league salaries. Beyond the limits of their incomes, the minor league owners have no incentive to break away from the structure of organized baseball. The American Association, Jack Dunn, and the Pacific Coast League all anticipated financial gain from greater independence. The current minor league executives have the best of all worlds. The Player Development Contract precludes serious losses, and the attraction of owning a baseball team promises great profits whenever one chooses money over glamor.

The current minimum salary in the majors is well over $50,000. Even a few years at that base salary would make a permanent return to the minors unappealing. A few major league veterans are willing to go back down, but the odds that a league could be sustained through such players is too remote to consider seriously.

Should the bubble burst for the major leagues—as it could for any spectator sport in America—a new economic order might permit or encourage independent minor leagues, but the wealth being generated today in the major leagues puts them on another planet as businesses.

THE BALANCE BETWEEN the business and the game of baseball goes to the heart of the sport's integrity. For purists, the game should be played according to rules that are revered as eternal and inspired. Except for the nefarious designated hitter, the game has remained essentially unchanged for nearly a century.

The modern setting of baseball has troubled some fans. Domed stadiums and artificial turf change baseball into a related but distinct game. It still looks like baseball, but so does softball. The scheduling of the All-Star Game and the World Series at night has been a blow to those who believe that the game is best played during the daytime. The addition of lights to Wrigley Field was another mistake of the same order. The clang of aluminum bats in the college game is too corrupting to discuss.

The purist's ethic is not without some force. Weekend World Series games may return to a day schedule, and relatively few night games are now slated for the Cubs. In a sartorial improvement, the Braves have abandoned the double-knit multicolored uniform for a return to their traditional white flannel.

The purist's game may have peaked in the early 1950s. Integration had dramatically improved several teams, ball parks had yet to be replaced with stadiums, television was still a novelty, and the major leagues contained their familiar sixteen entries. But the game's popularity was forcing changes in business arrangements that had been constant through the century.

Baseball's integrity concerns the relationship between those commercial adjustments and the essence of the game, and it is precisely on that point that the minor leagues have done rather well. Their commercial adjustments have done far less damage to the game than those of the major leagues have.

At all levels, baseball should be biased against change. Charlie Finley's proposals for orange baseballs and designated hitters and runners seem to reflect a fear of the game's nature. This fear dictates that fans at the park must be blasted with rock music after a third out lest they become restless watching the teams change sides. In a game with relatively little offense, boredom, it is thought, is the great enemy.

Changes such as the DH are deplorable not so much because they rob the game of the tough choice of whether to pinch-hit for a terrific pitcher who is a run behind. The travesty is that the DH is a contrivance to provide more action in a game whose appeal rests in its reflection and planning. Few fans have had the chance to play professional baseball, but we all believe we could manage better than that fellow in the dugout. We need the quiet moments that the game offers to refine our second-guessing to an art.

Motley uniforms, plastic grass, domed stadiums, and obnoxious sound systems are some of the business adjustments that sap the integrity from baseball. Ultimately they represent a breach of trust between owners and fans. The executives believe that fans prefer incessant stimuli through a version of baseball to the more subtle pleasures of the game itself. To make the implication explicit, the major leagues have let their integrity erode while the minors have found it again.

At first glance that opinion is nonsense. The minors not only provide rock music, they offer rock concerts to boost attendance. A few major league owners may be salivating over wild-card playoffs, but the minors have held them for fifty years. Major league parks may shatter the eardrums between innings, but the minors provide every kind of carnival antic to entertain the crowd. Raffles, lucky programs, and sing-alongs are among the more high-brow diversions. Without a doubt, the minors have cornered the market on the tinniest kind of boosterism. Whither integrity?

The saving grace for the minors is that the Babbitry is all in good fun. Minor league baseball is precarious at its core. It exists in most towns by a financial hair that could break at any

time for any number of reasons beyond the control of anyone
on the team or in the community.

The one certainty of the minors is that the good times will
not last. Does your team finally have a great player in the
dawn of a brilliant career? Hurry to the park, because he will
move up before you learn his middle name. Does your son
plan on trying out for the locals after high school? Tell him to
look for a day job because the league may realign before graduation. Does your business expect greater exposure now that
your town has a club in the high minors? Do not cut your
advertising budget because you could be back in Class A next
year.

The antics at the park are a kind of perpetual Irish wake. The
beloved team or player will inevitably leave, so their brief time
with the fans is celebrated with abandon. What appears to be
tacky in minor league promotions is simply a recognition that
all those in the park are not going to be together long enough
to have to bother with refinement. They have gathered because
baseball is fun.

We know that a traveling circus is a shoestring operation, so
we do not complain when a barker cons us out of a dollar.
Instead, we enjoy discovering what the scam is. But we do not
invest on Wall Street for the same reason. Hucksters in thou-
sand-dollar suits do not need the money; they are only greedy.

Unfortunately, major league baseball has lost its sense of
humor just as the minors have found theirs. When Walter
O'Malley or Branch Rickey cried poverty through their jowls
and cigars, it was a good show. They could not possibly have
thought that anyone believed them. Veeck was only being
honest when he described himself as a hustler.

When the modern major league owners complain about their
financial straits, they are offensive rather than charming because they appear to be sincere. They really do seem to believe
that they are pitiable. When they bemoan the high salaries to
which they themselves agreed, their whining is simply embar-
rassing. Like petulant children, some major league owners
threaten to run away from home if they are not given new

stadiums by cities that lack resources to care for suffering people who could not afford even bleacher seats.

The majors can point to their increased attendance and television revenues as signs that baseball is booming, and there is no question that the numbers are up. Some of this gain stems from greater competition and the emergence of new stars. But this growth is jeopardized by problems at baseball's foundation.

The major league owners continue to offer their privileged status as the ultimate value in the game. The players have successfully scoffed at that posture since the Seitz ruling established free agency. The minor league owners seem similarly unwilling to apologize for their new wealth. If city officials decide to stop being intimidated about stadiums, they too can be freed from the tyranny of the preposterous.

The financial stakes in the major leagues have reached such dimensions that lawsuits attend every facet of the business. To find the game, the fan must pore through battles over stadium construction, drug testing, the Basic Agreement, gambling, expansion, and television policies.

In contrast, money in the minors is needed for survival, not for another Rolls. The game is far more accessible and far more fun without the distractions of litigation. For most of us, life is challenging enough. When we turn to baseball for relaxation, we do not want to find millionaires who claim to be suffering more than we are. Hence, the fresh air of the minor leagues.

The minor leagues also offer a unique contribution in sparing baseball from one of the most degrading features of player development. Professional football and basketball use colleges and universities to perform the service that the minors provide. Some athletes are disguised as college students when they may not have mastered the curriculum of elementary school. Colleges themselves allow such corruption because they are trapped in the same financial prison that strips the integrity of so many institutions that our culture calls successful. College baseball is a minor sport compared to football and basketball, but it is also less corrosive to the purpose of higher education.

The minor leagues enhance the dignity of a great high school athlete who does not happen to be particularly bright. In the minors he can be a great prospect, and he can grow in his craft. The same young man in football or basketball must assume the role of a college student and know that he is considered by many who cheer him to be a dunce and a fraud.

THE INTEGRITY OF the minor leagues is impressive compared to that of other spectator sports, but we should not think that the minors monopolize virtue. If colleges could make as much money from baseball as basketball, we could expect more doctored transcripts and phony degrees. If Class-A teams could get $100 million subsidies from their city governments, few would turn them down. If minor league execs were lionized as some major league owners are, their heads would also be turned.

A reasonable amount of virtue has combined with some economic realities and some fortunate accidents to put minor league baseball in a very special place. The game that is now extolled in movies and books has become a repository of what is beautiful about baseball.

When the financial hysterics of the majors at last subside, those leagues may again find in the minors a source of rescue. The relief next time should not come from power games fueled by greed and suspicion, but from the rediscovery that baseball is a gift to be shared and enjoyed by players, owners, executives, and fans.

Like most gifts, this one resides where one would not expect it. In the smaller towns beyond the networks and the metropolitan dailies, baseball is enriching America, and the country is again celebrating its good fortune.

# NOTES

Chapter One

   1.  Robert Obojski, *Bush Leagues* (New York: Macmillan, 1975), 4.

   2.  Harvey Frommer, *Primitive Baseball* (New York: Macmillan, 1988).

   3.  Harold Seymour, *Baseball: The Early Years* (New York: Oxford University Press, 1989), 94.

   4.  Obojski, *Bush Leagues*, 8.

   5.  Society for American Baseball Research, *Minor League Baseball Stars*, vol. 1 (Manhattan, KS: Ag Press, 1984).

Chapter Two

   1.  David Voigt, *American Baseball*, vol. 1 (University Park: Penn State Press, 1983), 230.

2. Bill James, *The Bill James Historical Baseball Abstract* (New York: Villard Books, 1986), 38.

3. Eugene Murdock, *Ban Johnson* (Westport, CT: Greenwood Press, 1982), 39.

4. See James, *Historical Baseball Abstract*, 80–85.

5. A. D. Suehsdorf, "Honus Wagner's Rookie Year," *The National Pastime*, Winter 1987, 11–17.

6. Lawrence S. Ritter, *The Glory of Their Times* (New York: Morrow, 1984), 20–33.

7. Donald Honig, *Baseball America* (New York: Macmillan, 1985), 37–38.

8. *The Sporting News*, 19 October 1901, 2.

Chapter Three

1. John B. Foster, *A History of the National Association of Professional Base Ball Leagues* (National Association of Professional Baseball Leagues, 1926), 33.

2. Ibid., 29.

3. Robert Finch, L. H. Addington, Ben M. Morgan, eds., *The Story of Minor League Baseball* (Columbus, OH: The Stoneman Press, 1952), 18–20.

4. Ibid., 16.

5. Edward Michael Ashenback, *Humor Among the Minors: True Tales from the Baseball Brush* (Chicago: M. A. Donohue and Co., 1911), 38.

6. Ibid., 40.

7. Alfred H. Spink, *The National Game* (New York: Wehman Bros., 1910), 367.

8. Ashenback, *Humor*, 146–48.

9. Ibid., 57–58.

10. Steven A. Riess, *Touching Base: Professional Baseball and American Culture in the Progressive Era* (Westport, CT: Greenwood Press, 1980), 27.

11. Ibid.

12. Ibid.

13. Ibid., 28.

14. Foster, *National Association*, 81.

15. Ibid., 80.
16. Ibid., 81.

Chapter Four

1. Robert Creamer, *Babe* (Evanston, IL: Holtzman Press, 1974), 70.
2. Ibid., 75–76.
3. David Chrisman, *The History of the International League,* vol. 1 (privately published: 1981), 18.
4. Ibid., 25.
5. Ibid., 31.

Chapter Five

1. Murray Polner, *Branch Rickey* (New York: Signet, 1982), 65–66.
2. Ibid., 78.
3. Ralph Kiner with Joe Gergen, *Kiner's Korner* (New York: Arbor House, 1987), 24.
4. Ira Irving, "The Far-Reaching Results of 'Farm Baseball,'" *Baseball Magazine,* January 1929, 345.
5. Red Smith, "Pepper Martin v. Philadelphia," in *The Ultimate Baseball Book,* ed. Daniel Okrent and Harris Lewine (Boston: Houghton Mifflin, 1988), 170.
6. Ibid., 158.
7. Polner, *Branch Rickey,* 112.
8. Chrisman, *International League,* 1:62.
9. Ibid., 86–87.
10. Polner, *Branch Rickey,* 113.
11. Ibid., 149.
12. J. G. Taylor Spink, *Judge Landis and 25 Years of Baseball* (St. Louis: Sporting News, 1974), 202.

Chapter Six

1. Bill Veeck, *Veeck as in Wreck* (New York: Signet, 1986), 54.
2. Ibid.

3. Eugene Murdock, "They Called Him Unser Choe," *Baseball Research Journal* 1977:42.

4. Ibid., 43.

5. Veeck, *Veeck*, 74.

6. Ted Williams, *My Turn at Bat* (New York: Simon and Schuster, 1988), 50.

7. Ibid., 53.

8. Stew Thornley, *On to Nicollet: The Glory and Fame of the Minneapolis Millers* (Minneapolis: Nodin Press, 1988), 55.

9. For another look at the Dodgers' and Giants' moves, see Neil Sullivan, *The Dodgers Move West* (New York: Oxford University Press, 1987).

10. Thornley, *Nicollet*, 65.

Chapter Seven

1. Ronald Mayer, *The 1937 Newark Bears: A Baseball Legend* (East Hanover, NJ: Vintage Press, 1985), 11.

2. Obojski, *Bush Leagues*, 49.

3. Finch et al., *Minor League Baseball*, 31.

4. Ibid., 37.

5. Ibid., 37–38.

6. Finch et al., *Minor League Baseball*, 28.

7. Harry James O'Donnell, "Are the Minor League Skies Clearing?" *Baseball Magazine*, October 1933.

8. Finch et al., *Minor League Baseball*, 28.

9. Ibid., 33.

10. O'Donnell, "Minor League Skies," 512.

11. Chrisman, *International League*, 1:88.

12. Ibid.

13. Mayer, *Newark Bears*, 29.

14. Ibid., 23–24.

15. David Klein, *On the Way Up: What It's Like in the Minor Leagues* (New York: Julian Messner, 1977), 124–25.

Chapter Eight

1. Bill O'Neal, *The Texas League 1888–1987: A Century of Baseball* (Austin, TX: Eakin Press, 1987), 21–22. This chapter relies on O'Neal's fine work for basic historical information about the Texas League.

2. James, *Historical Baseball Abstract*, 130.
3. O'Neal, *Texas League*, 43.
4. Ibid., 246–47.
5. Ibid., 247.
6. Robert McConnell, "Three Shots of Rye," *Baseball Research Journal* 1980:81.

## Chapter Nine

1. Furman Bisher, "Last Blow to the Minors," *Baseball Digest*, September 1963, 55.
2. John E. Spalding, "Unknown and Phenomenal: Minor-League Batting Champions," *Baseball Research Journal* 1987:68–71.
3. George W. Hilton, "The Evangeline Scandal of 1946," *Baseball Research Journal* 1982: 101–02.
4. Finch et al., *Minor League Baseball*, 34.
5. Ibid.
6. John Steadman, "Poignant Memories in the Minors," *Baseball Digest*, May 1955, 69.
7. Don C. Trenary, "Everything Happens in the Minors!" *Baseball Digest*, August 1935, 35.
8. Ben Fanton, "How It Was in Old Days of Class 'D' Baseball," *Baseball Digest*, March 1981, 88.
9. Gerry Hern, "There Are Still *Too Many* Minors," *Baseball Digest*, April 1954, 45.
10. Ibid., 46.
11. L. H. Addington, "Minor League Expansion," *Baseball Magazine*, June 1941, 329.

## Chapter Ten

1. James Delaney, Jr., "The 1887 Binghamton Bingos," *Baseball Research Journal* 1982:110.
2. Robert Peterson, *Only the Ball Was White* (New York: McGraw-Hill, 1984), 79.
3. Warren Brown, "Baseball Echoes from the Pacific Coast," *Baseball Magazine,* July 1919, 155–56.
4. Ibid., 156.

5. Peterson, *Only the Ball*, 169.

6. Donn Rogosin, *Invisible Men: Life in Baseball's Negro Leagues* (New York: Atheneum, 1987), 31–32.

7. Ibid., 172.

8. Ibid., 179–80.

9. Jules Tygiel, *Baseball's Great Experiment: Jackie Robinson and His Legacy* (New York: Oxford University Press, 1983), 88–89.

10. Polner, *Branch Rickey*, 174.

## Chapter Eleven

1. Gerald Tomlinson, "A Minor-League Legend: Buzz Arlett, the 'Mightiest Oak,'" *Baseball Research Journal* 1988:14.

2. Ibid.

3. Ibid., 16.

4. Society for American Baseball Research, *Minor League Baseball Stars*, vol. 2 (Manhattan, KS: Ag Press, 1985), 11.

5. Al Wolf, "Coast Deal a Long Way Off," *Baseball Digest*, October 1947, 18.

6. H. G. Salsinger, "Here's P.C.L.'s Side," *Baseball Digest*, May 1948, 43.

7. Ibid.

8. Ibid., 44.

9. Al Wolf, "P.C.L. Jittery over Own Ultimatum," *Baseball Digest*, November 1951, 11–12.

10. James Crusinberry, "Pacific Coast League Impressions," *Baseball Magazine*, June 1951, 277.

11. Kevin Connors and Chuck Sexauer, "I'll Stick with the Coast League," *Sport*, July 1952, 22.

12. Ibid., 24–25.

13. Bill Conlin, "Crisis in the Coast League," *Baseball Digest*, March 1954, 72.

14. Obojski, *Bush Leagues*, 158.

## Chapter Twelve

1. Senate Committee on Interstate and Foreign Commerce, *Broadcasting and Televising Baseball Games*, 83d Cong., 1st sess., 1953.

2. Ibid., 13.
3. Ibid., 10–11.
4. Ibid., 20.
5. Ibid., 25.
6. Ibid., 30.
7. Polner, *Branch Rickey*, 253–54.
8. Lowell Reidenbaugh, *Take Me Out to the Ball Park* (St. Louis: The Sporting News, 1983), 124.
9. John Holway, "Stop Killing the Minors," *Baseball Magazine*, October 1956, 28.
10. Ibid.
11. Ibid., 29.
12. Gordon Cobbledick, "Cure for Minors: Hometown Stars," *Baseball Digest*, March 1959, 65–66.
13. Obojski, *Bush Leagues*, 30.

Chapter Thirteen

1. Randy Mobley, telephone interview with author, 5 May 1989.
2. Bill Cutler, telephone interview with author, 5 May 1989.
3. Carl Sawatski, telephone interview with author, 5 May 1989.
4. Jimmy Bragan, telephone interview with author, 5 May 1989.
5. Joe McIlvaine, interview with author, Shea Stadium, 19 April 1989.
6. Charlie Blaney, interview with author, Vero Beach, FL, 16 March 1988.
7. Frank Cashen, interview with author, Shea Stadium, 19 April 1989.
8. Harry Dalton, telephone interview with author, 9 May 1989.

# BIBLIOGRAPHICAL NOTE

My PRINCIPAL SOURCES of statistical information for the entire history of minor league baseball are Robert Obojski's *Bush League* (New York: Macmillan, 1975) and the two volumes of *Minor League Baseball Stars* compiled by the Society for American Baseball Research (SABR).

Harold Seymour's superb histories have been reissued, and the first volume, *Baseball: The Early Years* (New York: Oxford University Press, 1989), is a great help in sorting out the organizational turmoil of the nineteenth-century game. *American Baseball: From the Gentleman's Sport to the Commissioner System* (University Park: Penn State Press, 1983) by David Voigt is another fine work of that period, as is Peter Levine's *A. G. Spalding and the Rise of Baseball* (New York: Oxford University Press, 1985).

Some terrific books from that first era that should be republished include *The National Game* (New York: Wehman Bros., 1910) by Alfred H. Spink; *America's National Game* (New York: American Sports Publishing Co., 1911) by Albert G. Spalding; *History of Baseball in California and Pacific Coast Leagues 1847–1938* (Oakland, 1938) by Fred W. Lange; and *Humor Among the Minors: True Tales from the Baseball Brush* (Chicago: M. A. Donohue and Co., 1911) by Edward Michael Ashenback. A later work that also deserves a wider audience is H. D. Robins's *American Baseball Needs Four Major Leagues* (Los Angeles: Western Technical Press, 1947).

The two publications of the National Association of Professional Baseball Leagues, the 1926 history by John Foster and the 1952 version by Robert Finch, L. H. Addington, and Ben Morgan, are romanticized and biased, but they are useful for showing the frame of mind of top minor league officials.

Harold Seymour's second volume, *Baseball: The Golden Age* (New York: Oxford University Press, 1971), includes excellent chapters on the Federal League and the rise of the farm systems. David Voigt's *American Baseball: From the Commissioners to Continental Expansion* (University Park: Penn State Press, 1983) offers an interesting perspective on that same period.

In addition to the biographies of Branch Rickey, valuable information about the Cardinal farm system can be found in Donald Ray Andersen's doctoral dissertation, *Branch Rickey and the St. Louis Cardinal Farm System: The Growth of an Idea* (Ann Arbor: University Microfilms International, 1975).

League and team histories include David Chrisman's *The History of the Virginia League (1900–1928; 1939–1951)* (Bend, OR: Maverick Publications, 1988) and *The History of the Piedmont League (1920–1955)* (Bend, OR: Maverick Publications, 1986). Roger Kahn's *Good Enough to Dream* (New York: Doubleday, 1985) is a delightful book about the Utica Blue Sox.

Richard Beverage is the author of two books about PCL

teams: *The Angels: Los Angeles in the Pacific Coast League, 1919–1957* (Placentia, CA: Deacon Press, 1981) and *Hollywood Stars: Baseball in Movieland 1926–1957* (Placentia, CA: Deacon Press, 1984). *The Last Rebel Yell* (Lynn Haven, FL: Seneca Park Publishing, 1986) by Ken Brooks is a history of the Alabama-Florida League. *Innings Ago* (Kansas City: Normandy Square Publications, 1987) by Jack Etkin offers the recollections of some of the men who played for the Kansas City Blues, the Monarchs of the Negro Leagues, and the Athletics.

*50 Golden Years in the American Association of Professional Baseball Clubs 1902–1951* (Minneapolis: Syndicate Printing Co., 1951) by Robert French is the authorized history of that famous league.

*Only the Ball Was White* (New York: McGraw-Hill, 1984) by Robert Peterson inspired subsequent work by Donn Rogosin, Jules Tygiel, and others on the Negro Leagues. *The Pitcher* (New York: Prentice-Hall, 1988) by John Thorn and John Holway add some useful information about Satchel Paige.

SABR's *Baseball Research Journal* includes many valuable articles about the minors, especially:

"Nick Cullop, Minor League Great" by L. Robert Davids, BRJ 1975

"From the Bushes to the Bigs" by Vern Luse, BRJ 1976

"First Great Minor League Club" by Joseph Overfield, BRJ 1977

"A Vote for Dunn's Orioles" by Al Kermisch, BRJ 1977

"The Newark Bears" by Randy Linthurst, BRJ 1977

"The 1934 Los Angeles Angels" by W. R. Schroeder, BRJ 1977

"The 1920–25 Fort Worth Panthers" by E. Vern Luse, BRJ 1977

"They Called Him Unser Choe" by Eugene Murdock, BRJ 1977

"Performance of Perry Werden" by Raymond J. Nemec, BRJ 1977

"Minor League Baseball in Rocky Mount" by L. Smith, BRJ 1978

"The 17 Inning No Hitter" by Jack Rudolph, BRJ 1978

"Offerman Stadium in Buffalo" by Joseph Overfield, BRJ 1979

"All Negro Minor League Team" by Robert Hoie, BRJ 1979

"The Dallas Hams of 1888" by Harry Jebsen, BRJ 1979

"The 1903 Hudson River League" by Vern Luse, BRJ 1979

"When Joe Bauman Hit 72 Home Runs" by Bart Ripp, BRJ 1980

"Three Shots of Rye" by Robert McConnell, BRJ 1980

"The Hollywood Stars" by Stephen Daniels, BRJ 1980

"Minor League Hall of Fame Game" by Ed Brooks, BRJ 1981

"An Explosive Beginning" by Bart Ripp, BRJ 1982

"A Few Historic Minor League Ballparks" by R. Graber, BRJ 1982

"Lefty George" by George Tomlinson, BRJ 1983

"Millers Topped Minors in Odd Protests" by S. Thornley, BRJ 1984

"Research of Minors Yields Major Finds" by V. Luse, BRJ 1984

"Buzz Arlett" by Gerald Tomlinson, BRJ 1988

Other valuable information from SABR can be found in their publication *Nineteenth Century Stars*, issued in 1989; and *The National Pastime*.

*Baseball Magazine* and *Baseball Digest* are two sources for contemporary accounts of the minors' history. Pertinent articles from those publications include:

Addington, L. H., "Baseball—And the Minor Leagues," *Baseball Magazine*, August 1934

Addington, L. H., "Minor League Oddities of 1936," *Baseball Magazine*, November 1936

Addington, L. H., "The Minor League Frolic of 1937," *Baseball Magazine*, January 1938

Addington, L. H., "Minor League Expansion," *Baseball Magazine*, June 1941

Anderson, Rick, "P.C.L. Expects to Survive Loss of Seattle, San Diego," *Baseball Digest*, May 1968

Barnard, E. S., "What is Wrong with Minor League Baseball?" *Baseball Magazine*, November 1930

Barrow, Edward, "What's the Matter with the Minors?" *Baseball Magazine*, May 1917

Bell, Ed, "Big Doings in the Minor Leagues," *Baseball Digest*, August 1976

Birtwell, Roger, "Breeding Ground for Big League Managers," *Baseball Digest*, May 1979

Brown, Warren W., "A Few Innings from the Pacific Coast," *Baseball Magazine*, February 1920

Brosnan, Jim, "What It's Like in the Minors Now," *Baseball Digest*, February 1968

Bucey, Tim, "Minor League Stardom Doesn't Guarantee Success in Majors," *Baseball Digest*, March 1976

Carmichael, John P., "Are C and D Loops Really Needed for Major Prepping?" *Baseball Digest*, February 1960

Carpenter, Charles F., "The Tri-State League Explained," *Baseball Magazine*, September 1908

Claire, Fred, "Make Way for the Coast League," *Baseball Magazine*, July 1955

Cobbledick, Gordon, "Cure for Minors: Hometown Stars," *Baseball Digest*, March 1959

Conlin, Bill, "Crisis in the Coast League," *Baseball Digest*, March 1954

Crusinberry, James, "Pacific Coast League Impressions," *Baseball Magazine*, June 1951

Cummings, Joseph, "What's the Matter with the Eastern League?" *Baseball Magazine*, November 1909

Davids, Robert, "Youth Always Served in the Majors," *Baseball Digest*, February 1974

Duncan, C. William, "The Blue Ridge League: Breeder of Ball Players," *Baseball Magazine*, July 1928

Durant, Al, "The Professional Minor Leaguer," *Baseball Magazine*, April 1914

Dwyer, William, "Where the American Association Is Failing," *Baseball Magazine*, June 1912

Elderkin, Phil, "Farming for Profit," *Baseball Digest*, September 1968

Ermatinger, J. A., "The American Association," *Baseball Magazine*, July 1909

Fairweather, Thomas, "The Sioux City Champions," *Baseball Magazine*, June 1909

Fanton, Ben, "How It Was in Old Days of Class 'D' Baseball," *Baseball Digest*, March 1981

Freeburg, Dwight, "Who Said Minor League?" *Baseball Magazine*, January 1940

Gambino, Diane, "Minor League Experience—How Necessary Is It?" *Baseball Digest*, June 1976

Gerber, Max, "Columbus Rediscovers the Game," *Baseball Digest*, June 1959

Gordon, Dick, "They Majored in Triple-A Ball," *Baseball Digest*, May 1963

Gordon, Dick, "The Northern League Baseball Cradle Empty Now," *Baseball Digest*, July 1972

Green, Howard L., "There's Laziness in the Minors," *Baseball Magazine*, April 1952

Gregory, L. H., "P.C.L. Managers in the Majors," *Baseball Digest*, May 1951

Harzy, Walter, "Meandering through the Minors," *Baseball Magazine*, August 1942

Hern, Gerry, "There Are Still *Too Many* Minors," *Baseball Digest*, April 1954

Holway, John, "Stop! Killing the Minors," *Baseball Magazine*, October 1956

Hope, Bob, "One-Season Minor League Records Are—Awesome!" *Baseball Digest*, November 1984

Irving, Ira, "The Far Reaching Results of 'Farm' Baseball," *Baseball Magazine*, January 1929

Irving, Ira, "Baseball Farms in 1930," *Baseball Magazine*, January 1931

Irving, Ira, "Here and There in the Minors," *Baseball Magazine*, June 1936

Kelleher, George B., "Decisive Year for Springfield," *Baseball Magazine*, June 1952

Kofoed, J. C., "One Chance in a Thousand," *Baseball Magazine*, February 1914

Kofoed, J. C., "Mighty Sluggers in the Minor Circuits," *Baseball Magazine*, July 1920

Kofoed, J. C., "Base Stealing in the Minors," *Baseball Magazine*, August 1922

Levy, Sam, "Braves Farm Bill: $200,000," *Baseball Digest*, July 1948

Lewis, Franklin, "Here's the Difference between the Majors and Minors," *Baseball Digest*, July 1954

Livingston, Joe, "How Sam Wolfson Saved the Jacksonville Braves," *Baseball Magazine*, November–December 1954

Maher, Charles, "Trip with a Class A Club," *Baseball Digest*, December 1966

Mangum, Fred, "Reminiscences of the South Atlantic League," *Baseball Magazine*, March 1921

Martin, A. H., "The Pacific Coast League," *Baseball Magazine*, September 1909

McAuley, Ed, "Teachers-Pilots Big Farm Need," *Baseball Digest*, February 1950

McAuley, Ed, "The Farms Also Want to Win," *Baseball Digest*, May 1959

McDermott, Joe, "The Story of the American Association," *Baseball Magazine*, March 1912

Mehl, Ernest, "The Phillies Make Farming Pay," *Baseball Digest*, February 1960

Minshew, Wayne, "Most Colorful Guy in the Minors," *Baseball Digest*, September 1965

Murphy, Charles Webb, "A Square Deal for the Minor Leagues," *Baseball Magazine*, October 1919

Overfield, Joseph, "Gibraltar of the Minors," *Baseball Digest*, June 1958

Phelon, William A., "What Are We Going to Do about the Minors?" *Baseball Magazine*, June 1913

Pollock, Ed, "Rookie Hurlers Win Big League Berths in Minors: Tebbetts," *Baseball Digest*, June 1955

Pollock, Ed, "Few Bat Champs from Top Minors Called to Majors," *Baseball Digest*, June 1956

Richman, Milton, "It's Usually Four Years to Majors," *Baseball Digest*, November 1947

Robinson, Murray, "Bonus Kids Rip Minors' Morale," *Baseball Digest,* August 1958

Rumill, Ed, "The Braves Go in for Farming," *Baseball Magazine,* May 1945

Sanborn, Irving E., "Raising Baseball Stars for Future Markets," *Baseball Magazine,* March 1926

Siegel, Eric, "Baseball's Lowest Rung—The Rookie League," *Baseball Digest,* November 1974

Smith, Red, "It's Farm Now for Bonus Babies," *Baseball Digest,* February 1951

Steadman, John, "York, Pa., Majors in Minors," *Baseball Digest,* October–November 1962

Steadman, John, "Minor Leagues—Are They Headed for Extinction?" *Baseball Digest,* July 1973

Steadman, John F., "Poignant Moments in the Minors," *Baseball Digest,* May 1955

Steadman, John F., "Bus League Career Man," *Baseball Digest,* June 1960

Stockwell, R. F., "Sorrows of a Bush League Umpire," *Baseball Magazine,* April 1932

Totten, Hal, "Help Ahead for the Minors," *Baseball Digest,* November–December 1954

Trenary, Don C., "Everything Happens in the Minors!" *Baseball Digest,* August 1958

Tuttle, W. C., "Baseball's Great Minor Circuits," *Baseball Magazine,* January 1937

Ward, John J. "Echoes of the Minor World's Series," *Baseball Magazine,* December 1932

Wilson, C. M., "The Junior World's Series," *Baseball Magazine,* December 1931

Wilson, C. M., "Big Leaguers Endorse the Junior Campaign," *Baseball Magazine,* July 1932

Wolf, Al, "Coast Deal a Long Way Off," *Baseball Digest,* October 1947

Wolf, Al, "It's Tougher in Minors: Dykes," *Baseball Digest,* April 1948

Wolf, Al, "P.C.L. Jittery over Own Ultimatum," *Baseball Digest,* November 1951

Wolf, Al, "Coast League's No Ghost League!" *Baseball Digest*, January–February 1956

Young, Charles, "Minors in Major Difficulty," *Baseball Digest*, January 1952

*The Sporting News* is, of course, another publication rich in material about the minor leagues—especially in the days before *TSN* discovered other sports. The one serious complication to reviewing that material is the absence of an index.

*Baseball America* provides the best current coverage of minor league baseball. Their annual directory is a great aid in getting the information necessary to contact any team or league office in the minors.

# INDEX

Canadian-American League, 172–173
Canseco, Jose, 263
Cantley, John, 176
Cape Breton Colliery League, 173
Cardinals, St. Louis
  Gashouse Gang of 1930s, 100–103
  B. Rickey's role with, 95–103, 132
Carlyle, Hiram, 87
Carlyle, Roy, 90
Carolina League, 260
Cashen, Frank, 265, 266–267
Castro, Fidel, 130, 131
Cedar Rapids case, 112, 114
Central International League, 173
Cepeda, Orlando, 245
Chandler, Happy, 205, 219
Charleston, Oscar, 190, 203, 274
Chase, Hal, 54
Chatham, Buster, 179
Chrisman, Davd, 88, 142
Cicotte, Eddie, 47
Civil rights movement, 201
Clabaugh, Moose, 179
Claire, Fred, 226–227
Clamdiggers, Providence, 76
Clark, Dan, 90, 104
Clarke, Nig, 147, 152
Classification system, xi, 15, 42, 136
  class-AA status, 58, 259–261
  Pacific Coast League, 222, 227
  in reorganization of 1960s, 254
  Texas League, 152
  Triple-A league, 256–259
Cobb, Bob, 219–223
Cobb, Joe, 88
Cobb, Ty, 47, 119, 134, 190
Coleman, Jerry, 184
College baseball, 281
Collins, Jim "Ripper," 105, 106, 108
Comiskey, Charles, 19, 25, 26, 36, 37
Comiskey Park, 124
Congressional hearings on baseball,
  236–237, 238–240
Conley, Snipe, 154
Conlin, Bill, 225–226
Connelly, Tom, 89
Connors, Kevin "Chuck," 224–225
Connors, Mervyn, 179, 211
Continental League, 241–243
Cooper, Harold, 257, 263, 265, 270
Copper-Country Soo League, xi,
  168–169
Corruption in baseball, 8
  in black leagues, 197, 207
  Black Sox scandal, 57, 64, 69, 181, 182
  Houma Indians, 180–181
  Pitts case, 181–182
Cotton States League, 32, 170
Cravath, Gavvy, 56
Crawford, Sam, 190
Crues, Bob, 119, 179
Cuba, baseball in, 130–131, 171, 188,
  190, 199

Cubs, Chicago, 37, 62, 102, 116, 144, 269
Cueto, Manuel, 88
Cullop, Nick, 121, 211
Cummings, William Arthur "Candy," 12
Cutler, Bill, 258, 263, 264, 268

Dahlgren, Babe, 146, 216
Dalton, Harry, 270–271
Dandridge, Ray, 196
Dean, Dizzy, 102–103, 162, 166
Demaree, Frank, 216
Demons, Des Moines, 138
Deposit rule, 136
Derringer, Paul, 106
Designated hitter rule (DH), 248, 279
DeWitt, C. B., 152
Dickey, Bill, 196
Dickson, Hickory, 154
DiMaggio, Joe, 143, 216
Dittmar, Carl, 216
Dixie Series, 158–159
Doby, Larry, 205
Dodgers, Brooklyn, 116, 170, 202, 210,
  223, 227
Dodgers, Los Angeles, 227, 246, 264, 269
Donald, Atley, 146
Douthit, Taylor, 100, 101
Draft policies, 9, 10, 63, 110
  exemptions from, 65, 76, 91–92, 108,
    218, 220
  National League abuse of, 28–29
Dressen, Charlie, 116, 227
Dunn, Jack, 60–61, 63, 71–86, 94, 97, 99,
  106
  compared to B. Rickey, 99, 107–108
Dunn, Jack, Jr., 73, 81
Durham, Louis "Bull," 56
Durocher, Leo, 101, 116

Eagles, Newark, 203–205
Earnshaw, George "Moose," 83, 84
Eastern Championship Association, 15
Eastern Colored League, 197
Eastern Interstate League, 188
Eastern League, 20, 22, 58, 134, 259
Eastern Michigan League, 172
East Texas League, 176
East-West All-Star Game, 198
Eckhardt, Ox, 213, 214–215, 216
Egan, Ben, 76, 88
Essick, Bill, 143
Evangeline League, 169, 180–181
Exporters, Beaumont, 162
Expos, Montreal, 244, 246

Farm system, 19, 28, 85, 89, 93–114, 276
  advocacy of minors as wards of the
    majors, xi, 85, 237
  Cardinals, 98–103, 161–163
  career of Branch Rickey, 93–98
  conflicts between Rickey and Landis
    over, 103–104, 109–113
  deciding whether to join, 135–137